JOURNAL FOR THE STUDY OF THE NEW TESTAMENT
SUPPLEMENT SERIES
58

Executive Editor
David Hill

JSOT Press
Sheffield

NONE BUT THE SINNERS

Religious Categories in the Gospel of Luke

David A. Neale

Journal for the Study of the New Testament
Supplement Series 58

To Christine

Copyright © 1991 Sheffield Academic Press

Published by JSOT Press
JSOT Press is an imprint of
Sheffield Academic Press Ltd
The University of Sheffield
343 Fulwood Road
Sheffield S10 3BP
England

Printed on acid-free paper in Great Britain
by
Billing & Sons Ltd
Worcester

British Library Cataloguing in Publication Data

Neale, David A.
   'None but the Sinners': religious categories in the
   Gospel of Luke.—(Journal for the study of the New
   Testament supplement series. ISSN 0143-5108)
   I. Title II. Series
   226.4

ISBN 1-85075-314-8

CONTENTS

PART II

CONCLUSION 191

ACKNOWLEDGMENTS

Many years of preparation, planning and study are required for the production of a doctoral thesis, and my own case has been no exception. Along the way this support and encouragement of so many has played an important part in bringing this project to a rewarding culmination. To those who have smoothed the way I would like to extend my gratitude.

As a mentor and friend Dr L.C.A. Alexander guided my work at the University of Sheffield with skill and patience. Dr Andrew Lincoln and Dr Philip Davies at Sheffield made time in their busy schedules to read and discuss various aspects of the work as it progressed, as did Dr P.S. Alexander of the University of Manchester. In its thesis form the work was improved by the careful reading and critical comments of the external examiner, Professor Leslie Houlden, King's College London. The responsibility for its shortcomings remains, of course, entirely my own. For financial assistance thanks are due to the Tyndale Foundation in Cambridge and the University Higher Degrees Committee of the University of Sheffield for the provision of an Overseas Research Grant.

Above all, my wife Christine and sons Matthew and Thomas have sacrificed comforts, time and energy to make this project possible. It is to them that I owe the deepest thanks.

The subject of Jesus and the 'sinners' has been a fascinating field of study and I can only hope that this monograph will contribute in some small way to the effort to understand the one for whom their fate was such a concern.

ABBREVIATIONS

ANRW	*Aufstieg und Niedergang der römischen Welt,* ed. W. Haase, 1979.
Ant.	*Antiquities,* Josephus
Apoc. Elij.	*Apocalypse of Elijah*
Apoc. Sed.	*Apocalypse of Sedrach*
APOT	*Apocrypha and Pseudepigrapha of the Old Testament,* ed. R.H. Charles, 1913.
b.	Babylonian Talmud
BAG	*A Greek English Lexicon of the New Testament and Other Early Christian Literature,* by W. Bauer, trans. by W.F. Arndt and F.W. Gingrich, 1975.
BDB	*A Hebrew and English Lexicon of the Old Testament,* by F. Brown, S. Driver, C. Briggs, 1951.
Bib	*Biblica*
BJRL	*Bulletin of the John Rylands Library*
BZ	*Biblische Zeitschrift*
CBQ	*Catholic Biblical Quarterly*
CRIANT	Compendia Rerum Iudaicarum ad Novum Testamentum
CTM	*Concordia Theological Monthly*
EncJud	*Encyclopaedia Judaica,* 1971.
1 En.	*1 Enoch*
2 En.	*2 Enoch*
ERW	*Early Rabbinic Writings,* by H. Maccoby, 1988.
2 Esd.	*2 Esdras*
ETal	*Encyclopedia Talmudica,* 1969.
ETL	*Ephemerides Theologicae Lovanienses*
ExpT	*Expository Times*
Gk. Apoc. Ezra	*Greek Apocalypse of Ezra*
HeyJ	*Heythrop Journal*
HJP	*The History of the Jewish People in the Age of Jesus Christ,* by E. Schürer (ed. G. Vermes, F. Millar and M. Black, revised 1979).
HST	*History of the Synoptic Tradition,* by R. Bultmann, 1972.
HTR	*Harvard Theological Review*
HUCA	*Hebrew Union College Annual*

Int	*Interpretation*
JBL	*Journal of Biblical Literature*
JBR	*Journal of Bible and Religion*
JJS	*Journal of Jewish Studies*
JQR	*Jewish Quarterly Review*
JR	*Journal of Religion*
JSJ	*Journal for the Study of Judaism*
JSNT	*Journal for the Study of the New Testament*
JSS	*Journal of Semitic Studies*
JTS	*Journal of Theological Studies*
JTTJ	*Jerusalem in the Time of Jesus,* by J. Jeremias, 1967.
Jub.	*Jubilees*
LAE	*Life of Adam and Eve*
LTQ	*Lexington Theological Quarterly*
m.	*Mishnah*
1 Macc.	*1 Maccabees*
2 Macc.	*2 Maccabees*
NovT	*Novum Testamentum*
NTS	*New Testament Studies*
NTT	*New Testament Theology: The Proclamation of Jesus,* by J. Jeremias, 1971.
OTP	*Old Testament Pseudepigrapha,* ed. J.H. Charlesworth, 1983.
Pr. Man.	*Prayer of Manasseh*
Pss. Sol.	*Psalms of Solomon*
PRS	*Perspectives in Religious Studies*
1QH	Hôdāyôt (Thanksgiving Hymns)
1QS	Serek hayyaḥad (Rule of the Community)
Ques. Ezra	*Questions of Ezra*
RLGT	*Rabbinic Literature and Gospel Teachings,* by C.G. Montefiore, 1970.
SPG	*Studies in Pharisaism and the Gospels,* by I. Abrahams, reprint 1976.
Sib. Or.	*Sibylline Oracles*
TynBul	*Tyndale Bulletin*
TD	*Theology Digest*
TDNT	*Theological Dictionary of the New Testament,* ed. G. Kittel and G. Friedrich, 1964–76.
T. Abr.	*Testament of Abraham*
T. Benj.	*Testament of Benjamin*
T. Isaac	*Testament of Isaac*
T. Jud.	*Testament of Judah*
UJE	*Universal Jewish Encyclopedia,* 1948.
USQR	*Union Seminary Quarterly Review*
VT	*Vetus Testamentum*

Vis. Ezra	*Visions of Ezra*
Wis.	Wisdom of Solomon
y.	*Talmud de Jerusalem (Palestinian Talmud)*
ZAW	*Zeitschrift für die alttestamentliche Wissenschaft*
ZKG	*Zeitschrift für Kirchengeschichte*
ZNW	*Zeitschrift für die neutestamentliche Wissenschaft*

The subject of this study is 'sinners' in the Gospel of Luke. In all the synoptics we find a saying in which Jesus expressed his mission in terms of a call to 'sinners': 'I came not to call the righteous, but sinners . . .' Luke in particular emphasizes the importance of Jesus' relation to 'sinners' and, as we shall see, they are a central feature of the Galilean ministry in his Gospel. Two simple facts demonstrate this point: the group identified as 'sinners' appear more often in Luke than in any other Gospel, and he utilizes their presence in his story in a more highly developed way than the other Gospel writers. For Luke, 'sinners' provide the backbone of controversy that drives his Gospel forward. They are also the key point of contention which distinguishes how Jesus differs from his co-religionists, the Pharisees.

My interest in this topic was initially stimulated by the chapter entitled 'Sinners' in E.P. Sanders's book, *Jesus and Judaism*. Further reading and reflection on the issues raised there led to a conviction that there was a need for more research into this important but largely ignored facet of the Christian tradition. Who, indeed, were these 'sinners?' Since Jesus, or at least the Gospel writers, defined his mission in terms of the call and rescue of 'sinners', their identification must certainly be an important aspect of the study of the historical Jesus. In the Gospel records the respective attitudes of Jesus and the Pharisees towards the 'sinners' are a constant source of disputation and conflict. It thus seems worthwhile to enquire further about the cause and nature of this conflict.

Part I of this book is primarily devoted to a historical analysis of the issue of the 'sinners'. Since the Pharisees play such a prominent role in the Gospel tradition about 'sinners', Chapter 1 seeks to place the phenomenon of Pharisaism in its proper social and religious context in the pre-70 period. The investigation will focus on recent developments that have changed the way Pharisaism is viewed by some scholars and will then proceed to assess the implications this has for our subject. In Chapter 2 the relation of the rabbinic concept of the *'ammei ha-aretz* to that of the 'sinner' will be examined. The need to explore this issue arises, not from the biblical material itself, but from the tendency of scholarship to describe Jesus' conflict with the Pharisees in terms of the later rabbinic notion of the *'ammei ha-aretz*. Chapter 3 will examine material concerning the 'sinners' in the Old Testament, Apocrypha, Pseudepigrapha and rabbinic literature with a view towards uncovering the linguistic, historical and conceptual background of the term. Finally, I will propose some ideas about the nature and use of this type of language and its importance for the construction of a religious ideology. The purpose of Part I is ultimately to place my investigation of the 'sinners' in Luke's Gospel on the firmest possible footing with respect to history and the literature of this period.

Part II offers an analysis of the notion of the 'sinner' in a particular literary context, the Gospel of Luke. Initially, the study of 'sinners' in Luke was to have been an extension of the historical approach of Part I. However, as the study progressed, it became apparent that the real significance of Luke's 'sinner' material was to be found in the way he used this group as an element in his story. Luke's treatment has many salient literary qualities and appears not to be, as it were, a guide to the historical 'sinner'. Ironically, it was the historical emphasis of Part I that made this so apparent. The investigation of the 'sinner' from a historical perspective caused the distinctive Lucan treatment of the theme to emerge in high relief.

As with the gospel genre in general, the interplay between history and story is complex in Luke. A 'gospel' is an account of events shaped into a story from a particular ideological point of view. Just as with 'history', a gospel is something of a hybrid literary form, consisting of both historical data and narrative interpretation; fact and ideological perception meld to produce an apologetically convincing story. Methodologically, historical and literary analysis combine to produce a result unobtainable by a single method. If, for example, certain aspects of the 'sinner' motif are shown to have no satisfactory historical basis, then their explanation as a product of literary exigency is all the more necessary. Conversely, historical-critical investigation can serve as guard against the tendency of the literary approach to detach a story from its historical setting. In Part II we will see how one writer has skilfully brought the category of the 'sinners' into play as a key element in a dramatic story of rescue.

The scholarly literature on the subject of Pharisees and 'sinners' is considerable, but a great deal of the work has been bound by certain pre-suppositions. Most contemporary scholars dealing with the subject have followed a twofold description of the historical 'sinner' which was first set out by Joachim Jeremias. He described the 'sinner' as the notoriously immoral and/or the members of the rabbinically designated 'despised trades'. Quite often authors still merely give a nod to Jeremias and then pass over the subject without further discussion. The result has been a lack of in-depth thinking about the 'sinners', who were, after all, according to the Synoptic evangelists, the avowed target group of Jesus' mission. It has simply been assumed that a notion which has contributed so much to the modern understanding of Jesus was well understood.

One long-held assumption has been that the proper way to approach the question of 'sinners' in the Gospels is from the perspective of history. That is, since the Gospels appear to portray Jesus as interacting with a seemingly identifiable social group called 'sinners', there in fact must have been just such a group. Furthermore, it is argued that the actual historical referents of the term 'sinners' could be recovered by recourse to early rabbinic (and even modern!) presuppositions about what constitutes 'moral' and 'immoral' behaviour. Yet, does this approach adequately explain or grapple with the significance of the role of these 'sinners' in the Gospel tradition? Is not the use of terms such as 'righteous' and 'sinner' primarily a reflection of the ideological perspective of the story teller? Such terms, it would seem, are not derived from the vocabulary of history but from the vocabulary of belief. As such, the proper meaning of the term 'sinner' should be sought, not in history, but in the ideological nature of this sort of language; a language which conceives of reality in terms of a twofold moral universe, a dichotomy of good and evil.

For Luke the dictates of the Gospel story have necessitated that he employ and shape the tradition-material available to him in a certain way. At the level of story, Jesus is the main character, the prophet sent from God. The 'sinners' provide the ideal issue to highlight the radical nature of his mission and the scope of his call and are the issue around which conflict develops with those presented as the representatives of official Judaism, the Pharisees. These Pharisees, in turn, serve the purpose of setting Jesus' conduct in contrast to that purportedly dominant form of Judaism and showing Jesus' superiority to it.

This is not to suggest that genuine historical realities did not, at some level, underlie the Gospel tradition of Jesus in conflict with the Pharisees over 'sinners'. Jesus' coterie may well have included toll collectors or other undesirable types, and some religionists may have objected to this aspect of the ministry. Each Gospel contains these features and it thus seems probable that such associations were a part of Jesus' ministry. But the question under consideration here is whether these events and associations originally had the significance later assigned to them by Luke. Would an observer of Jesus and his activities have pointed to fellowship with 'sinners' as a central feature of his ministry? Would this observer have characterized Jesus as having been polarized in an ideological conflict with a socially dominant and religiously degenerate Jewish sect? These features of the Gospel story are more the product of an ideological interpretation of events and traditions than a straightforward report of unambiguous incidents in Jesus' life. The 'sinners' are just one of Luke's discrete religious categories in which past events and ideas were crystallized into a concrete social reality for the sake of his Gospel story.

PART I

Chapter 1

PHARISAISM IN CONTEXT

The portrait of the Pharisees in the Gospels of the New Testament is quite simple in its basic outlines. In general the Pharisees are presented as a single group which appears to dominate the religious scene of Jesus' day; they seem to represent almost an 'official' Judaism. The Pharisees often appear at key points in the text to challenge and oppose Jesus on aspects of his teaching and conduct. When Jesus heals on a sabbath or tells a parable it is often the 'Pharisees' who step forward to contest the propriety of his words or actions. When Jesus associates with 'toll collectors and sinners', it is the 'Pharisees' who take umbrage. The net result of this portrayal is that the Galilean teacher is seen to have been at odds with the religious leaders of his day. Essentially, these 'Pharisees' serve as a foil to demonstrate the way in which Jesus differed from his contemporaries. The Gospel of Luke is no exception in this regard and the 'Pharisees' are Jesus' chief antagonists in chs. 5–19 of the book. It is this feature of Luke's Gospel which gives rise to our interest in the Pharisees here.

To what extent does Luke's portrayal correspond to that which is actually known about the Pharisees in this period? Does this picture of Pharisaism have a foundation in history or were these 'Pharisees' only a polemical tool in the hands of the evangelist? Perhaps they were simply the adversaries currently being confronted by the church at the time the Gospel of Luke was written; an enemy whose presence was then super-imposed back onto the story of Jesus. Or did Jesus actually have conflict with a sect whose influence was somehow determinative for Jews in general at that time, as the Gospels seem to imply?

The purpose of this first chapter is to set the Pharisees of Jesus' day in their historical context as accurately as the present state of scholarship will allow. In the past twenty years there has been a paradigmatic shift in the understanding of the role of Pharisaism in Palestinian culture of the pre-70 period. The objective of this chapter is not to mount an entirely new investigation into this very difficult topic; many of the basic issues are still the subject of considerable debate.[1] The intention here is to set forth and document the fundamental questions of that paradigmatic shift and take a position on these issues. The decisions taken here will then guide hermeneutical decisions at key points in the later chapters of the investigation. Ultimately, the purpose here is to set out a reasonably accurate account of pre-70 Pharisaism against which Luke's own depiction of the Pharisees can be measured.

Thus, I begin with a survey of recent developments in scholarship about early Judaism and the relative position of Pharisaism in Palestine in this period. The resulting picture will be one of considerable complexity and, above all, diversity. Following this, the question of the extent of Pharisaic influence will lead us to enquire about several other issues. Were the Pharisees a strictly exclusive sect or were they broadly influential lay interpreters of Scripture and oral tradition? Do the forms and methods of religious expression popular in Jesus' day provide a basis for elucidating the relationship between Jesus and the Pharisees? How have the events and literature of the early rabbinic period influenced thinking about this subject? This chapter and the

1. On the Pharisees in general see the dictionary articles by A. Michel and J. Lemoyne, 'Pharisiens', *Dictionnaire de la Bible, Supplément*, VII (ed. Henri Cazelles and André Feuillet; Paris: Letouzey & Ané, 1966), col. 1022-115; and R. Meyer and H.F. Weiss, 'Φαρισαῖος', *TDNT*, IX, pp. 11-48. Among the older monographs, L. Finkelstein, *The Pharisees: The Sociological Background of their Faith*, I (2 vols.; Philadelphia: The Jewish Publication Society of America, 1938 [2nd edn, 1940]) and R.T. Herford, *The Pharisees* (Boston: Beacon Press, 1924); also J.Z. Lauterbach, 'The Pharisees and their Teachings', *HUCA* 6 (1929), pp. 69-139. More recently, the revised E. Schürer, *The History of the Jewish People in the Age of Jesus Christ*, II (ed. G. Vermes, F. Millar and M. Black; 3 vols.; Edinburgh: T. & T. Clark, 1979), pp. 388-403; J. Jeremias, *Jerusalem in the Time of Jesus* (Philadelphia: Fortress Press, 1967), pp. 246-67; E.E. Urbach, *The Sages: Their Concepts and Beliefs* (trans. I. Abrahams; Cambridge, MA: Harvard University Press, 1987). Among the many journal articles see E. Rivkin, 'Defining the Pharisees: The Tannaitic Sources', *HUCA* 40 (1969), pp. 205-49; S. Zeitlin, 'The Pharisees', *JQR* 52 (1961–62), pp. 97-129; R. Marcus, 'The Pharisees in the Light of Modern Scholarship', *JR* 23 (1952), pp. 153-64. Also see 'First-Century Pharisaism' in D. Hagner's *The Jewish Reclamation of Jesus* (Grand Rapids: Academie Press, 1984), pp. 171-90.

remainder of Part I will show that the religious environment in which Jesus lived was an extremely diverse and fluid one where lines were not so easily drawn between saints and sinners.

Jesus, the Pharisees and 'Normative Judaism'

A reference to 'Pharisee' in any modern dictionary will confirm that the view of Pharisaism which has passed into the modern imagination is one of hypocrisy, self-righteousness and sanctimony. The unfortunate truth of course is that this conception is due largely to the depiction of the Pharisees in the Gospels. This negative definition of Pharisaism has come to form part of the basis for understanding the historical Jesus. Jesus is conceived as being the opposite of all the negative attributes of the Pharisees and they, in turn, are the black background against which Jesus' own character shines forth. In the final turn of this hermeneutical circle, this view of Pharisaism has itself passed into our historical understanding of the religious milieu of Jesus' day. The Pharisees of the Gospels have thus been 'historicized' and our understanding of Jesus' identity has been based in part on an unquestioned acceptance of the Gospel depiction of Pharisaism.

In the past two decades, however, scholarly interest in what is now called 'early Judaism'[1] (c. 330 BCE to Hadrian, 138 CE) has challenged long-held beliefs about Palestinian Judaism in the pre-70 period. It was characteristic of older scholarship to view the Judaism of the rabbinic literature as a clear window on the pre-70 milieu and to hold that halakhic Pharisaism was 'normative' for the time of Jesus. A ten-

---

1. Thus the title of the recent work by Robert A. Kraft and George W.E. Nickelsburg, *Early Judaism and its Modern Interpreters* (Philadelphia: Fortress Press, 1986). The introductory essay traces the history of post-World War II scholarship in early Judaism, pp. 1-30. It is no coincidence that this upsurge in scholarly interest has occurred simultaneously with the increase in the study of the inter-testamental literature. As J.H. Charlesworth notes in the introduction to his *Old Testament Pseudepigrapha*, 'The simplistic picture of Early Judaism should be recast; it certainly was neither a religion which had fallen into arduous legalism due to the crippling demands of the Law, nor was it characterized by four dominant sects. A new picture has been emerging because of ideas preserved in the documents below' (ed. J.H. Charlesworth [2 vols.; New York: Doubleday, 1983], I, p. xxxix). See further his 'A History of Pseudepigrapha Research', in *ANRW* II.19.1 (ed. Wolfgang Haase; Berlin: de Gruyter, 1979), pp. 62, 87-88.

dency to view the Judaism of the post-exilic period right through to the time of the Tannaim with a certain homogeneity can be seen, for example, in Emil Schürer's *A History of the Jewish People*.[1] For Schürer, post-exilic Judaism, Pharisaism and rabbinic Judaism were all synonymous and as a result he could describe Pharisaism as the 'legitimate and typical representative of post-exilic Judaism'.[2] Similar views can be traced among other scholars.[3]

Needless to say, this acceptance of the dominance of Pharisaism was often combined with a generally negative appraisal of the religious value of the movement. Thus, a foundation was laid for viewing Jesus as having created a new and revolutionary piety in fundamental opposition to his Jewish roots. This conception of the Judaism of Jesus'

---

1.   This is true even in the revised edition of 1979, in spite of the editors' efforts to nuance Schürer's views more carefully (see Vermes's own comments on Schürer's work in *Jesus and the World of Judaism* [London: SCM Press, 1983], pp. 58-73). So Schürer wrote, 'As in its attitude towards biblical law, so in its religious and doctrinal views, Pharisaism essentially represented the standpoint of later rabbinic Judaism' (*HJP*, II, p. 391). Also, 'No peculiarity emerges from this characterization of Pharisaism which might distinguish it from Judaism in general during the period of the Second Temple. Regarded as a spiritual orientation, it was simply identical with the trend adopted by the main body and the classical representatives of the post-exilic Jewry' (pp. 395-96). Compare p. 389 n. 20, for the views of the editors who quote Neusner; 'Such a portrait is based on hindsight, i.e. on a view of the past evolution formulated after the triumph of the Pharisaic school of thought at Yavneh and Usha'.

2.   Schürer, *HJP*, II, p. 400; for a classic statement of this view see F.C. Burkitt, 'Jesus and the "Pharisees"', *JTS* 28 (1927), p. 392.

3.   So also G.F. Moore, *Judaism in the First Centuries of the Christian Era*, I–III (Cambridge, MA: Harvard University Press, 1927; reprint 1946). The term 'Judaism' is one Moore uses with imprecision, it being the name he applies to Jewish religion from Ezra to the Amoraim. Moore understands the difficulty in using the name so broadly (e.g. I, p. 14) but differs from more recent understandings of pre-70 Judaism by positing a development of 'normative' Judaism that appears to gloss over the upheaval of the period. Moore asserts that the goal of a normative Judaism 'was not reached without many conflicts of parties and sects and more than one grave political and religious crisis, but in the end the tendency which most truly represented the historical character and spirit of the religion prevailed, and accomplished the unification of Judaism' (I, p. 1). For a critique of Moore's view of Judaism and its influence see J. Neusner's '"Judaism" after Moore', *JJS* 31 (1980), pp. 141-56, esp. 142, 148-49. See also the survey of scholars in this tradition by Hagner, *The Jewish Reclamation of Jesus*, pp. 182-84.

day was one which believed, as Morton S. Enslin has described it, that Judaism had

> sadly decayed or deteriorated into an arid and barren legalism, under
> which Jesus had suffered and against which Paul had fulminated. . . It
> was from this sad decay of what had once been a noble religion that, like a
> fragrant lily amazingly blooming from the muddy bottom of a stagnant
> lake, Jesus had appeared 'in the fullness of time', to stand in absolute
> contrast to this rigid and intolerable system.[1]

In this view the religious milieu in which Jesus ministered was characterized by casuistry, intolerance and hair-splitting legalism; a black
background indeed. And while such thinking has been abandoned by
most scholars[2] it should not be presumed that Gospel studies have become entirely free of these presuppositions.[3]

That the Pharisees[4] were perhaps viewed as an important and
influential force in the religious milieu of Jesus' day is not necessarily

---

1.   So Enslin describes the views of Schürer, W. Bousset and F. Weber in his
prolegomenon to I. Abrahams's *Studies in Pharisaism and the Gospel* (New York:
Ktav, 1967; reprinted in one volume from two originally published in 1917 and 1924
by Cambridge University Press), pp. v-xxiv.

2.   See G. Vermes, 'Jewish Studies and New Testament Interpretation', *JJS* 31
(1980), pp. 9-10; also the excursus by D.A. Hagner, 'First Century Pharisaism' in
The Jewish Reclamation of Jesus, p. 171. But see further Robert Wild, 'The
Encounter Between Pharisaic and Christian Judaism: Some Early Gospel Evidence',
NovT 27, 2 (1985), pp. 105-24. Wild states, 'This view of Pharisaic and religious
dominance was widely assumed in the past and still makes its appearance with regu-
larity in some of the standard introductions to the New Testament Literature' (p.
104).

3.   Some post-war 'lives of Jesus' may be cited as examples: 'there developed,
on the ground of Pharisaism and the scribal teaching connected with it, that
formalistic legalising of the law, and a corresponding detailed technique of piety, to
which Jesus' message stands in sharp contrast' (G. Bornkamm, *Jesus of Nazareth*
[New York: Harper & Row, 1960], p. 40). Ben Meyer describes Jesus as 'appealing
to the stubborn fund of religious good sense which the *halaka* inhibited but failed to
extinguish' (*The Aims of Jesus* [London: SCM Press, 1979], p. 150). Other
examples of this attitude will be seen in the chapters following.

4.   The meaning and origin of the name is obscure. The root is most likely
p^erûshîm and means 'separated', but whether this is in a negative or positive sense is
unclear. See further A.I. Baumgarten, 'The Name of the Pharisees', *JBL* 102
(1983), pp. 411-28; E. Rivkin, 'Defining the Pharisees', pp. 205-49; H.F. Weiss,
'Φαρισαῖος', *TDNT*, IX, pp. 12-16.

in doubt.[1] This does not mean, however, that they would have been the chief arbiters of religious observance and conscience in the period. They almost certainly were not. In a seminal article written over thirty years ago Morton Smith advanced the view that the Pharisees had limited influence in this period.

> If there was any such thing, then, as an 'orthodox Judaism', it must have been that which is now almost unknown to us, the religion of the average 'people of the land'. But the different parts of the country were so different, such gulfs of feeling and practice separated Idumea, Judea, Caesarea, and Galilee, that even on this level there was probably no more agreement between them than between any one of them and a similar area in the Diaspora. And in addition to the local differences, the country swarmed with special sects, each devoted to its own tradition. . . As for the major philosophic sects—the Pharisees, Sadducees, and Essenes—the largest and ultimately the most influential of them, the Pharisees, numbered only about 6000, had no real hold either on the government or on the masses of the people, and was, as were the others, profoundly Hellenized.[2]

The main features of this assessment (except perhaps for the emphasis on Hellenization) have been confirmed by more recent research.

> Whereas rabbinic Judaism is dominated by an identifiable perspective that holds together many otherwise diverse elements, early Judaism appears to encompass almost unlimited diversity and variety—indeed, it might be more appropriate to speak of early Judaisms.[3]

1.   From the perspective of Josephus the Pharisees were, 'extremely influential among the townsfolk; and all prayers and sacred rites of divine worship are performed according to their exposition' (*Ant.* 18.15). The Sadducees, however, 'submit. . . to the formulas of the Pharisees, since otherwise the masses would not tolerate them' (*Ant.* 18.17). See further S. Safrai, 'Jewish Self-government', in *The Jewish People in the First Century* (CRIANT, Sec. 1; ed. S. Safrai and M. Stern in co-operation with D. Flusser and W.C. van Unnik; 2 vols.; Philadelphia: Fortress Press, 1974), I, pp. 386, 396, 401; II, pp. 892-93.

2.   Morton Smith, 'Palestinian Judaism in the First Century', in *Israel: Its Role in Civilization* (ed. M. David; New York: Harper & Brothers, 1956), pp. 67-81; this quotation is from p. 81. Smith credits the mistaken conception of the dominance of Pharisaism to the 'natural prejudice' (p. 74) of the rabbinic material and the pro-Pharisee tendency of *Antiquities* (see pp. 74-78). For further observations on the care necessary in the use of rabbinic sources see P.S. Alexander, 'Rabbinic Judaism and the New Testament', *ZNW* 74 (1983), pp. 237-46; and below, Chapter 2.

3.   Kraft and Nickelsburg, *Early Judaism*, p. 2. So also Marcel Simon: 'Ritualistic, scriptural, and doctrinal deviations came together in multifarious

The resulting picture of variety, religious ferment and vitality in Judaism in this period makes Jesus' relation to his society in general and to the Pharisees in particular all the more difficult to ascertain.

What was the extent of Pharisaic influence among the general populace? The question centres to a considerable degree on whether the Pharisees were an exclusive sect or a widely popular lay movement. The answer to this question will be of pivotal importance for our view of Jesus' relationship to the Pharisees and the significance of any conflict that arose. If the Pharisees were the chief arbiters of popular religion and Jesus was found to be in opposition to them, then his was at least a minority and perhaps a rebel position. Jesus would have been one who departed from the accepted path of the religion of his day by not submitting to Pharisaic teaching. On the other hand, if the Pharisees were a small exclusionary sect and did not have broad influence over the masses then the picture changes. In that case it would seem very natural to think of Jesus as clashing with Pharisees about matters that were quite likely debated among many factions of pious Jews, some sectarian and some not. In this scenario Jesus becomes one participant in the midst of a vigorous and multi-form religious debate about the proper direction and focus of Jewish faith. This must surely be closer to the truth and a review of recent thinking on the sectarian nature of Pharisaism bears this out.

The Pharisaic institution of the *haburah* figures centrally in the notion of Pharisaism as an exclusive sect. While not all Pharisees were members of a *haburah*, a strict association for observance of ritual purity and tithing, the principal distinctions of the *haburah* and the Pharisaic way of life were essentially the same.[1] The primary concern

combinations, defining a whole gamut of movements and groupings that we too often assume to be of secondary importance in Jewish religious life. . . Everything was still in a state of flux in this infinitely complex phenomenon that was Judaism around the beginning of the Christian era', *Jewish Sects at the Time of Jesus* (Philadelphia: Fortress Press, 1967), pp. 12-13; and Charlesworth, 'it is obvious that Judaism was not monolithically structured or shaped by a central and all-powerful "orthodoxy"' (*OTP*, I, p. xxxix).

1.   Whether the Pharisees and the *haberim* are to be equated is a matter of controversy. The point is not crucial to our argument here, but see the discussion by J. Bowker, *Jesus and the Pharisees* (Cambridge: Cambridge University Press, 1973), pp. 1-15. On the conditions for entering a *haburah* and the basic principles of membership see J. Neusner, 'The Fellowship in the Second Jewish Commonwealth',

was the extension of priestly holiness to all of life and thus the desire to take all ordinary food in a state of ritual purity. Second was the desire strictly to observe the tithing of all food.[1] These ideals governed one's participation in an association[2] and dominated, in general, the Pharisaic way of life.[3]

The constraints of such a life led inevitably to a real separation between the practitioner and the non-observant. Such people, says Neusner,

> distinguished themselves from the common society by their strict adherence to ritual laws which separated them in crucial relationships of daily life. Thus members cast up a barrier between themselves and the outsider, who was by definition a source of ritual defilement.[4]

This life was not for the many but for those few who could summon the commitment to follow its requirements. New members would advance by stages to a more thorough observance of the many and intricate halakhoth.[5] If a novice wished to advance no further than a particular stage of observance this was permitted.[6] There were members at various levels of faithfulness and to be less than fully observant was acceptable.[7] But such concessions to those who could not commit themselves fully to the disciplines of all the halakhoth show that this

---

HTR 53 (1960), pp. 125-42; see further P.H. Peli, 'The *Havurot* that Were in Jerusalem', *HUCA* 55 (1984), pp. 55-74.

1. Neusner collects the relevant texts in 'Fellowship', pp. 130-32; see further J. Jeremias's appendix, 'The Pharisees', in *JTTJ*, p. 247-67. See also Chapter 2 below.

2. Neusner, 'Fellowship', pp. 127-28.

3. Neusner claims, 'Approximately 67% of all legal pericopae deal with dietary laws: ritual purity for meals and agricultural rules governing the fitness of goods for Pharisaic consumption [i.e. tithing]' (*The Rabbinic Traditions about the Pharisees before 70*, III [Leiden: Brill, 1971], p. 304).

4. Neusner, 'Fellowship', p. 125. Urbach agrees, saying that the daily routine of the Pharisaic sect member was of such a nature that it created 'class and sectarian polarity' (*Sages*, p. 584). See also R. Meyer, 'Φαρισαῖος', *TDNT*, IX, p. 19; and again Urbach, 'The Sages', *EncJud* 14, p. 642.

5. *M. Hag.* 2.7 is the classic text about levels of observance. Again see Chapter 2 below and A. Oppenheimer, *The 'Am Ha-aretz: A Study in the Social History of the Jewish People in the Hellenistic-Roman Period* (Leiden: Brill, 1977), pp. 61-62.

6. Neusner, 'Fellowship', p. 129.

7. Consider, for example, the 'disciples of the Pharisees' of Mk 2.18 who might represent this category.

way of life was arduous and by no means for everyone. The fundamental nature of a life lived on this basis was separation from the non-observant; neighbour from neighbour and sometimes family member from family member.[1] The line between sectarian and non-sectarian remained readily distinguishable.[2]

It must be remembered, however, that those who undertook such a life were a very small percentage of the population as a whole.[3] Furthermore, the observance of sectarian practice was a supererogatory undertaking that was essentially a matter of personal conscience for the devotee. While a sectarian no doubt viewed him or herself as set apart, this involved no widely recognized social or class differentiation.[4] Pharisees could be rich or poor, excessively strict in observance or only marginally so, residents of town or country. In any case, their relatively small number and diverse praxis militated against the exercise of a broad social influence.

Not all have interpreted the nature of Pharisaism in this fashion, and some scholars have preferred to understand the movement as a broadly influential one which had the support of the masses.[5] In this view the Pharisees are understood less as a 'sect' and more as a 'party'[6] of lay interpreters of Scripture and tradition whose views

1. *T. Dem.* 3.9, for a *ḥaber* whose wife is not observant: 'It is as if he dwells in the same cage as a serpent'. See further *b. Bek.* 30b-31a; *b. Ket.* 71a; Neusner, 'Fellowship', pp. 138-39.

2. See C. Rabin, 'The Novitiate', in *Qumran Studies* (Oxford: Oxford University Press, 1957), pp. 16-21.

3. According to Josephus, the Pharisees numbered only 6000 (*Ant.* 17.42; see Jeremias, *JTTJ*, p. 252). For a population of between 600,000 to 1,000,000 this works out to less than 1% (Jeremias, *JTTJ*, p. 205).

4. See further Chapter 2.

5. This view is based primarily on the evidence of Josephus, *Ant.* 13.288, 399-411; 15.2-4; 18.15-17. The problem with this view is that it fails to take into account Josephus's contrary portrait in *War* where the Pharisees do not figure prominently. See M. Smith ('Palestinian Judaism', pp. 75-78) for the case against Josephus. Cf. D. Schwartz who more recently has questioned Smith's findings: 'Josephus and Nicolaus on the Pharisees', *JSJ* 14 (1983), pp. 157-71.

6. E.g. Ellis Rivkin, *A Hidden Revolution* (Nashville: Abingdon, 1978); E.P. Sanders, *Paul and Palestinian Judaism* (Philadelphia: Fortress Press, 1983, second printing), p. 156: 'the Pharisees are better called a party than a sect. . . a party is a group which believes itself to be right and which wishes others to obey or agree, but which does not exclude dissenters from "Israel"'. See further the discussions of this

were widely esteemed. But this position encounters a dilemma when its proponents attempt to synthesize two views and say that the Pharisees were *both* widely influential and an exclusive sect. Sanders, for example, argues that the Pharisees were unable broadly to influence Jewish religious opinion[1] but then still calls them 'lay experts in the law'.[2] Likewise, Jeremias seems to be of two minds about the Pharisees. On the one hand he stresses, 'we must never lose sight of the fact that they [the Pharisees] formed *closed communities*' (his emphasis), but then he later describes them as the 'people's party' and asserts that the people 'unreservedly' followed them.[3] Or consider, for example, E. Schürer's definition of the Pharisees:

> This exclusiveness of Pharisaism justifies in any case its description as a sect, αἵρεσις, the term applied to it in the New Testament (Acts 15.5; 25.5) and also by Josephus. But at the same time, it was the legitimate and typical representative of post-exilic Judaism.[4]

We cannot, it would seem, have it both ways. Strict exclusionists would not have been broadly influential among non-sectarians who would have had little concern for that strict way of life. Non-sectarians rarely care what sectarians think about them.[5] This is not to say that Pharisees were completely without admirers or influence among the general populace. Nor is it *impossible* that the Pharisees both shunned fellowship with outsiders and were the heroes of the common

---

dichotomy among scholars in S.J.D. Cohen's 'The Significance of Yavneh: Pharisees, Rabbis, and the End of Jewish Sectarianism', *HUCA* 55 (1984), pp. 30-31; G. Porton, 'Diversity in Postbiblical Judaism', in Kraft and Nickelsburg, *Early Judaism* , pp. 69-70; H. Maccoby, *Early Rabbinic Writings* (Cambridge: Cambridge University Press, 1988), pp. 12-16.

1. E.P. Sanders, *Jesus and Judaism* (Philadelphia: Fortress Press, 1985), p. 193.

2. Sanders argues his position *contra* Neusner in *Jesus and Judaism*, p. 388 n. 59. See further the criticism of Sanders's views on the Pharisees by P.S. Alexander in his review of *Jesus and Judaism* (*JJS* 37 [1986], pp. 103-106). Alexander describes Sanders as 'vague' on the real role and identity of the Pharisees and points out that Sanders leaves them in a 'sociological limbo' (p. 104).

3. Jeremias, *JTTJ*, cf. p. 247 to p. 266.

4. Schürer, *HJP*, II, p. 400.

5. Would the masses of Israel been particularly disturbed about their excommunication by the Essenes (see Simon, *Jewish Sects*, p. 13) or a non-Pharisee about the exclusivist mind-set of the Pharisee?

people. But it would seem that the two notions are, if not mutually exclusive, at least very much contradictory. The sectarian's way of life must inevitably have isolated him or her from the non-sectarian Jew.

The exact nature of Pharisaism in this period will remain a matter of debate for some time. The final resolution of the problems must await a complete form- and redaction-critical treatment of the rabbinic sources concerned.[1] But for the present the Pharisees are best viewed as a small 'sect' who did not rule religious life in the time of Jesus but were one voice among many competing for the allegiance of the common Jew. They were not a monolithic 'official' presence in Palestinian society in Jesus' day.[2]

Form and Method of Religious Expression in Early Judaism

The diversity inherent in early Judaism shows that the picture of Jesus as one standing alone against an 'orthodox' Judaism of his time is unrealistic. It is doubtful whether the term 'orthodox' can even be applied to any facet of Judaism in this period. Furthermore, Jesus' voice was not the only one raised in a call summoning followers to a particular path.[3] This is not to say there was nothing extraordinary about his teaching and deeds; that is not the issue here. What is under consideration is the relationship that might have existed between Jesus and one particular group, the Pharisees. Thus it is at least necessary to ask what he might have had in common with these fellow religionists. I will not single out views of Torah or eschatology or some other specific doctrine to compare Jesus with his contemporaries. Instead, I

---

1.   A task only begun by Neusner's study of the traditions about the Pharisees before 70 already quoted above.

2.   This would be true in particular of Galilee, as Sean Freyne's recent discussion of the subject shows. See the chapter 'Galilean Religious Affiliations in the First Century', in *Galilee, Jesus and the Gospels* (Philadelphia: Fortress Press, 1988), pp. 176-218, esp. pp. 207, 212; and G. Vermes, 'Jesus and Galilee', in *Jesus the Jew* (Philadelphia: Fortress Press, 1973), pp. 42-57, esp. p. 57. The Galileans were not, however, unconcerned about Jewish observance; again Freyne, *Galilee*, pp. 186, 190, 200. See further E.M. Meyers, 'The Cultural Setting of Galilee; The Case of Regionalism and Early Judaism', *ANRW*, II.19.1, pp. 686-701 and Oppenheimer, *The 'Am Ha-aretz*, pp. 200-17.

3.   E.g. Acts 5.35-37.

will look more generally to the methods and forms of religious expression current at that time and consider Jesus' use of them; in regard to his teaching method Jesus was very much a part of the ways of his time.

Two modes of expression in Jewish oral law in this period were halakhah and haggadah.[1] These categories are, of course, those of the rabbinic literature but we adopt them here as methods of religious expression which, if not fully developed in the pre-70 period, certainly had their roots there.[2] Midrash was a third method of exposition of the oral law but this is best understood as a sub-category of halakhah and haggadah since it was essentially a method, i.e. the exegetical method, of arriving at halakhic and haggadic material.[3]

The definition of halakhah offered by Jacob Neusner will serve as our initial guide to the importance and function of halakhic tradition:

> A legal, or halakhic, tradition is a saying or story about the way something is to be done, a statement intended to have practical effect and carry

---

1.   Neusner offers these two categories with midrashic exegesis viewed as a sub-category of haggadah (*Pharisees*, III, p. 43); likewise in the definition of oral law, M. Herr, 'Agadah', *ETal*, I, p. 168. Others, however, prefer three categories. So Safrai: halakhah, haggadah and midrash (*The Jewish People*, II, p. 959) and Moore: halakhah, midrash halakhah and midrash haggadah (*Judaism*, I, p. 132). Perhaps J. Bowker put the difference most clearly: 'Midrash describes the way in which both sorts of material were collected together by being attached to the text of scripture' (*The Targums and Rabbinic Literature* [Cambridge: Cambridge University Press, 1969], p. 40).

2.   With regard to halakhah we have the effort of Neusner to extract a picture of the Pharisees from the pre-70 halakhic prescriptions. His method is based mainly on sayings with attribution to pre-70 sages, Neusner believing that it is impossible to date unattributed sayings with any degree of certainty. Nevertheless, halakhic sayings clearly date from the pre-70 period. Haggadic sayings are often without attribution in the rabbinic corpus but that does not mean such material cannot at times be very old (Maccoby, *ERW*, p. 14). Style is often the only indicator. Although it lacks a healthy suspicion of rabbinic attribution, the article by Bernard Bamberger is still valuable ('The Dating of Aggadic Material', *JBL* 67 (1949), pp. 115-23, esp. p. 121.)

3.   So M. Herr, 'Midrash', *EncJud*, XI, p. 1507. See also J. Newman, *Halachic Sources: From the Beginning to the Ninth Century* (Leiden: Brill, 1969), p. 14 and the helpful explanation of the development of the term 'Midrash' offered by Maccoby, *ERW*, pp. 22-25.

normative authority, or an inquiry into the logic or legal principle behind
such a rule.[1]

The development of halakhah was always in accordance with majority
rule[2] and its concern was to form binding judgments about matters not
expressly addressed in the text of Scripture. It sought to establish fixed
forms of observance which would settle matters of ordinary life in
strict fidelity to the law. As such, it carried legal force and a normative authority.[3] It is important to appreciate that the process by which
it developed was a disputational one. The ruling of a certain Rabbi
would be quoted as precedent and then modified or contradicted by
another. Eventually, the view of one or the other would gain prece-
dence. Two processes were at work simultaneously: (1) the addition of
new regulations from exegesis, and (2) the ongoing fermentation of
new traditions which revised or supplanted older practices. In this
way rabbinic Judaism was able from its earliest days to adapt itself to
the changing life situation of Jewish society.[4]

Halakhah is entirely precautionary in principle. Its main purpose is
to prevent the breaking of the law; thus the famous saying of *m. Ab.*
1.1: 'to set up a fence around the law'. The dietary laws of the Mishnah, for example, are given in order that one may not transgress the
rabbinic canons of ritual purity and tithing. Halakhah proscribes activity in order that the law may not be broken.[5]

Precision in the definition of haggadah is more difficult to attain and
we survey several attempts to define it.[6] Some explain it quite nar-

---

1.   Neusner, *Pharisees*, III, p. 5.

2.   For example, *b. Shab.* 39b, 'Wherever you find two (scholars) differing and
a third one tipping the balance (in favour of one of them), the Halakhah is according
to the words of the one tipping the balance'.

3.   Stephen Westerholm has coined an apt phrase for the halakhoth when he calls
them a 'statutory codification of the divine will' (*Jesus and Scribal Authority* [Lund:
Gleerup, 1978], pp. 79-80). On the authority of halakhah see Maccoby, *ERW*, p.
20.

4.   This is the process as set out by Schürer; see 'Halakhah and Haggadah',
HJP, II, pp. 339-55. See further the discussion by Maccoby, *ERW*, pp. 8, 17-22.

5.   It is clear that the discussion of halakhah cannot go far in relation to our
current subject without attempting to establish the extent to which the halakhoth of
the rabbinic literature pertain to the pre-70 period. The issue will be dealt with more
directly in Chapter 2 where some actual texts will be treated.

6.   The word 'haggadah' may derive from the Aramaic $n^e gad$, meaning 'to

rowly as mere story telling or fanciful exegesis;[1] but while haggadah certainly includes this aspect it is not a comprehensive description. It is more common to define haggadah very broadly as that which is 'non-halakhic' or 'non-legal'. J. Newman defines haggadah this way: 'Every aspect that finds its way into the general store of folklore, including conduct; anything, in fact, that is not strictly legal and contained in talmudic literature, is referred to as Aggada'. It may be 'of an ethical, homiletic, moral and legendary nature' and 'covers mainly post-biblical sayings and legends'.[2]

The purpose of haggadah is didactic and it is concerned with 'moral and ethical teachings dealing with the problems of faith and the art of living'.[3] This basic view of the nature of haggadah is seen in the following definition:

> Haggadah is hard to define precisely since it ranges over a number of areas: theology, religious philosophy, ethics, practical wisdom, historical legend, biblical non-halakic exegesis, speculations on messianic times, etc. In general, it comprises all aspects of the oral Law which are not Halakah.[4]

The development of haggadah was not bound by rigid methods. Two elements combined in the realm of the doctrinal to produce haggadic material. The first was a study of Scripture that derived a theology from imaginative exegesis, allegorical exposition and interpreta-

flow', i.e. haggadah 'causes the hearts of men to flow' and be attracted to God and Torah; Herr, 'Agadah', *ETal*, I, p. 169; cf. *t. Hag.* 14a. More often it is said to derive from the Hebrew form of the same three radicals meaning 'declare, expound, make known' (BDB, p. 616) or perhaps from the Hebrew *'aggâdâh/haggâdâh* meaning 'narrative' (Herr, 'Aggadah', *EncJud*, I, p. 354).

1.   E.g. Samuel Sandmel in his article 'The Haggadah within Scripture', *JBL* 80 (1961), p. 110. Sandmel sets the whole question of biblical sources in a different and provocative light when he suggests that what appear to be different sources for variant traditions in both OT and NT actually are haggadic re-tellings of a single source (p. 114).

2.   *Halachic Sources*, p. 14. So also H. Strack, *Introduction to Talmud and Midrash* (New York: Atheneum, 1969), p. 7; see also Bowker, *The Targums*, p. 48.

3.   Herr, 'Aggadah', *EncJud*, I, pp. 356ff.

4.   Safrai, *The Jewish People*, II, p. 959. So also Neusner: 'An aggadic tradition is a saying or story about a moral, theological, or historical matter, without direct legal consequence, bearing no immediate, practical effect, and carrying no normative authority' (*Pharisees*, III, p. 43).

tion by analogy to other Scripture. The second was a more free-wheeling supplementation of scriptural material with original material.[1] It is important to appreciate the non-systematic nature of haggadic exposition and the lack of impetus to produce an organized 'theology'. The purpose of haggadah was not to establish a doctrinal orthodoxy but to inspire and energize the faith of the ordinary believer.[2] It is to this category that the teaching style of Jesus should be assigned.

The differences between halakhic and haggadic forms of religious expression are readily evident. They advance on entirely different forms of appeal. Halakhah seeks to establish itself as normative and is expressed in disputational pericopae that conclude with a normative ruling. It is essentially legal in nature and purpose. On the other hand, haggadah encompasses a very broad scope of religious interests and is free to range over a wide landscape of theological, exegetical and historical issues. It does not claim normative authority but relies on its own moral and persuasive content to present its message. Thus we see that within the complex of early Judaism there were two modes of religious expression that were constituent parts of a single religious perspective.

The importance of the distinction between halakhah and haggadah becomes clear when the spheres of life in which they were promulgated are considered. A commitment to strict observance of halakhic prescriptions would, of necessity, affect every aspect of one's daily life. This would have been true of a Pharisee in Jesus' day. When halakhic canons were to be observed about the purity of food or the avoidance of impurity in general, a simple excursion into the market place could become a matter fraught with complexity. Such concerns

---

1. As Schürer puts it, 'The free creations of phantasy linked up with the results of learned enquiry. . . This investigative and continuously creative theological activity, extending over the whole field of religion and ethics, gave to the religious ideas of Israel in the inter-Testamental era a stamp of imagination on the one hand and of scholasticism on the other' (*HJP*, II, p. 352). It is this haggadic philosophy which underlies the corpus of inter-testamental literature with its legend, wisdom, eschatology and apocalypse. Thus, there is an underlying unity between the largely halakhic rabbinic Judaism and the more haggadically oriented inter-testamental literature. They are, in form and philosophy, two different expressions of a single religious sytem.

2. See Maccoby, *ERW*, pp. 21-22.

could even extend to the sphere of the family since not all would necessarily undertake the same obligations of observance.

Haggadah, on the other hand, was religion for the masses. Maccoby describes the difference between halakhah and haggadah as that between schoolhouse and synagogue. Haggadah was the main element in synagogue homiletics[1] and popular teaching whereas halakhic teaching was the province of the sages and their inner circles of disciples; the latter was technical in nature and content, the former easily accessible and popular.[2] It was haggadah which nourished the non-sectarian[3] and the forms in which it was presented were those that were readily understandable to all; parables, allegories, metaphors, aphorisms, prayers and polemic.[4] These were of course the teaching tools of Jesus.

Jesus and the Haggadah

While consideration of the 'halakhah' occurs with some frequency in discussions of Jesus and the Pharisees, it is surprising that the concept of haggadah has had comparatively little mention.[5] Haggadah is cer-

1. Maccoby (*ERW*, pp. 19-20) claims that preaching was organized around the Jewish calender; see also Safrai, *The Jewish People*, II, pp. 932-33, 959, and A. Finkel, 'The Pericopes' Text and the Homily', in *The Pharisees and the Teacher of Nazareth* (Leiden: Brill, 1964), pp. 149-55.

2. Finkel, *The Pharisees*, pp. 149-55. In *b. Sot.* 40a two rabbis are lecturing, one on halakhah and one on haggadah and the gemara tells how the former lost his audience to the latter!

3. 'In aggadic thoughts and expositions the masses found comfort and became fortified to bear their lot with courage and hope. Aggada therefore became an important factor in Jewish life and served as a vital pillar for Jewish survival' (Newman, *Halachic Sources*, p. 33).

4. Newman, *Halachic Sources*. See also Bowker, *The Targums,* pp. 40-47. Also, Brad Young has noted, 'Not everyone could have appreciated or understood the technicalities of halachic instruction but agadic teaching had wide appeal that could speak to the less educated and yet often would also engage the mind of the scholar. . . ' (*Jesus and his Jewish Parables* [New York: Paulist Press, 1989], pp. 3-4).

5. For example, Joseph Klausner in his classic Jewish treatment of Jesus in *Jesus of Nazareth* (London: Allen & Unwin, 1925; reprint 1947), pp. 259-72, places Jesus within Judaism as the 'Pharisaic "Rabbi"' whose parables were so attractive' (p. 276) but he never makes a connection to haggadah. So also a more modern

tainly the proper category in which to place the ethical and parabolic
instruction of Jesus and as a teacher it seems likely that he would have
been a recognizable figure within the context of his own time: a haggadist *par excellence*.[1] Indeed, Brad Young in his recent book, *Jesus
and his Jewish Parables*, calls Jesus a 'master of the agadah'.[2]

Jewish treatment, Geza Vermes's *Jesus the Jew*, says, 'Since halakhah became the
corner-stone of rabbinic Judaism, it is not surprising that despite their popular
religious appeal, Jesus, Hanina, and the others, were slowly but surely squeezed out
beyond the pale of true respectability' (p. 82). Jesus is a representative of
'charismatic Judaism' but Vermes never discusses halakhah and haggadah. One may
search modern 'new quest' books with a similar result. See Bornkamm, *Jesus of
Nazareth*, pp. 100-109; B. Meyer, *The Aims of Jesus*, pp. 149-53. In his discussion
of Jesus as a religious type in *Jesus and Judaism*, pp. 237-40, E.P. Sanders never
broaches the subject of this important distinction. Stephen Westerholm in his chapter
'Jesus and the Sages of the Halakhah' (*Jesus and Scribal Authority*, pp. 126-32)
rather disappointingly fails to describe Jesus as an haggadist even though he
describes the haggadic approach accurately (esp. p. 130). In Sean Freyne's treatment
of Jesus as a 'type' (*Galilee, Jesus and the Gospels*, p. 260), he all but describes the
haggadist when he says Jesus' wisdom had 'folk and gnomic as well as aphoristic
qualities which are rooted in human experience. . . ' But surprisingly, Freyne
continues, 'Jesus fits none of the recognized teaching types in Judaism. . . ' (p.
261).
    1.   Haggadah had its specialists but the rabbinic portrayal of Yohanan ben Zakkai
as a master of both halakhah and haggadah was perhaps the ideal. See Neusner's *A
Life of Rabban Yohanan ben Zakkai* (Leiden: Brill, 1962), p. 26; cf. also *b. San.*
38b.
    2.   B. Young, *Jesus and his Jewish Parables*, p. 3. In his extensive book on the
subject of the nature of Jesus' parables, D. Flusser has asserted, 'Die Gleichnisse
Jesu gehören zweifellos zur Gattung jüdischer Gleichnisse. . . [sie] gehören zum
älteren, klassichen Typus der jüdischen Gleichnisse, der auch nach der Zeit Jesu
weiter gepflegt wurde' (*Die rabbinischen Gleichnisse und der Gleichniserzähler
Jesus* [Bern: Peter Lang, 1981], pp. 11, 14). Similarly, see also B.B. Scott, *Hear
Then the Parable* (Minneapolis, MN: Fortress Press, 1989), pp. 7-19. Two older
scholars made the direct connection between Jesus and haggadah: Leo Baeck,
'Haggadah was the common ground and inevitably the battle ground between
Christians and Jews' ('Haggadah and Christian Doctrine', *HUCA* 23 [1950], p.
557); and Samuel Cohen, 'The Place of Jesus in the Religious Life of his Day', *JBL*
48 (1929): 'As a Haggadist, too, he was listened to with great joy. The Haggadists
were great favorites with the people' (p. 95; also p. 108). Between these older views
and those very recently expressed I have found few attempts to characterize Jesus'
teaching along haggadic lines. The parables of Jesus were certainly not, as Jeremias
asserted, 'something entirely new' (*The Parables of Jesus* [trans. S.H. Hooke;

An example of how halakhic and haggadic teaching combine in the New Testament has been proposed by David Daube.[1] The fourfold question format of Mk 12.13-37a (Mt. 22.23-46; Lk. 20.27-44 and 10.25-28) resembles that of the Passover Haggadah and *b. Nid.* 69bff. All portray four questions based on an interest in: (1) halakhah; (2) a *boruth*, 'vulgarity', a question designed to embarrass a teacher; (3) a question of *derekh eretz*, principles of a moral life; (4) haggadah, in this case a non-legal question of a seeming contradiction in Scripture. In Mark we have: (1) the halakhic question of the legality of paying tribute to Caesar (Mk 12.13-17); (2) the mocking question of the woman with seven husbands in the resurrection, a *boruth* (Mk 12.18-27); (3) the question of the Great Commandment, an example of *derekh eretz* (Mk 12.28-34); (4) the non-legal/haggadic question of the identity of David's son (Mk 12.35-37).[2] With regard to the question of paying taxes to Caesar, Jesus answers the question, not like a lawyer, but like a haggadic master with non-legal, aphoristic language: 'Render to Caesar the things that are Caesar's, and to God the things that are God's'. For Jesus the question is not to be answered on a legal basis, but on considerations of a higher, cosmic nature.[3] In the question of the woman with seven husbands, Jesus answers with the characteristic doctrinal freedom of the haggadist. The answer is independent of any appeal to canonical Scripture, 'For when they rise from the dead, they neither marry nor are given in marriage'. This example may teach us more about the method which governed the Marcan redaction of these traditions than the agenda of Jesus; nevertheless, it is an interesting example of how haggadah and halakhah combine in the Gospel record. If this way of teaching is indeed characteristic of Jesus then his style leans to the haggadic.

The point of this attempt to connect Jesus to the methods of reli-

London: SCM Press, 1963], p. 12).

1. D. Daube, *The New Testament and Rabbinic Judaism* (London: The Athlone Press, 1956), pp. 158-69.

2. Notice that the four questions of Mark are separated from the Last Supper narrative only by the Olivet Discourse. Thus the connection of the fourfold format to the Passover Haggadah may indeed have been in the author's mind.

3. See further Klaus Wengst's interesting treatment of this passage. He also observes that this statement by Jesus is not a legal ruling on the Roman *imperium* (*Pax Romana and the Peace of Jesus Christ* [trans. J. Bowden; London: SCM Press, 1987], pp. 58-59).

gious expression of his own time is to show that he should not be seen as one who brought a new approach to religion;[1] rather, he was part of the middle stream of his time in terms of method. This fact should have a profound impact on how we view the reports of Jesus' conflict with Pharisees in the Gospels. Disputation among competing segments of that religious milieu was the norm not the exception, and determining who was 'right/wrong' or 'in/out' was no simple matter. The question always remains, 'right or wrong in comparison to what standard?' In the Gospels the 'Pharisees' and 'sinners' cannot be taken at face value as terms which lead to a definitive description of the complex religious milieu in which Jesus lived (as my later chapters will also confirm). The view of early Judaism as full of vitality, disputation and various modes of religious expression should govern our thinking about this period. Jesus was one participant in an ongoing and vigorous public debate about the proper direction and emphasis of Judaism in his day.

Yavneh and the Gospels

Other factors must be taken into account as we consider the portrayal of the Pharisees in the Gospels. There can be little doubt that the emergence of the Pharisees as the dominant force at Yavneh in the wake of the destruction of the Temple influenced the way the Gospels (at least the later ones, Matthew, Luke and John) portrayed the Pharisees.[2] This is probably part of the answer to the question of why the Pharisees are singled out as the main adversaries of Jesus during his public ministry.[3] The Gospel writers were, after all, attempting to

---

1.   In Jesus' teaching we can speak of 'distinctiveness but not uniqueness' (Scott, *Hear Then the Parable*, pp. 14ff.).

2.   See the section 'Luke's Pharisees', Chapter 4, for the way in which Matthew and Luke tend to introduce the Pharisees into controversy stories over against Mark.

3.   See the Jewish scholars I. Abrahams, *SPG*, p. xxii and J. Lauterbach, 'The Pharisees and their Teachings', *HUCA* 6 (1929), pp. 72-75, for two very apt and early representations of this view. Lauterbach says: 'But the Gospel writers, knowing no other Jewish leaders and teachers than those of the Pharisee group of their own times imagined that the conditions of their own times also prevailed in the times of Jesus' (p. 74). For a more recent argumentation of the attribution of controversy stories to a church setting see A. Hultgren, *Jesus and his Adversaries* (Minneapolis, MN: Augsburg, 1979), esp. pp. 86-87; also E.P. Sanders, *Jesus and*

present a convincing message, not a historically balanced view of Pharisaism in the modern sense. This refraction of the historical perspective at the point of the written Gospel has been compounded for the modern interpreter by another entirely independent factor: the biases of the corpus of early rabbinic Judaism itself.

While many of the traditions of the Mishnah pre-date the destruction of the Temple, it was nevertheless formulated and finally redacted in the post-destruction period under the influence of first the Yavnean and then the Ushan academies. Yet the Mishnah presents itself as the unrivalled representative of Judaism from the earliest times. *M. Aboth* ch. 1, for example, represents the history of the Jewish people in terms of a continuous line of development from Moses at Sinai to Rabban Simeon b. Gamaliel.[1] The rabbis saw themselves as preserving and expanding the very law of Moses, even when Torah made no comment on the subject of their traditions.[2]

The view of Judaism presented in the Mishnah has several distinct characteristics. The Mishnah is a halakhic document; a compilation of halakhic disputations that sought to overcome decades of controversy from the pre-70 period.[3] In the wake of the destruction of the Temple, Judaism entered a time of consolidation and retrenchment, and the absence of a central cultus brought about a strong impetus for a new centre of authority. The normalization of halakhic observance met this need and the academy at Yavneh undertook the task of turning Judaism to a new focus.[4] Eventually the primacy of halakhic observance

---

Judaism, p. 264.

1. See also *m. Yad.* 4.3; there R. Eliezer says, 'for I have received a tradition from Rabban Johanan b. Zakkai, who heard it from his teacher, and his teacher from his teacher, as a Halakhah given to Moses from Sinai. . . '

2. On this see further Bruce Chilton, *A Galilean Rabbi and his Bible* (Wilmington, DE: Michael Glazier, 1984), pp. 22-23, especially his treatment of *b. Men.* 29b. See also P.S. Alexander, *Textual Sources for the Study of Judaism* (Manchester: Manchester University Press, 1984), pp. 1-2.

3. Especially between the traditions of the houses of Hillel and Shammai (Neusner, *Pharisees*, II, p. 4).

4. Thus in *m. Ab.* 3.12 a saying attributed to R. Eleazar of Modiim at about the time of the Bar Cochba revolt says that if a man 'discloses meanings in the Law which are not according to the Halakhah, even though a knowledge of the Law and good works are his, he has no share in the world to come'. Rabbi Eliezer ben Hyrcanus, the distinguished pupil of Yohanan ben Zakkai, was excommunicated for failing to adhere to the Yavnean line on halakhah (see J. Neusner, *A Life of Rabban*

as the religious method of choice became canonized in the final redaction of the Mishnah. For a time all other forms of religious observance and literature fell by the wayside, at least in terms of any sort of representation in the literature of early rabbinic Judaism.[1] It is remarkable that, with the exception of Jesus ben Sirach, the great quantity of apocryphal and pseudepigraphic literature of Judaism is nowhere referred to in the whole of the rabbinic literature.[2] The Mishnah tells us nothing of other influential strains of religious thinking prevalent in the Judaism of the late Second Temple period nor does it relate anything of substance about various views on the canon, doctrine, other sects, the messiah or the tumultuous politics of the period.[3] The Mishnah's almost sole concern with halakhah has obscured our perceptions of what Judaism was like before 70 CE. The omission of much of the variety and diversity inherent in Judaic religion in the pre-70 period by the early rabbinical schools has made more difficult the task of reconstructing the richness, colour and vitality that must have surely characterized the Judaism of Jesus' day.

How has this affected the reading of the Gospels? It has been presumed that the Mishnah's self-portrait as normative halakhic Judaism was fully representative of Judaism not only in the time of the Mishnah but that of Jesus as well. The Pharisees, as the authors of early rabbinic Judaism, have thus been thought of as also representing a 'normative', almost solely halakhic religion in Jesus' day. The Gospel portrait of the Pharisees as the pre-eminent religionists of the day who are often adamant about seemingly minor points of observance has dovetailed with the halakhic agenda of the Mishnah and the exalted

Johanan ben Zakkai, pp. 177-79). Urbach observes, 'The supervision of Halakhic decision, introduced by Rabban Gamaliel, led him not only to denounce severely the Sages who continued to stand for freedom in Halakhic ruling, but even to punish them' (*Sages*, pp. 600-601, 604).

1.   The study of haggadah probably never ceased but was officially frowned upon. Even in the third century some Amoraim prohibited the study of haggadah thinking it might lead to neglect of the halakhah (*y. Ber.* 3.4). Even so, one third of the Babylonian Talmud is haggadic.

2.   Herford, *The Pharisees*, pp. 179, 185. *M. San.* 10.1 reads, 'These are they that have not share in the world to come:. . . he that reads the heretical books'. This is probably a reference to at least portions of that literature which we now call 'intertestamental'. See Rabin, in Safrai and Stern, *The Jewish People*, I, p. 1015.

3.   Neusner, *Pharisees*, III, pp. 247-48, 304-305.

status it accords itself. As a result there has been a tendency to think that we know very well who the Pharisees of Jesus' day were and the nature of their importance relative to Judaism in general. But neither the widespread practice of rabbinic halakhoth nor the position of the Pharisees as a central authority can be assumed for the pre-70 period. When this is taken together with an appreciation of the inherent polemical bias of the Gospel material itself it becomes apparent that the role of the Pharisees in Jesus' day was probably much less prominent and clear-cut than the Gospels themselves would lead us to believe. Our assessment of the conflict between Jesus and the Pharisees in the Gospel of Luke must take these realities into account and an appreciation of the difficulties will help us cast a more critical eye on the Gospel portrait of the religious milieu in which Jesus ministered.

Chapter 2

THE *'AM HA-ARETZ*:
TITHING AND THE PURITY OF FOOD

The material in Luke's Gospel which speaks of 'sinners' is dominated by Jesus' conflict with the Pharisees over the issue of table-fellowship and the general impropriety of associating with 'toll collectors and sinners'. 'Why. . .' the Pharisees enquire, 'do you eat with toll collectors and sinners?' (Lk 5.31; cf. 7.33ff., 15.1-2, 19.7). The full treatment of this theme in Luke's Gospel will be reserved for Part II;[1] suffice it to say here that the subject is of considerable importance in chs. 5–19 of Luke. As a prologue to that discussion it is first necessary to consider one aspect of the background and origin of the supposed offence given by Jesus' activities in this area. What exactly was the offence caused by Jesus' association at table with these 'sinners?' Is there a reasonable historical explanation for the phenomenon as it arises in the Gospels? Since discussions of this subject often make reference to the concept of the *'ammei ha-aretz* ('the people of the land'), we now turn our attention to this aspect of the question.

The *'am ha-aretz*[2] (the singular form, meaning 'a person of the

---

1. See esp. Chapter 5 below.
2. See the modern treatments: Aharon Oppenheimer, *The 'Am Ha-aretz: A Study in the Social History of the Jewish People in the Hellenistic-Roman Period* (Leiden: Brill, 1977); I. Landman, ''Am Ha-aretz', in *The Universal Jewish Encyclopedia*, I, pp. 215-17; Urbach, *The Sages*, pp. 584-88, 632-39; Safrai, *The Jewish People*, II, pp. 794, 819-21, 923; C.G. Montefiore, *Rabbinic Literature and Gospel Teachings* (New York: Ktav, 1970), pp. 6-15; G. Alon, *Jews, Judaism and the Classical World* (trans. I. Abrahams; Jerusalem: Magnes Press, 1977), pp. 207-16; I. Abrahams, ''Am Ha-aretz', in C. Montefiore, *The Synoptic Gospels*, II (London: Macmillan, 1927), pp. 647-69; C. Rabin, 'The Novitiate', pp. 1-21. Strack and Billerbeck have an extensive treatment of the rabbinic texts in their treatment of Jn 7.49 (*Kommentar zum Neuen Testament aus Talmud und Midrasch* [Munich: Beck, 1924], pp. 494-519). Some of the older 'sociological' treatments

land') is the outcast, the 'sinner' if you will, of the rabbinic corpus. The imprecations against the *'am ha-aretz* reflect the various meanings the term can convey. In some contexts it refers to their lack of Torah learning and neglect of the sages. At other times it is a term of reference for those who display a lack of piety and religious concern in general; something like the modern term 'boor'. Quite often however, the term *'ammei ha-aretz* refers to those who fail to observe sectarian standards of of tithing and purity.[1] This last meaning is the primary concern in this chapter.

The table had special significance among Jewish sectarians as the focal point for the extension of priestly purity into the whole of life.[2] This involved a commitment to the scrupulous tithing of food and, for some, the consumption of ordinary meals in a state of ritual purity normally required only of the priesthood.[3] More generally, there was a widespread belief in the ancient world that communion at table represented an expression of intimate fellowship; thus one's table companions were always a matter of concern.[4] In the rabbinic literature the *'ammei ha-aretz* are those with whom the scrupulous (*haberim*) should avoid contact in such matters.

now seem less useful, but see S. Zeitlin, 'The 'Am Ha-aretz', *JQR* 23 (1932), pp. 45-61; Herford, *The Pharisees*, I, pp. 24-37. The *'ammei ha-aretz* as known in the Old Testament is a subject area largely unrelated to the enquiry here; see e.g. E.W. Nicholson, 'The Meaning of *'Am Ha-aretz* in the Old Testament', *JSS* 10 (1965), pp. 59-66; A. Gunneweg, ''Am Ha-aretz—A Semantic Revolution', *ZAW* 95 (1983), pp. 437-40.

1. See the summary of meanings and associated texts in Strack–Billerbeck, *Kommentar*, II, pp. 494ff.

2. The Pharisees, says Neusner, 'were primarily a society for table-fellowship, the high point of their life as a group' (*Pharisees*, III, p. 318). Late Second Temple Pharisaism was a 'cult-centred piety, which proposes to replicate the cult in the home, and thus to effect the Temple's purity laws at the table of the ordinary Jew, and quite literally turn Israel into a "kingdom of priests and a holy nation"' (Neusner, 'The Formation of Rabbinic Judaism: Yavneh from A.D. 70 to 100', in *ANRW*, II.19.2, p. 23). See also M. Borg, *Conflict, Holiness and Politics in the Teachings of Jesus* (New York: The Edwin Mellon Press, 1984), pp. 80-81.

3. Borg, *Conflict, Holiness and Politics*, pp. 80-81; see also *m. Dem.* 2.2-3.

4. See further below, Chapter 5.

The 'Am Ha-aretz *and the New Testament*

The importance of table-fellowship in Luke and the Gospel tradition in general is paralleled by an overarching concern with the same topic in the early rabbinic literature. This commonality of interest has often led scholars to interpret New Testament conflict between Pharisees and Jesus over the 'sinners' in the light of rabbinic teaching on table-fellowship.

Some scholars feel the conflict between the Pharisees and *'ammei ha-aretz* in the rabbinic literature best explains the protests which Jesus' fellowship with 'sinners' aroused among the Pharisees in the Gospels. Joachim Jeremias, for example, held that the 'masses' in the time of Jesus were equivalent to the *'ammei ha-aretz* of the rabbinic literature. In the opinion of the Pharisees, according to Jeremias, these people did not observe religious laws to an acceptable standard. The Pharisees 'drew a hard line' between themselves and the *'ammei ha-aretz*[1] and believed that 'access to salvation' was blocked for such people.[2] It was to these ostracized 'masses' that Jesus made his appeal. In effect, for Jeremias, the non-Pharisee was an *'am ha-aretz* and an *'am ha-aretz* was excluded from salvation (that is, was a 'sinner') in the view of the Pharisees as the ruling religious elite.[3] But the problem does not end there. A further confusion arose when Jeremias then equated the 'sinners' of the Gospel tradition with the *'ammei ha-aretz*. Jeremias goes on, 'the people as a whole' (now understood as the *'ammei ha-aretz*) accepted the 'yoke of a contempt based on religious superiority. . . To this desire we may trace, partly at least, the motive to follow Jesus among those who "travailed" and were "heavy laden", were the "publicans" and "sinners"'.[4] In moving between references

1. Jeremias, *JTTJ*, pp. 259, 266-67; so also H.F. Weiss, 'Φαρισαῖος', *TDNT*, IX, p. 19: 'they saddled this non-Pharisaic majority with the uncomplimentary name of 'Am ha-'Ares'.

2. J. Jeremias, *New Testament Theology: The Proclamation of Jesus* (trans. J. Bowden; London: SCM Press, 1971), p. 112.

3. Jeremias, *JTTJ*, p. 259: the 'masses, the *'am ha-aretz*. . . did not observe the demands of religious laws as they [the Pharisees] did, and in contrast to whom the Pharisees considered themselves to be the true Israel'.

4. Jeremias, *JTTJ*, p. 267. For another early expression of this thinking see W.H. Raney, 'Who Were the "Sinners"?', *JR* 10 (1930), pp. 578-91. Montefiore held that the 'sinners' of the Gospels were 'similar' if not identical to the rabbinic class of the *'am ha-aretz* (*The Synoptic Gospels*, II [London: Macmillan, 1927], p.

to the 'people as a whole' on the one hand and the 'sinners' on the other, Jeremias blurred the lines between the 'people', the *'ammei ha-aretz* and the 'sinners'. The net effect was that Jesus' mission was understood by Jeremias as a call for the liberation of the masses (who were all 'sinners') from Pharisaic oppression, a mission which was one of 'unparalleled risk'.[1] Nor has this view been without influence in more recent years. One modern treatment of Jesus' relationship to his contemporaries contains this observation:

> The church from the beginning—from the original followers of Jesus on—was made up largely from 'people of the land' (*'am ha-aretz*) who were considered 'sinners' in the estimation of the Pharisees.[2]

E.P. Sanders, however, has dismantled the notion that Jesus addressed his message to a public which was despised and castigated as outcasts by the ruling religious elite.[3] The public did not, says Sanders, consist of yearning *'ammei ha-aretz* who felt themselves excluded from Israel. This conclusion is based on his belief that, (1) the Pharisees did not control religious life to the extent that they were able to exclude *anyone* from Israel, and (2) the Pharisees did not believe that all non-Pharisees were 'lost' but simply that they were not

668).

1.   Jeremias, *JTTJ*, p. 267; see also Jeremias, *New Testament Theology: The Proclamation of Jesus*, p. 118: Jesus' mission was a 'slap in the face to all the religious feelings of the time'.

2.   Hultgren, *Jesus and his Adversaries*, pp. 86-87. Comment on Jn 7.49 in particular has followed this line of thinking, largely due to Strack and Billerbeck's extensive excursus on the *'ammei ha-aretz* at this passage in their commentary (*Kommentar*, pp. 494ff.). See e.g. R.E. Brown, *The Gospel According to John*, I (Garden City: Doubleday, 1966), p. 325; G. Beasley-Murray, *John* (Waco, TX: Word Books, 1987), pp. 119-20. For examples in the treatment of Luke see W. Hendriksen, *The Gospel of Luke* (Edinburgh: The Banner of Truth Trust, 1978), p. 304; G.B. Caird, *The Gospel of St Luke* (London: A. & C. Black, 1968), pp. 95-96; W.F. Arndt, *St Luke* (St Louis: Concordia, 1956), pp. 167, 346. See also Isaac Landman, ''Am Ha-aretz', *UJE*, I, p. 217.

3.   See *Jesus and Judaism*, pp. 174-211. Sanders's discussion is convincing and need not be repeated here. Before Sanders this view was held by M. Smith ('A Comparison of Early Christian and Early Rabbinic Tradition', *JBL* 82 [1963], p. 171 and 'Palestinian Judaism in the First Century', p. 73). But Smith's application of the name *'am ha-aretz* to the 'masses' in Jesus' day is anachronistic. More recently, Sanders's view is supported by the work of Stephen Westerholm, *Jesus and Scribal Authority*, p. 70, and Maccoby, *ERW*, pp. 71, 95-96.

haberim. Both the first chapter of this study and subsequent findings here confirm Sanders's judgment on both points. Jeremias's view that Jesus' mission was the announcement of forgiveness for the masses in the face of Pharisaic opposition to their redemption must be laid aside.

Still, confusion persists as to whether the issue of table-fellowship and the general denigration of the 'sinner' in the Gospels by the Pharisees should be understood from the perspective of rabbinic utterances about the unobservant. Could not the concerns of purity, tithing and fellowship with respect to the *'ammei ha-aretz* still be the same root issues that are at stake in the Gospels? Is the cause of conflict the same in both bodies of literature? In order to answer this question we must first know who these *'ammei ha-aretz* were. Do they provide the key to understanding the 'sinners' of the Gospels? This is the question which brings us to a fresh examination of the rabbinic traditions about the *'ammei ha-aretz.*

The most extensive modern treatment of the rabbinic material on this subject is Aharon Oppenheimer's book, *The 'Am Ha-aretz.* His collection of the passages on the *'ammei ha-aretz* is exhaustive and the selection of texts for treatment here is, in part, indebted to that work. While Oppenheimer's book is an indispensable guide to the rabbinic literature on this topic, it suffers from several limitations in terms of its usefulness. First, there is almost no reference by Oppenheimer to work by modern non-Israeli scholarship in this area. Oppenheimer fails to connect his study to the general body of scholarship and this would have been its greatest value.[1] Also, Oppenheimer is somewhat 'traditionalist' with regard to dating and attribution of rabbinic materials.[2] He will often identify a tradition or tractate as 'early' without any supporting critical discussion. The problem of dating is notoriously difficult and we might have wished for a more substantive con-

---

1.   See the critique by G. Porton, 'Diversity in Postbiblical Judaism', in Kraft and Nickelsburg, *Early Judaism,* p. 70: 'he virtually ignores modern non-Israeli scholarship'. Hans G. Kippenberg (review of A. Oppenheimer's *'Am Ha-Aretz, JSJ* 9 [1978], pp. 230-31) also severely criticizes this aspect of Oppenheimer's book.

2.   Says Porton, 'he seems to ignore the possibility that the later rabbinic collections may not contain evidence of the same value as the earlier collections' ('Diversity'). Shayne D. Cohen (review of A. Oppenheimer's *'Am Ha-Aretz, JBL* 97 [1978], pp. 596-97) is almost scathing in his review of Oppenheimer on this point, describing his approach as guilty of a 'rabbinocentric bias'.

tribution from Oppenheimer in this respect.[1] The treatment of attributions in this analysis will generally follow the method of J. Neusner.
Neusner holds that attribution to a named master may be cautiously
considered as an indication of the general period of formulation of a
tradition.[2] It is not to be thought that an attribution necessarily pre-
serves the exact words of a rabbi or that the tradition was even composed by the named tradent. Neusner states, 'I do not believe we have
any way of verifying whether a person to whom a saying is attributed
actually said it'.[3] Nevertheless, when traditions are found in the
mouths of sages of various generations it is possible to trace a logical
development and so discover which material is earlier and which is
later.[4] The recovery of the *ipsissima verba* is not important for our

1.   There is no clearer statement of the fundamental problems occasioned by
dating and attribution in the rabbinic corpus than Neusner's response to Urbach's
book, *The Sages*, in the article, 'The Formation of Rabbinic Judaism: Yavneh
(Jamnia) from A.D. 70 to 100', in *ANRW*, II.19.2, pp. 3-16. See also P.S.
Alexander's 'Rabbinic Judaism and the New Testament', *ZNW* 74 (1983), pp. 237-
46; R. Booth's section entitled 'The Dating and Assessment of Rabbinic Material', in
Jesus and the Laws of Purity (Sheffield: JSOT Press, 1986), pp. 130-50; H.
Loewe's excursus in C.G. Montefiore and H. Loewe, *A Rabbinic Anthology*
(Cleveland: The World Publishing Company, 1963), pp. 707-13.
2.   Neusner says, 'The simplest possible hypothesis is that the attributions of
sayings to named authorities may be relied upon in assigning those sayings to the
period, broadly defined, in which said authorities flourished' ('The Formation of
Rabbinic Judaism', in *ANRW*, II.19.2, p. 14; see also pp. 8-16). For further details
on Neusner's methodology see Anthony J. Saldarini's '"Form-Criticism" of
Rabbinic Literature', *JBL* 96 (1977), pp. 263-69, and Booth, *Jesus and the Laws of
Purity*, pp. 137-40.
3.   Neusner, *ANRW*, II.19.2, pp. 13-14. By way of comparison, see Urbach
for the traditionalist 'philological-historical' approach to rabbinic exegesis (*Sages*,
pp. 17-18). He speaks of the 'elucidation of the sources on the basis of a reliable and
clarified text against the historic background in which they originated and grew' (p.
17).
4.   Neusner, *ANRW*, II.19.2, p. 14. In his book *From Politics to Piety*
(Englewood Cliffs, NJ: Prentice–Hall, 1973), Neusner says, 'After 70 AD traditions
about a man were shaped by his immediate disciples and discussed by people who
actually knew him. Remarks made out of context, in other settings, frequently
provide attestation that a living tradition of what a master had said and done was
shaped very soon after his death, and even during his lifetime. They often supply a
terminus ante quem. That does not mean the master actually said and did what the
disciples and later contemporaries claim, but it does mean we stand close to the mas-

purposes. However, when attribution occurs in a chain of tradition it can often serve as a general guide for dating. On the other hand, a tradition may be earlier than the time of the named master and dismissal of the possibility of mishnaic tradition containing pre-70 material must be avoided. Being too trusting of rabbinic attributions is no worse an error than dismissing their usefulness as a guide to dating altogether.

In any case, assertions about close dating are not of determinative importance here. To anticipate my findings, it will be seen that the understanding of the *'ammei ha-aretz* was never clearly defined *at any time*, even granting the complete reliability of attributions. Certain aspects of the rabbinic treatment of the *'ammei ha-aretz* do date from before the destruction. The point here, however, is that if the definition of the *'ammei ha-aretz* was uncertain in the post-70 period, then this must have been all the more so in the time of Jesus.

Tithing and the Purity of Food: General Considerations

Before turning to the rabbinic texts themselves it will be necessary to place our discussion on a firm footing with respect to the conflict over tithing and the observance of ritual purity between the *haberim* and the *'ammei ha-aretz*. Otherwise, the concept of the *'ammei ha-aretz* cannot be properly appreciated.

The concern over the issue of food in the rabbinic literature[1] must be understood by means of a basic distinction between the concerns over (1) tithing, and (2) the eating of all food in a state of ritual purity normally reserved for priests. One who undertakes to scrupulously observe tithing regulations is known as a *ne'eman* ('one who is

ter' (p. 42). So also H. Loewe, 'The Dating of Rabbinic Material', in Montefiore and Loewe, *A Rabbinic Anthology*, p. 713.

1.   The subject is the primary concern of the first division of the Mishnah entitled Zeraim and its equivalents in the Tosefta and Talmuds. Of the eleven tractates of Zeraim, the Babylonian Talmud has gemara only on the tractate Berakoth (Oaths) since the rules of tithing did not apply where it was composed, i.e. outside the land of Israel. *M. Kel.* 1.6: 'The Land of Israel is holier than any other land. Wherein lies its holiness? In that from it they may bring the Omer, the Firstfruits, and the Two Loaves, which they may not bring from any other land.' See also *b. Kidd.* 36b; *m. Dem.* 2.1; and the introduction to the Seder Zeraim in the Soncino edition of the Babylonian Talmud, pp. xix-xx.

trusted'—in Danby translated as 'trustworthy'). One who undertakes not only to tithe but also to eat their ordinary food in a state of ritual purity is known as a *ḥaber* (translated by Danby as 'Associate').[1] Both undertakings were supererogatory. The former because the separation of tithes was the obligation of the farmer, not the purchaser;[2] the latter because no biblical law commands the ordinary Jew to eat everyday food in ritual purity.

Tithing itself was, of course, a biblical injunction based on observance of the commandments found in Num. 18.8-32 and Lev. 27.30-33.[3] The presentation of the tithe to the priests was an integral part of the system established by God for the maintenance of the cult.

> And behold, I have given you [i.e. the priests] whatever is kept of the offerings made to me, all the consecrated things of the people of Israel; I have given them to you as a portion, and to your sons as a perpetual due.[4]

The tithes were made in five forms:

(1) The heave offering, or *terumah*, an amount that could be quite small, was usually about one sixtieth to one fortieth of the harvest.[5]

(2) The first tenth, which was originally given to the Levites, was given to the priests in the late Second Temple period. It was forbidden that the food of these first two tithes be consumed by any but the members of the priesthood.

(3) The *terumah* of the tithe was a tenth separated by the Levites and given to the priests (Num. 18.25).

(4) A second tenth was separated and was to be consumed in a state of ritual purity in Jerusalem at the time of one of the feasts in years one, two, four and five of the sabbatical cycle. This was the only biblical injunction to eat food in a ritually

---

1.   The distinction is based on *m. Dem.* 2.2-3; see the discussion below, 'The *'Am Ha-aretz* and Table-fellowship'. H. Maccoby's description of the distinction cannot be improved upon; see *ERW*, pp. 68ff.; see also Oppenheimer, *'Am Ha-aretz*, pp. 151ff.; Meyer, 'Φαρισαῖος', *TDNT*, IX, p. 18; Montefiore and Loewe, *A Rabbinic Anthology*, p. 138.

2.   Maccoby, *ERW*, p. 68.

3.   See Safrai, *The Jewish People*, II, pp. 818-25 for a complete treatment of the subject.

4.   Num. 18.8; cf. Deut. 18.4.

5.   *M. Ter.* 4.3; Deut. 26.1-4, 10; see also Maccoby, *ERW*, p. 97.

pure state that applied to all of Israel.[1] If the produce could
not be carried to Jerusalem it could be sold and the money
consecrated for the purchase of food when the pilgrim ar-
rived in the holy city.[2]

(5) In years three and six of the sabbatical cycle the second tithe
was designated the 'poor man's tithe' and distributed locally
(Deut. 14.28ff.; 26.12). In the seventh year of the sabbatical
cycle no tithes were due.

This state of affairs is reflected in the rabbinic injunctions that deal
with the legal basis for the 'suspicion' of the non-payment of tithes.
Obviously, there was no way to know if food offered for sale had
been properly tithed; and unless the merchant was considered
'trustworthy', the scrupulous regarded their produce as 'suspect' (i.e.
'demai').[3] Many of the *'ammei ha-aretz* did in fact separate tithes[4] but
the necessity of being sure meant that the scrupulous took a routinely
sceptical view. This is important because it demonstrates that this
tithing was a matter, not of biblical law for the non-farmer, but of
conscience for those who wished to be scrupulous.[5] To consider
someone as 'suspect' did not imply moral condemnation; it was simply
a way to ensure that one's own undertaking was not violated.

A merchant's produce was not suspect, however, with respect to all
the tithes and not all five needed to be separated from suspect produce.
The *terumah* was not suspect since this was a 'light exaction' and could
be satisfied by giving the priest a single grain of wheat.[6] Nor was anyone suspect with regard to the first tithe or the poor man's tithe. Le-
gally, it was incumbent upon the Levite or the poor person to prove
that these tithes had not been separated and they were presumed to
have been given until proven otherwise. Thus, only the *terumah* of the

1. See *m. Ma'as. S.* 1.1; 5.6-9; Deut. 12.17-18; 14.22-26; Safrai, *The Jewish
People*, II, pp. 818, 823-24.

2. Deut. 14.26; *m. Ma'as. S.* 3.3.

3. *M. Dem.* 2.2-3; 4.1-7; *m. Ma'as.* 2.1; *b. Ber.* 47b; *b. Sot.* 48a; *b. Ned.* 20a;
b. Mak. 17a; *t. Dem.* 2-5; *et al.*

4. Some Rabbis were of the opinion that the *'ammei ha-aretz* were trustworthy
in their tithing; *b. Shab.* 23a, 'The majority of *'ammei ha-aretz* tithe [their produce]';
b. Mak. 17a; *b. Bez.* 35b; *b. Men.* 31a; *b. Git.* 61a; *m. Mak.* 6.3. See Oppenheimer,
'Am Ha-aretz, pp. 67-68.

5. *M. Dem.* 4.6.

6. See Danby, *The Mishnah*, p. 20 n. 9.

tithe (i.e. one hundredth of the produce) and the second tithe (one tenth) in years one, two, four and five of the sabbatical cycle were under suspicion. Someone who undertook to ensure that the biblical injunctions on tithing had been met would separate the *terumah* of the tithe and the second tithe from any produce that was purchased from a suspect source.

The concept of 'demai' produce was first established by Johanan the high priest in the late Maccabean period:

> whoever purchases fruits from an *'am ha-aretz* must separate the first and second tithes therefrom.[1]

It was this concern that circumscribed fellowship at table with the *'am ha-aretz*, as seen in the famous mishnah:

> He that undertakes to be trustworthy. . . may not be the guest of an *'am ha-aretz*.[2]

Throughout the late Second Temple period the tithing regulations were widely ignored by the general population of Jews.[3] As the pronouncement of Johanan shows, a distinction was being made at a very early stage about tithing, and trusting to the farmer was not considered sufficient. By the time of Jesus non-observance was so widespread that Josephus reports that the high priests were sending servants to the fields to collect the tithes.[4] Not only had economic pressure in general militated against the separation of tithes[5] but other factors contributed to the decline in observance. The Torah stipulated that tithes should be separated for the benefit of the priests and Levites since they were prohibited from owning land (Num. 18.31-34), but now many priests and Levites had themselves become landowners, some quite wealthy.[6] As a result the rationale for the payment of tithes had lost much of its force among the people. Additionally, since

---

1. *B. Sot.* 48a. Probably Johanan Hyrcanus I (134–104 BCE). The quote here is the indirect discourse of the Amoraim and thus the term *'am ha-aretz* is no doubt anachronistic. See also *m. Sot.* 9.10; *m. Ma'as. S.* 5.15; and Oppenheimer, *'Am Ha-aretz*, pp. 75-76.

2. *M. Dem.* 2.2.

3. Safrai, *The Jewish People*, II, pp. 586, 824.

4. *Ant.* 20.181, 206.

5. Safrai, *The Jewish People*, II, p. 586.

6. Safrai, *The Jewish People*, II, pp. 824, 587.

priests and Levites served only in rotation, usually two weeks a year, they were usually otherwise employed and not solely dependent on the tithes and heave-offerings. Even some high priests held other employment.[1] In view of these realities it would seem that the Pharisaic insistence on strict observance of tithing regulations set them quite apart from the general populace. And since the practice of bringing all tithes to the Temple for central distribution had long since been abandoned,[2] tithing was a matter of conscience for which there was little impetus except personal discipline.

This description should help us obtain a more realistic understanding of the nature of the criticism of the *'ammei ha-aretz* in rabbinic literature for the failure to tithe. If tithing seems a complicated matter[3] this may go some way towards the appreciation of why many failed to be entirely scrupulous. When we further consider the supererogatory nature of the act it is clear that someone who elected not to undertake these obligations would not have been considered an outcast or excluded from Israel. They were simply not 'trustworthy' in the technical sense of the word. From a non-sectarian point of view the charge against the *'ammei ha-aretz* for failure to tithe was not a particularly grave one.

Some Rabbinic Texts on the 'Am Ha-aretz

I turn now to an analysis of a selection of rabbinic texts that discuss the *'ammei ha-aretz* in relation to food and table fellowship. The purpose is not to set out a complete form- or tradition-critical treatment of all such passages. To my knowledge this has not yet been undertaken[4] and the task lies well beyond the scope of this brief chapter. The aim here is a more modest one: to bring together some of the most significant rabbinic texts on the subject in order to answer sev-

---

1.   Safrai, *The Jewish People*, II, pp. 824, 587.

2.   Oppenheimer, *'Am Ha-aretz*, pp. 36-38.

3.   *B. Mak.* 17a, 'The Rabbis take the view that the *'ammei ha-aretz* are mistrusted about it [tithing], because it involves trouble, and as the separation of the due means some trouble to them, they will not set it apart'.

4.   While the criticisms of Oppenheimer by Porton, Kippenberg and Cohen are fitting, it should, in fairness, be noted that no one else has done what they criticize Oppenheimer for failing to do.

eral questions.[1] Did the practice of the *'ammei ha-aretz* regarding food actually set them apart as an identifiable social group and, if so, was this the case in the time of Jesus? Can the rabbinic texts on the *'ammei ha-aretz* and food help in any way to explain Jesus' relationship with the Pharisees? Finally, what is the nature of the information these passages yield?

Because of the complexity of the material and the numerous references involved it is perhaps best to describe how the discussion will progress. I will begin with an early text which deals with the eating of the second tithe in purity and then proceed to other texts dealing generally with eating in purity. Next, texts pertaining to table-fellowship are considered.[2] Finally, I will analyse a key talmudic passage, *b. Ber.* 47b, which contains elements of all of the above and will serve to bring the analysis together. Sections will be subtitled throughout to help keep the inquiry on track. Also, where appropriate, the mishnah on which a gemara or baraita is based will be given in addition to the gemara or baraita itself.

Perhaps one of the earliest rabbinic references to the *'ammei ha-aretz* is *b. Sheb.* 16a, a gemara purporting to describe conditions in the days of the Second Temple which deals with the biblical injunction that the second tithe be eaten in Jerusalem in a state of ritual purity by all Israel (Deut. 14.22ff.).

> Come and hear: Abba Saul said: There were two meadows on the Mount of Olives, the lower and the upper; the lower was consecrated with all these; the upper was not consecrated with all these, but by the returned exiles, without King and without Urim and Tummin; the lower one which was properly consecrated; the illiterate ['*ammei ha-aretz*] entered there, and ate there sacrifices of a minor grade of holiness, but not the second tithe.[3] And the learned [*haberim*] ate there sacrifices of a minor grade of

---

1. I have, to the best of my knowledge, read all of the rabbinic texts which deal with the issue of the *'ammei ha-aretz*, although one can never be sure with the rabbinic corpus. The texts treated here are those which have been prominent in the literature and which, in my opinion, contain the most revealing treatment of the *'ammei ha-aretz*.

2. All these items apply to the so-called *'am ha-aretz le mitzvot*; see Oppenheimer's Chapter 3, 'The 'Am ha-aretz le mitzvot and the 'Am ha-aretz la Torah', pp. 67ff.

3. Compare the Soncino text here to Oppenheimer's text of the gemara, *'Am Ha-aretz*, pp. 85-86. Oppenheimer cites there a variant of the Vienna MS which has

> holiness and also the second tithe. The upper one which was not properly
> consecrated; the *'am ha-aretz* entered there, and ate there sacrifices of a
> minor grade of holiness, but not the second tithe. And the learned did not
> eat there either sacrifices of a minor grade of holiness or the second tithe.

The discussion occurs between Raba (Amora, who died in 375 CE) and
one R. Nahman (perhaps b. Hisda or b. Isaac, both Amoraim, living
around the fourth century also). R. Nahman reports the tradition of
Abba Saul (Tanna, 140–165)[1] who in turn reports conditions made
known to him by a tradition about a time when the Temple was
standing. The time is said to be after the consecration of the upper
parts of the Mount of Olives was established 'by the returned exiles,
without King and without Urim and Tummin'. The consecration of
the upper meadow contrasts with that of the lower which dates from
an even earlier period, and in consequence of which enjoys a higher
state of consecration, that is, one suitable for the consumption of second tithe.[2]

The *'ammei ha-aretz* did not appreciate the higher degree of consecration of the lower meadow, and thus would not eat second tithe
there but would eat only sacrifices of a minor grade in both meadows.
The 'learned' (*haberim*) understood the difference and knew it was
acceptable to eat second tithe in the lower meadow and that the upper
meadow was of insufficient consecration for even sacrifices of a minor
grade. In this case, the *'ammei ha-aretz* were actually more strict than
the *haberim* in regard to second tithe, believing that the only acceptable place for its consumption was within the city itself.[3] Their error
was based on their inability to appreciate the distinction in levels of
sanctity but they erred, not in leniency but in strictness. In any case
the whole matter was not a particularly grave concern: the *'ammei ha-*

---

the *'ammei ha-aretz* eating their second tithe also in the lower meadow. If this is the
correct reading it does not materially affect the interpretation since in both readings
the only failing of the *'ammei ha-aretz* was the eating of minor sacrifices in the upper
meadow.

1.   Not to be confused with Abba Saul b. Batnith (Tanna, 80–120 CE).

2.   The higher sanctity of the lower meadow is probably also to be attributed to
its proximity to the city. See *m. Kel.* 1.6-9 for the idea that the nearer a location is to
the Holy of Holies the higher the sanctity. The walls of Jerusalem represented a
special boundary of sanctity, thus the *'am ha-aretz* in this gemara would only eat
second tithe within the actual walls of the city.

3.   Deut. 14.23; cf. *m. Kel.* 1.8.

aretz simply did not observe the rules with a sophistication equal to that of the *haberim*. Nevertheless, they would not eat second tithe outside the city itself and this shows them to have been very concerned about observing the biblical injunction of eating second tithe 'before the Lord your God, in the place which he will choose' (Deut. 14.23).

The antiquity of the account seems quite certain since it is difficult to imagine a motive for the Amoraim to create such a tradition when the Temple had long since vanished.[1] However distant an echo, it is a tradition that must derive from the period when the Temple was still standing. Over 500 years separates the tradition from its final redaction and this no doubt accounts for the anachronistic use of the terms *'ammei ha-aretz* and *haberim*. Yet the passage would seem to preserve a genuine memory of the difference between those who were more scrupulous and those who were less.

In this passage, just as in *b. Sot.* 48b (the pronouncement on 'demai' produce by Johanan the high priest), the earliest representations of the *'ammei ha-aretz* are in regard to biblical obligations.[2] The issues are those the Bible enjoins on all Israel and no evidence of the much later issue of eating all food in a state of ritual purity is yet discernible.

An important mishnaic reference that deals with the eating of food in ritual purity is *m. Hag.* 2.7.[3] It is described by E. Rivkin as the text used by 'most scholars, both Jewish and non-Jewish, [to] construct

---

1. Oppenheimer says that Abba Saul, 'transmitted many historically authentic traditions relating to the days of the Second Temple', but does not elaborate (*'Am Ha-aretz*, p. 86).

2. Likewise *b. Ber.* 17a; *b. Shab.* 32a; *m. Ab.* 3.10, 5.10 which record non-sectarian (i.e. biblically based) conflicts between factions of Jews, observant and not so observant.

3. This mishnah is often cited as of central importance on the subject of ritual purity. See Oppenheimer, *'Am Ha-aretz*, pp. 60, 62, 87, 118, 125, 133, 156; E. Rivkin, 'Defining the Pharisees', *HUCA* 40-41 (1967–70), pp. 205-49; Herford, *The Pharisees*, pp. 30-32; Maccoby, *ERW*, pp. 205-23 and Rivkin, *A Hidden Revolution*, pp. 160-61, who both follow Büchler in maintaining that the Pharisees made these laws of ritual purity for the priests, not for the ordinary individual. While Maccoby's treatment of *m. Hag.* 2.7 was published after I had completed the first draft of this chapter, I was pleased to find many of my findings confirmed by his exceptionally clear treatment of this difficult text. On the whole, Maccoby has done New Testament scholars a service in his treatments of this text and *m. Dem.* 2 (*ERW*, pp. 67-74).

their definition of the Pharisees'.[1] The mishnah reads as follows:

> For Pharisees the clothes of an *'am ha-aretz* count as suffering midras-
> uncleanness; for them that eat Heave-offering the clothes of Pharisees
> count as suffering midras-uncleanness; for them that eat of Hallowed
> Things the clothes of them that eat Heave-offering count as suffering
> midras-uncleanness; for them that occupy themselves with the Sin-offer-
> ing water the clothes of them that eat of Hallowed Things count as suffer-
> ing midras-uncleanness. Joseph b. Joezer was the most pious in the
> priesthood, yet for them that ate of Hallowed Things his apron counted as
> suffering midras-uncleanness. Johanan b. Gudgada always ate [his com-
> mon food] in accordance with [the rules governing] the cleanness of Hal-
> lowed Things, yet for them that occupied themselves with the Sin-offering
> water his apron counted as suffering midras-uncleanness.

The meaning of *'am ha-aretz* in *m. Hag.* 2.7 requires some analysis.
The mishnah is set in Moed, the second division of the Mishnah, which
deals with the festivals. The tractate *Hagigah* deals with Deut. 16.16-
17: 'Three times a year all your males shall appear before the Lord
your God at the place which he will choose: at the feast of unleavened
bread, at the feast of weeks, and at the feast of booths'. In particular it
treats the voluntary offerings that were to be brought at the time of
the these festivals.[2] At *m. Hag.* 2.5–3.6, however, a meandering digression deals with the subject of the conveyance of uncleanness in
general;[3] thus the issues raised in 2.7 have a wider significance than
conduct at feasts. Maccoby has called *m. Hag.* 2.7 a 'conspectus of the
Mishnaic system of ritual purity'.[4]

The importance of the mishnah lies in the significance some scholars
have attributed to it as a guide to social stratification in early Judaism.
The matter of purity has been said to have set up an 'impassable religious barrier'[5] and to have created 'class and sectarian polarity'.[6] Op-

---

1.   Rivkin, *A Hidden Revolution*, p. 206.

2.   Cf. Exod. 23.14.

3.   The most important special regulation about the purity of food which applied
during festivals, i.e. that an *'am ha-aretz* did not transmit impurity with regard to
wine and dough (*b. Bez.* 11b; *b. Hag.* 26b), does not materially affect the discussion
of 2.5-7.

4.   See *ERW*, pp. 95-100.

5.   Herford, *Pharisees*, I, p. 26. See further the discussion by Sanders which
debunks this view (*Jesus and Judaism*, pp. 180-82, 188-94).

6.   Urbach, *Sages*, p. 584.

penheimer says, 'The consequence of this segmentation was the creation of barriers between one class and another. . .'[1] He further contends that this social stratification was dependent upon the 'circumstances prevailing at the time and the identity of the particular Sage who defined or discussed the *'am ha-aretz'*.[2] This last statement is surprising. It reveals a great deal about Oppenheimer's method of analysis and, in general, about the kind of thinking that underlies the above assertions about 'class distinctions' based on purity observance in early Judaism. Oppenheimer apparently believes that a single sage could establish or abolish a 'class' merely on the basis of his opinion about the *'ammei ha-aretz*. He stands the sociological task on its head. Whereas the normal method[3] of such analysis is to collect a broad range of data and then identify social categories and trends, Oppenheimer finds evidence of 'class distinctions' in the opinion of a single sage. No amount of sociological terminology can mask this error of method. Our examination of the pericope in *m. Hagigah* itself will further confirm that such pronouncements about 'social stratification'[4] based on purity observance are extremely tenuous.

We learn from *m. Hag.* 2.5 that food may be classed into five categories for the purposes of purity: unclean and four levels of purity.[5]

---

1. Oppenheimer, *'Am Ha-aretz*, p. 62.
2. Oppenheimer, *'Am Ha-aretz*, p. 69.
3. Philip Esler describes the sociological task in relation to biblical studies in his book *Community and Gospel in Luke–Acts: The Social and Political Motivations of Lucan Theology* (Cambridge: Cambridge University Press, 1987), pp. 6ff. He rightly points out a fundamental tenet of sociological analysis: 'a good typology is based upon as wide as possible a range of empirical data, and its resulting high level of generality will improve its usefulness when used in a comparative exercise upon a particular set of data' (p. 7).
4. Oppenheimer, *'Am Ha-aretz*, pp. 118, 125.
5. The grades of uncleanness are referred to in the Mishnah as first, second, third and fourth grade, the first being the 'lightest' and so progressing to the most grave impurity (e.g. *m. Toh.* 1). The more severe the impurity the more easily it is passed on. Thus, heave-offering can suffer contamination at three removes from the primary source of impurity (the so-called 'father of impurity', *m. Kel.* 1.1), whereas contamination would normally lose its force after passing to the second party (the so-called 'offspring of impurity'). Hallowed things can be rendered unclean at even four removes. See Danby, p. 714 n. 3; also the eighteenth-century formulation of those rules listed in Danby's Appendix IV, pp. 800ff., esp. 17b-c. See also Maccoby, *ERW*, pp. 97-98; Oppenheimer, *'Am Ha-aretz*, pp. 58-61.

> For [the eating of food that is] unconsecrated or [Second] Tithe or Heave-offering, the hands need but to be rinsed; and for Hallowed Things they need to be immersed; and in what concerns the Sin-offering water, if a man's hands are unclean his whole body is deemed unclean.

The first type of food mentioned is unconsecrated food (*ḥullin*), that is, food which is eaten without any attempt of observing purity. The second tithe[1] was eaten in the lowest level of purity (*Ma'as. S.* 2.2) and the biblical injunction stated that it was incumbent upon all Israel to eat their second tithe annually in Jerusalem in a state of ritual purity, albeit the lowest state.[2] The second level of purity was that required for the consumption of heave-offering (*terumah*). According to Num. 18.11-13 the heave-offering of the people of Israel was to be eaten by the priests and members of their families in a state of ritual purity. The third level was that of 'hallowed things'. These are the cereal, sin and guilt Temple offerings reserved from the fire and to be consumed only by priests and their sons in a most holy place (Num. 18.8-10) and are one degree more sensitive to impurity than heave-offering (*m. Hag.* 3.1). As one moved up the scale it became increasingly difficult to observe the requisite purity. The fourth and utmost degree of purity was that reserved for the priest who handled the Sin-offering water (Num. 8.7; 19.17-18). It is evident from *m. Hag.* 2.7 that these strictures, which according to the Scriptures applied only to the priests, were voluntarily assumed by those who wished to live according to such disciplines in everyday life.

> Johanan b. Gudgada always ate [his common food] in accordance with [the rules governing] the cleanness of Hallowed Things, yet for them that occupied themselves with the Sin-offering water his apron counted as suffering midras-uncleanness.

This is how the sages of the Babylonian Talmud understand the passage, referring repeatedly to 'unconsecrated food which was prepared according to the purity of hallowed things' in the gemara on *m. Hag.* 2.7.[3] It is against this background that the first portion of *m. Hag.* 2.7 is to be understood:

---

1.   There is no special level of purity assigned to the first tithe in the Mishnah. Thus, the 'tithe' is actually the second tithe as we see in *m. Hag.* 2.5, 6 and 7.
2.   Deut. 12.7; 14.22ff.; Lev. 27.30-33; *m. Ma'as. S.* 3.3, 9; cf. *m. Kel.* 1.8.
3.   *B. Hag.* 19b.

For Pharisees the clothes of an *'am ha-aretz* count as suffering midras-uncleanness; for them that eat Heave-offering the clothes of Pharisees count as suffering midras-uncleanness. . .

The term 'Pharisees' (*perushim*) is not used with reference to a sect but simply to those who customarily eat secular food at the level of purity required for second tithe.[1] The *'ammei ha-aretz* are those who make no supererogatory attempt with respect to the purity of their food. A Pharisee would nullify the first level of purity by coming into contact (midras- or 'pressure'-uncleanness) with the clothes of an *'am ha-aretz* and the remedy was a ritual immersion.[2] However, no 'class' distinction can be based on this state of affairs. The *'am ha-aretz* had done no wrong and the Pharisees' undertaking was an entirely voluntary act of religious devotion. To describe the contraction of midras-uncleanness in terms of social 'strata' attributes far too much sociological importance to what was simply a matter of individual religious conscience.[3] Above all, it is evident from the citation of the case of Johanan b. Gudgada, who ate at the level of purity required for 'hallowed things', that such a practice was not widespread. When understood from this perspective it is clear that the *'am ha-aretz* was not actually guilty of any wrongdoing, either moral or ceremonial. The failure of such a person to observe ritual purity with regard to ordinary food may well have been condemned by Pharisees but this was a matter of personal religious prejudice, not legal transgression. Nor did the failure to observe sectarian sensibilities constitute the *'ammei ha-aretz* as a separate social class.

Rabbinic acceptance of the definition of the *'ammei ha-aretz* in *m. Hag.* 2.7 was not unanimous however. The mishnah itself is unattributed and there is no way of establishing a date on internal considerations.[4] But differences of opinion were in evidence in the early Ushan period, as *b. Hag.* 19b attests. Commenting on *m. Hag.* 2.7 the gemara reads:

---

1. Maccoby, *ERW*, pp. 95-96; and see further Sanders, *Jesus and Judaism*, pp. 187-88; Rivkin, 'Defining the Pharisees', pp. 207-208.

2. *M. Hag.* 2.6.

3. Maccoby says, 'The idea that the ritual-purity laws made mutual trust, friendship and social intercourse impossible between the different sections of the community is thus incorrect' (*ERW*, p. 96).

4. Oppenheimer considers the tractate in general and this mishnah in particular to be pre-70 in date, but he offers no argumentation (*'Am Ha-aretz*, pp. 59, 87).

> According to whom will our Mishnah be? [Presumably] it is according to
> the Rabbis,[1] who distinguish between unconsecrated [food] and [Second]
> Tithe. But [then] how will you understand the second part [of the Mish-
> nah]? 'The garments of an *'am ha-aretz* possess midras-uncleanness for
> Pharisees; the garments of Pharisees possess midras-uncleanness for
> those who eat terumah': this will be according to R. Meir, who said that
> unconsecrated [food] and [Second] Tithe are [in this respect] the same.
> Thus the first part [of the Mishnah] will be according to the Rabbis and
> the second part according to R. Meir!. . . R. Mari said:. . . [the Mish-
> nah] does not teach it [i.e. Second Tithe] as a [special] degree [of purity].

The Amoraim drew upon a tradition from Rabbi Meir (Tanna,
140–165 CE) which did not accept the opinion that the garments of the
'ammei ha-aretz count as midras-uncleanness to a Pharisee. Rabbi
Meir held that the Pharisees did not eat their secular food in an acceptable state of purity: 'unconsecrated [food] and [Second] Tithe are
[in this respect] the same'. It was his view that the Pharisees, who, we
must presume, were in the habit of eating their secular food at the
level of purity required for second tithe, were counted as a source of
midras-uncleanness to those who ate at the appropriate level, that of
heave-offering.[2] R. Meir could not have agreed with the first half of
the statement that the clothes of the *'ammei ha-aretz* count as midras-
uncleanness to the Pharisee. In his thinking the Pharisee *and* the *'am
ha-aretz* are the same since neither observe a high enough state of
purity when eating secular food. Both are unobservant.[3]

The Amoraim resorted to a bit of source criticism to explain the
seemingly contradictory opinions.

> Indeed, the first part [of the Mishnah] is according to the Rabbis and the
> second part according to R. Meir.

Yet another opinion is that of R. Mari (II, Amora, 4th century) who
holds that the second tithe and the hallowed things constitute a single
category of purity.

---

1. Who are 'the Rabbis'? We do not know. R. Meir is, of course, the great
rabbi of the early Ushan period, c. 140–165. Since his position responds to an
existing tradition contained in that attributed to 'the Rabbis' it seems likely that the
mishnah is, in its basic content, at least extant from the early Ushan period or
perhaps even earlier. R. Mari is an Babylonian Amora of the fourth century.
2. Oppenheimer, *'Am Ha-aretz*, p. 59.
3. Cf. *m. Yad.* 4.6; *m. Sot.* 3.4.

But perhaps the reason why [the Mishnah] does not teach it [i.e. the Second Tithe] as a [special] degree of purity is because if it is like *terumah*, behold [the Mishnah] deals with *terumah*. . .[1]

Thus, there are three opinions as to the proper observance of the levels of purity. (1) The Rabbis held that there were three separate levels of purity: unconsecrated, second tithe and heave-offering. These were to be observed respectively by the *'am ha-aretz*, the Pharisees and 'others who eat at the heave level'. (2) R. Meir supported the view of two levels of purity, combining unconsecrated and second tithe in the first level with heave offering standing alone in the second. For R. Meir and *'am ha-aretz* and the Pharisees observed the first level and 'others who eat at the level of heave' observed the second level. (3) R. Mari placed unconsecrated food in a separate level observed only by the *'am ha-aretz* and combined second tithe and heave-offering in the second level for observance by both Pharisees and 'others who eat at the level of heave'.

It should now be apparent that such texts should not be used to ascertain discernible social groups in early Judaism. Not even the rabbis could agree on the meaning of the mishnah and the passage contains no information that would aid in the sociological task. Nevertheless, the following basic observations can be made on the basis of *m. Hag.* 2.7. First, some exceptional individuals ate unconsecrated food in ritual purity but this was not normal for everyone. More importantly, we note that confusion surrounded the attempt to define the *'ammei ha-aretz* in the middle of the second century CE. R. Meir, reacting to an earlier tradition, shows that the definition was a matter of debate from even before the Ushan period. Even if the Rabbis' views were early Yavnean in date it is almost impossible to conceive of their influence as being normative in the pre-destruction period.

The only thing we learn about the *'ammei ha-aretz* is that they did not even eat their secular food to the level of purity required for the second tithe, as did those who stood at the lowest level of observance, the 'Pharisees'. In failing to do so, however, the *'ammei ha-aretz* broke no law; nor does the text suggest this to be so. More importantly, none of the distinctions raised in the discussion were based on substantive social issues; instead, they revolve around tortuous arguments about various levels of purity which few but the sages could

---

1. *B. Hag.* 20a.

have appreciated. The only point of agreement consists in the placement of the *'am ha-aretz* at the bottom of the scale of observance. In
conclusion, this mishnah and its gemara lend no support to the assertion that the *'ammei ha-aretz* constituted an underclass. They are
rather what I have chosen to term a 'religious category' in a system of
religious thought which, as such, does not bear any direct connection
to concrete social realities.

The *'Am Ha-aretz and Table-Fellowship*

We now turn to some of the references to social intercourse with the
'ammei ha-aretz in an eating context because of their interest for the
issue of table-fellowship in the Gospels. Many references in the rabbinic literature deal with the social intercourse of the *haberim* with
the *'ammei ha-aretz*, but surprisingly few deal directly with the issue
of table-fellowship. Of about a hundred passages in the Babylonian
Talmud which expressly mention the *'ammei ha-aretz* only a few
speak of table-fellowship.[1] Likewise, of twenty-three references to the
'ammei ha-aretz in the Mishnah only *m. Dem.* 2.2-3 discuss fellowship
with an *'am ha-aretz* in one's house; and these do not mention the par-
ticulars of eating. *T. Dem.* 2.2 discusses accepting 'hospitality' from
an *'am ha-aretz*, as we shall see, but *t. Dem.* 3.7 is the only text which
explicitly discusses the *'am ha-aretz* and table-fellowship. The
difficulty arising from this paucity of material is compounded by the
fact that most of the pericopae are anonymous, thus the dating and development of tradition is uncertain.

Even the few references mentioned above do not give a consistent
picture of how table-fellowship with an *'am ha-aretz* should be handled. In the two references of *m. Demai* 2 the halakhah is opposed to
fraternizing with an *'am ha-aretz* in his or her house. First we have
m. Dem. 2.2,

> He that undertakes to be trustworthy (*ne'eman*) must give tithe from what
> he eats and from what he sells and from what he buys [to sell again]; and
> he may not be the guest of an *'am ha-aretz*. R. Judah [b. Ilai, Tanna, 140–
> 165 CE] says: Even he that is the guest of an *'am ha-aretz* may still be
> reckoned trustworthy.

M. Dem. 2.3 also prohibits being the guest of an *'am ha-aretz* but does

---

1.   They are *b. B. Bat.* 57b-58a; *b. Shab.* 13a; *b. Ned.* 20a; *b. Bek.* 43b.

not forbid receiving an *'am ha-aretz* as a guest in one's own house.

> He that undertakes to be an Associate *(haber)*. . . may not be the guest of
> an *'am ha-aretz* nor may he receive him as a guest in his own raiment.

Fellowship for the *ne'eman*, being only concerned with tithes, was prohibited in the house of the *'am ha-aretz* because he or she had no control over the tithing of the food. This, however, was no obstacle to having an *'am ha-aretz* as a guest in one's own house. Even the *ḥaber*, for whom both purity and tithing were at issue, could entertain an *'am ha-aretz*, the only stipulation being a change of raiment to prevent midras-uncleanness (the concern of *m. Hag.* 2.7). This proves that the only reason for avoiding the *'ammei ha-aretz* was the danger that they might give you untithed or impure food.[1] Midras-uncleanness was an issue, but only secondarily so. There is no implication that sitting at table with an *'am ha-aretz* was considered wrong or contaminating in a moral sense, it is simply an issue of one's own undertaking to avoid unclean or untithed food as a matter of religious conscience.[2]

T. Dem. 2.2 quotes the above mishnah and attributes it to R. Meir (Tanna, 140–165 CE), although in the Mishnah the attribution is the anonymous 'they'. The ruling was strict, as was the custom of R. Meir's halakhoth;

> He [the *'am ha-aretz*] would not be trustworthy in what concerns himself;
> how then could he be trustworthy in what concerns others?

In response to this position a view is given which softens the observance;

> They said to him, 'Householders have never refrained from eating with
> one another, nonetheless the produce in their own homes [viz., the homes
> of those who have undertaken to be trustworthy] is properly tithed'.[3]

---

1.   Maccoby, *ERW*, p. 69.

2.   Compare, on the other hand, 1QS 5.13-14 where table-fellowship is based on righteousness, for those who 'are not reckoned in his Covenant. . . They shall not enter the water to partake of the pure Meal of the saints, for they shall not be cleansed unless they turn from their wickedness: for all who transgress his word are unclean.' The translation is by G. Vermes, *The Dead Sea Scrolls in English* (New York: Penguin Books, 1962; reprinted 1986), p. 79.

3.   *T. Dem.* 2.2; quotations are from Jacob Neusner and Richard Sarason (eds.), *The Tosefta: Zeraim* (New York: Ktav, 1986), p. 82; without the versification.

In *t. Dem.* 3.7 a specific situation is dealt with.[1]

> A *ḥaber* who was seated at the banquet of an *'am ha-aretz* or at the feast of
> an *'am ha-aretz* [as a guest]—even if they see him take and eat
> immediately [viz., without first separating tithes], take and drink immedi-
> ately—this is not reason for presuming that everything has been tithed,
> [for] perhaps he tithed in his heart. If his son was seated next to him, he
> separates tithes for him [i.e., for that which his son eats, from the *ḥaber*'s
> own portion]. [If] someone else [was seated next to him], he does not
> separate tithes for him. . . Nonetheless they have said, 'All of these
> [actions] constitute a stumbling-block for others.'

Again, the only concern is the matter of whether the food has been
tithed. The idea that the *ḥaber* may have tithed 'in his heart' is
interesting, but even so, tithe must be physically separated for his son.
It would appear that in a difficult social situation a *ḥaber* could
suspend the need to tithe, but if desired, tithe could be separated right
from the plate. There is no attribution on this passage but the content
seems late, representing as it does, a softening of the earlier halakhoth
of *m. Demai*.

   B. Shab. 13a clearly shows that it is not the personal association
with the *'am ha-aretz* that bars table-fellowship but, again, the issue of
unfit food.

> A zab,[2] a parush, may not dine with a zab, who is an *'am ha-aretz*, lest he
> cause him to associate with him. But what does it matter if he does cause
> him to associate with him? Rather say [thus]: lest he offer him unclean
> food to eat.

In *b. Ned.* 20a the same view is expressed, 'do not frequent an *'am ha-
aretz* for eventually he will give you tebalim. . . ', that is untithed
food.[3] Maccoby has observed that the refusal of a *ḥaber* to eat with an
'am ha-aretz:

> would not lead to the breaking off of friendly relations. . . since there
> was no objection whatever to their sharing a meal at the house of the
> *ne'eman*, while the *'am ha-aretz* perfectly understood that their friend's
> vow precluded him from accepting invitations.[4]

---

1.   Neusner and Sarason, *The Tosefta*, p. 89.
2.   That is, one who has experienced a flux.
3.   So also *y. Shab.* 1.3c.
4.   Maccoby, *ERW*, p. 69.

Nor does the prohibition against eating 'imply any strong disapproval of his way of life, or stigmatize him as a sinner'.[1]

It remains quite uncertain how much, if anything, of what we have learned can be said to apply to the pre-70 period. None of the passages claim to derive from pre-70 masters but this, in itself, does not settle the matter. The passages reflect a period when the issue of table-fellowship was formally observed, but was moving toward a more lenient position. In the pre-70 period the canons of table-fellowship were probably *less* well defined than we find them here in these rabbinic passages. Most importantly, there is no evidence that rabbinic prohibitions concerning table-fellowship had anything to do with the *morality* of the participants; it was based entirely on the necessity of avoiding untithed or impure food and midras-uncleanness. If observant Jews disdained table-fellowship with people they considered morally inferior we cannot confirm it from the rabbinic material.

The 'classic' text that deals with the definition of the *'ammei ha-aretz* is *b. Ber.* 47b.[2] This passage describes the evolution of the term *'am ha-aretz* over a period of about 250 years.[3] The gemara moves from the earlier emphasis on tithing and purity to the second century

---

1.   Maccoby, *ERW*, p. 69. Nonetheless, cf. *b. B. Bat.* 57b-58a: 'The table of an *'am ha-aretz* is like a hearth with pots all round. What is the sign of the bed of a *talmud ḥakam*?—That nothing is kept under it save sandals in the summer season and shoes in the rainy season. But the bed of an *'am ha-aretz* is like a packed storeroom.' I would not wish to vouch for the tidiness of the *'am ha-aretz*! Cf. also *b. Ber.* 43b, 'the scholar. . . should not take a set meal in the company of the *'ammei ha-aretz*'. But this may be nothing more than a convention of good society. Oppenheimer (p. 21 n. 73) quotes *Massakhet Derekh Eretz* 3.1 in this connection: '*Talmidei ḥakhamim* are pleasant in company, and *'ammei ha-aretz* are unpleasant in company'.

2.   So I. Landman, '"Am Ha-aretz", *UJE*, I, p. 217. Oppenheimer treats the passage throughout his book, *'Am Ha-aretz*, pp. 1, 9, 67, 69, 80, 83, 97, 101, 122, 138, 171, 224, 226, 233, 237. See also Urbach, *Sages*, pp. 632-34; Montefiore, *RLGT*, p. 7. Cf. *b. Git.* 61a; *b. Sot.* 21b-22a; *t. 'Abod. Zar.* 3.10.

3.   The dating of the attributions are mostly second through fourth generation tannaim. Two attributions are anonymous, the 'Rabbis' and the 'Others'. R. Nathan b. Joseph is a Tanna of uncertain date (also known as Johanan b. Joseph). The halakhah is decided in favour of 'Others' by R. Huna who is an Amora (either Babylonian, c. 300 CE or Palestinian, c. 350 CE). Geographically, most are Palestinians yet the term may include a Babylonian authority; in any case the recording Amoraim are Babylonians.

animosity between the *talmidei ḥakamim* and the *'ammei ha-aretz*.[1]

B. Ber. 47b is a gemara on *m. Ber.* 7.1. The discussion in progress in the Mishnah relates, as the name of the tractate implies (lit. 'benedictions'), to the manner in which the *Shema'*, the *Tefillah* (lit. 'prayer', here meaning the Eighteen Benedictions) and the various routine and occasional prayers required for daily life are to be given. The mishnah on which this gemara is based reads:

> If Three ate together they must say the Common Grace. If one of them ate demai-produce, or First Tithe from which Heave-offering had been taken, or Second Tithe or dedicated produce that had been redeemed; if an attendant ate an olive's bulk of food or [if one that ate was] a Samaritan, they may be included [to make up the number needed] for the Common Grace.

A quorum of three, or *zimmun*, who gather for eating must say a common grace in which all join. The Talmud addresses the question of the proper constitution of a *zimmun*. We learn from the Mishnah that a Samaritan, or Cuthean,[2] can be included in a *zimmun*. The Talmud then asks:

> Wherein is he better than an *'am ha-aretz*, and it has been taught: an *'am ha-aretz* is not reckoned in for *zimmun*?

In the Talmud the Amoraim are puzzling over *m. Ber.* 7.1 and wondering why a Samaritan should be included for *zimmun* when an *'am ha-aretz* is not. Raba (Amora, 3rd–4th centuries CE) interprets the Mishnah to include the *'am ha-aretz* in *zimmun* according to the teaching of R. Meir (Tanna, 140–165 CE). This occasions a digression on the definition of an *'am ha-aretz*:

> Who is an *'am ha-aretz*? Anyone who does not eat non-sacred food in ritual cleanness. So R. Meir. The Rabbis, however, say: anyone who does not tithe his produce in the proper way. . . Our Rabbis taught: who is an *'am ha-aretz*? Anyone who does not recite the *Shema'* evening and morning. This is the view of R. Eliezer. R. Joshua says: anyone who does not put on *tefillin*. Ben 'Azzai says: anyone who has not a fringe on his garment. R. Nathan says: anyone who has not a *mezuzah* on his door. R. Nathan b. Joseph says: anyone who has sons and does not bring them up to the study of the Torah. Others say: even if one has learnt Scripture

---

1. Urbach, *Sages*, pp. 632-33; Landman, "'Am Ha-aretz', p. 217; Oppenheimer, *'Am Ha-aretz*, p. 17.

2. The residents of Cuthah (2 Kgs 17.24) whom the king of Assyria placed in the cities of Samaria in the place of the Israelites.

and Mishnah, if he has not ministered to the disciples of the wise, he is an
'am ha-aretz. R. Huna said: the *halachah* is as laid down by 'Others'.

Each of the definitions is cast in a similar form and they are
brought together in a balanced structure.[1] The disputes of R. Meir
(Tanna, 140–165 CE) and the 'Rabbis' (anonymous) over food and
tithing, together with those of R. Nathan b. Joseph (Tanna, date unknown) and the 'others' (anonymous) over the study of Torah and
ministering to the wise, form a parenthesis of the most important issues in the identification of the *'am ha-aretz*. In between are found the
four minor issues of observance put forward by 'our rabbis': the
Shema', R. Eliezer (b. Hyracanus; Tanna, 80–120 CE); the *tefillin*, R.
Joshua (b. Hananiah; 80–120 CE); the fringe, Ben 'Azzai (Tanna, 120–
140 CE); and the *mezuzah*, R. Nathan (Tanna, 140–165 CE).

The pronouncement of each sage is given in a formula ('anyone
who . . .') and the redactional activity of the Amoraic editors is evident in the way they have assembled sages from many generations in a
serial discussion of the definition of an *'am ha-aretz*. These are traditions that, in the view of the Amoraim, have ostensibly survived from
as early as the Yavnean period. It is not surprising that the dispute is
settled according to the opinion of the recording Amoraim (i.e.
'others').

The structure of the argument of *b. Ber.* 47b places two comparatively major points of contention (tithing vs. purity) at the beginning.
This agrees with what has already been observed about the earliness of
the tithing issue discussed above. Also the purity issue as we saw in *m.
Hag.* 2.7 was said to be at least Ushan in date and perhaps earlier,
although how much so we do not know. Following this four minor
definitions of *'am ha-aretz* are given: those who neglect *Shema'*,
tefillin, fringe and *mezuzah*. These seem inconsequential but are nevertheless proposed as aspects of what marks out the behaviour of an
'am ha-aretz. They are followed, again, by two major issues in the
definition of *'am ha-aretz* (study of Torah vs. serving the sages). It
would seem that the gemara does display a roughly accurate chronological progression from issues prominent in the early rabbinic period
(tithing and purity) to those of later importance (the conflict between

---

1.   My appreciation is given to P.S. Alexander for bringing this point to my
attention.

the learned, the *talmidei ḥakamim* and the unlearned, the *'ammei ha-aretz*).

What have we learned, however, about the positive identity of the *'ammei ha-aretz*? Again, very little it would seem. The definitions proposed in *b. Ber.* 47b also have an artificial sense of either/or about them. Someone concerned about tithing could well have been concerned about purity, and vice versa. Nor would it seem probable that anyone could base their whole notion of the *'ammei ha-aretz* on the saying of the *Shema'* or *tefillin*, or fringe, or *mezuzah*. Neither were the study of Torah and service to the sages contradictory practices.[1] It may be that each addition to the list is meant to augment those that preceded it, i.e the list is cumulative. In any case, all of this points to the fact that *b. Ber.* 47b is not an attempt at a precise definition of a 'social class'. Rather, the gemara represents the ruminations of Amoraic sages about subtleties of emphasis on matters of observance that held sway in various times and places. The gemara is not a guide to social stratification in early Judaism, but an academic disputation on the religious sensibilities of individual rabbis, all refracted through the viewpoint of the Amoraim.

Conclusion

The most striking aspect of *b. Ber.* 47b, and indeed all rabbinic texts about the *'ammei ha-aretz*, is that the definition of the *'ammei ha-aretz* is based on what they do *not* do. It is the lack of conformity to a supposed ideal role that identifies the *'ammei ha-aretz*. With the exception of the fact that some rabbis thought the *'ammei ha-aretz* were trustworthy in regard to tithing, we have little positive information about them. Indeed, the notion of the *'ammei ha-aretz* exists only as a negative abstraction, the chief function of which is to show how a *ḥaber*, or *talmid ḥakam* should *not* act. This is accomplished by holding forth the supposedly habitual bad behaviour of the *'ammei ha-aretz* as a negative example. It would not be an exaggeration to say that negative behaviour is the subject of virtually all of the rabbinic texts about the *'ammei ha-aretz*. The *'ammei ha-aretz* are not a social class but an idea—a concept that serves as a foil against which the rabbinists set

---

1. See G. Alon, *The Jews in their Land in the Talmudic Age*, II (Jerusalem: Magnes Press, 1984), p. 476.

their own behaviour and standards of conduct.

Our concern in examining this material has been to discern whether the practices of the *'ammei ha-aretz* in fact set them apart as a socially identifiable group. As far as the evidence indicates, this was not the case in the second century CE and was even less likely to be so in the time of Jesus himself. Moreover, to attempt to establish a sociological profile of the general Jewish public through the lens of rabbinic pronouncements on the *'ammei ha-aretz* is not only poor methodology but profoundly misleading.

The *'ammei ha-aretz* were simply those who, from a sectarian point of view (the only viewpoint we possess), did not observe certain supererogatory practices. But we have no evidence that broadly accepted class distinctions emerged from this situation. Jesus' ministry cannot be conceived in terms of liberating the masses from sectarian oppression because there was probably no such thing in the pre-70 period. As far as the evidence indicates, all ideas about Jesus 'rescuing' the *'ammei ha-aretz* are mere shadow boxing. In answer to the initial question, we have not found here the key that will unlock the relationship of Jesus to his contemporaries.

Chapter 3

THE QUEST FOR THE HISTORICAL 'SINNER'

In Chapters 1 and 2 I undertook an examination of some of the historical questions regarding Pharisaism and the *'ammei ha-aretz* in relation to the time of Jesus. This has prepared the way for an analysis of
Luke's Gospel presentation of Jesus' ministry around the matrix of
three character groups: Jesus, the 'Pharisees' and the 'sinners'. The
same interest now brings us to an examination of the term 'sinner' and
its significance in literature germane to the formation of the Gospel
tradition. The enduring importance of the historical Jesus question
has, as we have seen, led to a corresponding interest in the historical
nature of Pharisaism. Jesus had conflicts with the 'Pharisees' and so
we wish to know who the 'Pharisees' were. The same is true with respect to the 'sinners'; if Jesus came to 'call' them (Lk. 5.32), then the
quest for the historical 'sinner' is also of considerable importance.
The significance of the question lies, ultimately, in the light it sheds on
the person of Jesus himself. Thus we ask: who were the 'sinners'? If
they form a crucial element in Jesus' conflict with the Pharisees in the
Gospels then a historical explanation of that conflict requires their
identification. But, as we saw with the Pharisees and *'ammei ha-aretz*,
such an identification is not necessarily a simple matter. If the historical 'sinner' proves as difficult to recover as the others, then a solution
to the problem of the Gospel triangle of Jesus, the 'Pharisees' and the
'sinners' may continue to elude us.

The purpose of this chapter is to explore some of the past efforts to
come to terms with the concept of the 'sinners', and then to proceed to
an assessment of the subject in the primary literature outside the New
Testament. Material may be found there that will inform our appreciation of the Gospel usage of the term.

Some Modern Attempts at a Definition of the 'Sinner'

In one of his earlier works Jeremias set out a definition for the 'sinner' that has served as the basis for much of the scholarly discussion that has since taken place.[1] While in later works Jeremias appeared to blur the line between the 'masses' and 'sinners',[2] his original proposal for the specific attributes of the New Testament 'sinner' has become widely accepted and quoted. The appellation 'sinner', argues Jeremias, must be understood in terms of a value judgment by the people (not the Pharisees) and the key is its occurrence in the phrase 'toll collectors and sinners'. This points to a narrow, concrete meaning in which 'sinners' are understood in the same sense as the hated 'toll collectors'.[3] The significance of the term 'sinner', says Jeremias, is in its connotation of moral disrepute. Such a one might be (1) guilty of an immoral mode of life, or (2) a practitioner of one of the dishonourable vocations.[4] Both of these aspects are argued on the basis of rabbinic texts that link the 'toll collector' with an assorted rabble: robbers, prostitutes, pagans, swindlers, adulterers, moneychangers, etc. To this list of immoral types Jeremias also added the so-called 'despised trades' that are set out in various rabbinic lists.[5] It is this twofold definition of the 'sinner' as either morally disreputable or a despised tradesman that has carried so much influence among later scholars.

Others have followed Jeremias's lead in this basic view of the 'sinner'. Norman Perrin held that we should think in terms of three different kinds of 'sinners': (1) Gentiles for whom there was no hope

1. See J. Jeremias, 'Zöllner und Sünder', *ZNW* 30 (1931), pp. 293-300.
2. See the discussion above, Chapter 2, 'The *'Am Ha-aretz* and the New Testament'.
3. Jeremias, 'Zöllner und Sünder', pp. 293-95.
4. Jeremias, 'Zöllner und Sünder', p. 293; also Jeremias, *NTT*, p. 109. So also I. Abrahams, 'Publicans and Sinners', in *SPG*, p. 55: 'The "sinners" were thus not those who neglected the rules of ritual piety, but were persons of immoral life, men of proven dishonesty or followers of suspected and degrading occupations'. According to Rengstorf, *TDNT*, I, p. 327: 'ἁμαρτωλοί partly means those who live a flagrantly immoral life (murderers, robbers, deceivers etc.) and partly those who follow a dishonourable vocation or one which inclines them strongly to dishonesty'.
5. Jeremias, 'Zöllner und Sünder', pp. 295ff. This portion of his work appears in English as the chapter entitled, 'Despised Trades and Jewish Slaves', *JTTJ*, pp. 303-12. See further the discussion of the despised trades below.

of salvation; (2) Jews who could repent without much difficulty; (3) Jews who had 'made themselves as Gentiles' and for whom penitence, while not impossible, was almost 'insurmountably difficult'.[1] Perrin does not say what those Jews in the second group had done, or rather avoided doing, but they apparently were not notorious in their transgression. The third group are Jeremias's despised tradesmen and those who participated in particularly disreputable activities.[2] In a similar vein, Richard Horsley proposes three meanings for the term 'sinner': (1) those into whose hands Jesus is betrayed in the Gospel story (Lk. 24.7; Mt. 26.4; Mk 14.41), the 'priestly aristocracy who ruled Jewish society for the Romans'; (2) the average Jew who stands in need of repentance; and (3) the third group who, again, are the despised tradesmen (a category which Horsley criticizes; see below).[3]

Two other writers on the life of Jesus have also recently attempted definitions of the 'sinner'. Stephen Westerholm first repeats Jeremias's formula but then seems to conflate the issues of Pharisaic ritual purity and moral misconduct.[4] Westerholm asserts that Jesus 'did share the view of his contemporaries' that those who disregarded the scribal regulations on Pharisaic purity 'were sinners; they were the "sick" element of society, in greatest need of a physician'.[5] Westerholm does not appear to understand the supererogatory nature of the observance of the canons of Pharisaic purity. Marcus Borg says the term 'sinners' referred to 'an identifiable social group' and he sets out four criteria for inclusion: (1) despised tradesmen, (2) the flagrantly immoral, (3) the non-Pharisee, and (4) the Gentile.[6]

1. N. Perrin, *Rediscovering the Teaching of Jesus* (London: SCM Press, 1967), pp. 93-94.

2. Perrin, *Rediscovering*, pp. 93-94.

3. R. Horsley calls this third view the 'current consensus among New Testament scholars. . . ' (*Jesus and the Spiral of Violence: Popular Jewish Resistance in Roman Palestine* [San Francisco: Harper & Row, 1987], pp. 217-21).

4. See Westerholm, *Jesus and Scribal Authority*, pp. 69-71.

5. Westerholm, *Jesus and Scribal Authority*, p. 71.

6. Borg, *Conflict, Holiness and Politics*, pp. 83-84. More recently Borg writes: 'In particular, the emphasis upon the politics of holiness, combined with the economic pressure toward non-observance, produced a large group of "sinners" and "outcasts". The term "sinners" referred to an identifiable social group, just as the term "righteous" did: those who did not follow the ways of the fathers as spelled out by the Torah wisdom of the sages. The worst of the non-observant were the outcasts. We do not know the exact extent of the class, though it included the

The recent treatment of this subject by E.P. Sanders has stirred considerable comment. However, his conception of the 'sinner' is not actually much different from Jeremias's. He calls Jeremias's arguments on the despised tradesmen 'basically correct' but criticizes the tendency to take the use of such lists too far.[1] Furthermore, for Sanders, the 'sinners' are the *resha'im*, those who 'sinned wilfully and heinously and who did not repent'.[2]

Essentially, all of these definitions reflect two basic features that identify the 'sinners': they are flagrantly immoral and/or they belong to a despised trade. To this some add the Gentiles and the priestly aristocracy. It is difficult of course to arrive at a clear-cut definition for a notion that is so closely tied to the ideological perspective of the one who uses the term. Perrin succinctly observes that a 'sinner' was the one 'of whom the particular seer disapproved, or who disapproved of the particular seer!'[3] Still, we must question whether this basic twofold conception of the 'sinner' has sufficient value to justify its wide acceptance.

In response to the contention that 'sinners' were 'flagrantly' immoral or sinned 'wilfully' and were 'unrepentant', we could legitimately ask what this language really means. If it means they transgressed the 'provisions of the Torah'[4] it still remains to be discovered *what* provisions of Torah, and according to *whose* conception of Torah. We are still on no firmer ground historically than Perrin's maxim above. The whole argument seems to presume that there was a widely agreed conception of Torah and the specific obligations it laid upon all Jews. The centrality of Torah to Judaism is not in question; what is in question is what was meant by the 'law' or the 'Torah' by

---

notoriously "wicked" (murderers, extortioners, prostitutes, and the like), as well as members of certain occupational groups, membership in which made one as a "non-Jew". The outcasts were virtually untouchables, not very different from the lowest caste of the Hindu system. . . ' (*Jesus: A New Vision* [San Francisco: Harper & Row, 1987], pp. 91-92). I believe this reconstruction of the first-century social milieu to be wrong in all its parts.

1. E.P. Sanders, *Jesus and Judaism*, p. 178.
2. E.P. Sanders, *Jesus and Judaism*, p. 177.
3. Perrin, *Rediscovering*, p. 93.
4. Horsley, *Jesus and the Spiral of Violence*, p. 219; Borg, *Conflict, Holiness and Politics*, p. 84.

those who identify a 'sinner' as one who disregarded it.[1] Was it the
Pentateuch, and if so, which prescriptions were considered essential to
being 'in' Israel? It should not be doubted that some ancient Jews did
flagrantly transgress the 'law' but we do not know what they did or
who perceived those acts as 'flagrant'. As such, it seems particularly
hazardous to suggest, as does Borg, that such a definition could mark
out an 'identifiable social group' or that, as Jeremias says, there were
those who 'notoriously failed to observe the commandments of God
and at whom, therefore, everyone pointed a finger'.[2]

The suggestion that the rabbinic categories of despised trades can
supply the answer to this problem also requires some analysis. Sanders
has noted the rabbinic tendency to 'homiletical exaggeration' in such
matters[3] and Horsley has rightly criticized the dependence on these
lists.[4] The use of these lists for sociological analysis is certainly problematic, as a look at the rabbinic material itself will clearly show.

Jeremias offers several lists of despised trades gathered from the
Mishnah and Babylonian Talmud. The first list is based on *m. Kid.*
4.14 and deals with all known types of transport workers.[5] Such
workers were under suspicion of dishonesty because they transported
goods owned by others and this action occurred outside the owner's
supervision. Thus, there existed a basis upon which some rabbis felt
their conduct could never be considered above reproach. The mishnah
reads as follows:

> Abba Gorion of Zaidan says in the name of Abba Guria: a man should not
> teach his son to be an ass-driver or a camel-driver, or a barber or a sailor,
> or a herdsman or a shopkeeper, for their craft is the craft of robbers. R.
> Judah says in his name: ass-drivers are most of them wicked, camel-
> drivers are most of them proper folk, sailors are most of them saintly, the
> best among physicians is destined for Gehenna, and the most seemly
> among butchers is a partner of Amalek.

---

1.   See P.S. Alexander's analysis of this question in his article, 'Jewish Law in
the Time of Jesus: Toward a Clarification of the Problem', in *Essays on the Place of
the Law in Israel and Early Christianity* (ed. B. Lindars; Cambridge: James Clarke,
1988), pp. 44-58. See further D.E. Aune, 'Orthodoxy in First Century Judaism?',
JSJ 7 (1976), pp. 1-10.
2.   Jeremias, *NTT*, p. 109.
3.   E.P. Sanders, *Jesus and Judaism*, p. 178.
4.   See Horsley, *Jesus and the Spiral of Violence*, pp. 219-20.
5.   Jeremias, *JTTJ*, pp. 304ff.

The professions of *b. Kid.* 82a are in a similar category since they were also suspected of temptation to immoral behaviour. This was because their professions involved contact with women; they were goldsmiths, flaxcombers, handmill cleaners, pedlars, weavers, barbers, launderers, blood-letters, bath attendants and tanners. All of the above trades are 'suspected' of immoral behaviour by a sage. There is, however, quite a difference between rabbinic suspicion and a concrete social reality. In the mishnah above it was Abba Guria's[1] personal opinion that such trades were the 'crafts of robbers' and thus he would not like his son to enter them. Opinions differed however; R. Judah agreed about ass-drivers and physicians but thought that, on the whole, camel-drivers and sailors were a pretty tolerable bunch. Jeremias himself points to an equal amount of positive evidence on the opinions about such trades.[2] As we noted above, the opinion of one sage does not create a social class distinction. There is no evidence to suggest that these suspicions were widely held among the general public. The suggestion that such rabbinic prejudice points to an identifiable social group with whom Jesus' association might have been objectionable rests on illusion.

It is also contended that practitioners of some of the despised trades were deprived of their 'normal citizenship rights'.[3] One mishnah reads:

> And these are they which are not qualified [to be witnesses or judges]: a dice-player, a usurer, pigeon flyers, or traffickers in Seventh Year produce ... . R. Judah said: this applies only if they have none other trade, but if they have some other trade than that they are not disqualified.

Thus Perrin identifies 'dice players, usurers, pigeon flyers, traffickers in seventh-year produce' as among the 'worst' of the Jews and considered 'beyond hope, regarded, in fact, as Gentiles' and for whom repentance was considered 'almost insurmountably difficult'.[4] But such a conclusion is hardly supported by the mishnah. Some of those who participated in the above activities may have been genuinely disliked by some rabbis but generalizations about 'dice-players' as a class of people is not good historical analysis. Pigeon flyers, for example,

---

1. Variant, 'Saul', c. 140–165 CE.
2. Jeremias, *JTTJ*, p. 306.
3. Perrin, *Rediscovering*, pp. 93-94; Jeremias, *JTTJ*, p. 310.
4. Perrin, *Rediscovering*, p. 94.

were suspect for no other reason than because their fowl might feed on carrion while out of their sight.[1] It would be impossible for a *ḥaber* or a priest to keep carrier pigeons since handling them would render him or her unclean for the purposes of food. However, the offence could easily be removed by selling the pigeons; it is not at all 'insurmountably difficult'. Furthermore, the basis of suspicion derives entirely from the sectarian point of view which, we have already seen, was not shared by all.

The suspension of 'civil rights' imposed on such people does appear to have meant that they lost certain statutory legal rights in the opinion of some sages. The pigeon flyer could not 'bear witness' says R. Eliezer (*m. Ed.* 2.7), nor is the oath of the 'dice-player, usurer, pigeon-flyer, or a trafficker in Seventh Year produce' acceptable in a legal proceeding (*m. Sheb.* 7.4). Essentially, such individuals assume the status of a woman with respect to the law (*m. Ros. Has.* 1.8). But from this evidence Jeremias concludes that such people were 'despised, nay hated, by the people; they were *de jure* and officially deprived of rights and ostracized'.[2] Jeremias simply assumes that the occasional rabbinic prejudice exactly represented the prevailing public opinion.

The method by which all of this is connected to the New Testament 'sinner' is circuitous. 'Toll collectors', it is observed, are coupled in the rabbinic literature with various thieves (*m. Toh.* 7.6), robbers (*m. B. Kam.* 10.2; *m. Ned.* 3.4),[3] money-changers (*Derekh Eretz* 2), and murderers (*m. Ned.* 3.4). Since 'toll collectors' are coupled with 'sinners' in the New Testament, these 'sinners', it is argued, must be the equal of those coupled with 'toll collectors' in the rabbinic texts.[4] E.P. Sanders makes the exact same transference of the despised trades argument to the New Testament 'sinner' and concludes, 'Thus we

---

1. 'They may not rear fowls in Jerusalem because of the Hallowed Things nor may priests rear them [anywhere] in the Land of Israel because of [the laws concerning] clean foods' (*m. B. Kam.* 7.7).

2. Jeremias, *JTTJ*, p. 311.

3. Another mishnah shows an interesting double standard of some rabbis; prevarication in one's dealings with such types was considered acceptable: 'Men may vow to murderers, robbers, or tax-gatherers that what they have is a Heave-offering even though it is not a Heave-offering; or that they belong to the king's household even though they do not belong to the king's household' (*m. Ned.* 3.4).

4. Jeremias, *JTTJ*, p. 311; Perrin, *Rediscovering*, p. 94.

know in general terms who the wicked were. . .'[1] Upon examination, this unquestioned application of rabbinic material to the identification of the 'sinner' of Gospel tradition seems wholly unjustified.

Furthermore, the dating of this rabbinic material is much later than the New Testament period. The attributions generally purport to be no earlier than second generation tannaim (R. Eliezer, *m. Ed.* 2.7) and most are third generation or later (Akiba, Abba Saul, Abba Gorion). To read the conditions described in these pericopae back into the time of Jesus and suggest that they carried a normative societal status is anachronistic in the extreme. The 'despised trades' were not a clearly defined social category in Jesus' time and it seems unlikely that they ever existed in a substantive social form.

The Linguistic Evidence of the Greek Psalms and Other Primary Sources

If the rabbinic categories of the outcast have proven inadequate for our task of identifying the 'sinner', we must now look in the other chronological direction to the literature of the Second Temple period. The obvious starting point for the exploration of the semantic and conceptual heritage of the New Testament ἁμαρτωλός is the Septuagint. The almost complete absence of the word 'sinner' from any literature other than that of the Jews confirms that this is the place to begin.[2] It is also rather surprising that the term does not appear in the

---

1. E.P. Sanders, *Jesus and Judaism*, p. 178. While Sanders criticizes Jeremias's use of the lists, in the last analysis he wholly adopts Jeremias's definition of the 'sinner'. Thus Sanders assumes, like most others, that we actually know who these people were. See also B. Chilton, 'Jesus and the Repentance of E.P. Sanders', *TynBul* 39 (1988), p. 9.

2. A search on the Tyndale House TLG Ibycus confirms the finding of Rengstorf (*TDNT*, I, pp. 317-33) that only five instances of the word are known from classical Greek; from over 2100 occurrences from 800 BCE to 600 CE, I could find nothing to augment Rengstorf's list. In Aristophanes ἁμαρτωλός is used to describe an old fellow who is a κλέπτος καὶ πανοῦργος (*Thesmophoriazusae* 111). In Aristotle the mean between 'excess and defect' is the goal but one of the two is ἁμαρτωλότερον, i.e. misses the mean more than the other (*Nicomachean Ethics* 2.9.1-3). For Plutarch, 'the ignorant man always misses the mark (ἁμαρτωλόν) in everything, while the refined man does all things well' (*Moralia* 25c). In none of these does the meaning carry a religious sense. The grave inscriptions from Lycia, on the other hand, denote an offence to the gods without implying moral transgression.

Stoic literature, Josephus or Philo.[1] This fact is particularly surprising in view of Philo's intimate acquaintance with the Septuagint, where the term is used in abundance.

It has been proposed recently that the meaning of ἁμαρτωλός resides in its relationship to the Hebrew *resha'im* of the Masoretic text. Sanders calls *resha'im* a 'technical term' in the Old Testament for those who purposely sinned and refused to repent.[2] While contextually the *resha'im* of the Old Testament are too varied in nature to support a single meaning in a technical sense,[3] the basic equation of the *resha'im* and the ἁμαρτωλοί has merit. The *resha'im* are those beyond the pale in terms of salvation.

Of the 250 plus occurrences of *rasha'* and its cognates in the MT, the LXX used ἁμαρτωλός in seventy-three instances (29%).[4] Most revealing however, is the fact that of these seventy-three instances, sixty two (85%) occur in the Greek Psalms.[5] Obviously, if we are to learn about the 'sinner' in the Old Testament we will be primarily concerned with the semantic field of the Psalms. T.W. Manson noted many years ago that the 'sinners' theme is 'most frequent in the

---

E.g. 'let him [who desecrates this grave] be a sinner against the infernal gods' (*Corpus Inscriptionum Graecarum*, III, 4307; see also 4303). Also, 'If the ruler and the citizens do not carry out the sacrifice annually, let them be sinners in the sight of all the gods' (W. Dittenberger, *Orientis Graeci Inscriptiones Selectae*, I [Lipsiae: S. Hirzel, 1903], p. 91, ref. 55.31f.). The only other occurrences are Philodemus Philosophus, *De Ira*, p. 73 (Wilke), δοῦλοι ἁμαρτωλοί; and Eupolis, 24, Demianczuk Supplement Com. where it is a simple term of derision. See further, *TDNT*, I, p. 318.

1.   The stoics use φαῦλος ('worthless, bad, evil'), not ἁμαρτωλός, to signify one who stumbles from failing to failing (ἁμαρτάνειν); Rengstorf, *TDNT*, I, p. 319.

2.   E.P. Sanders, *Jesus and Judaism*, pp. 177-78.

3.   See B. Chilton, 'Jesus and the Repentance of E.P. Sanders', pp. 9-10.

4.   E. Hatch and H.A. Redpath, *A Concordance to the Septuagint*, I (Oxford: Clarendon Press, 1897–1906), pp. 64-65. *Rasha'* is also translated by: ἀσεβής (120×), ἄδικος (5×) and ἄνομος (32×).

5.   More generally, the occurrences of ἁμαρτωλός and the Hebrew word it translates are: 72× = *rasha'*, wicked; 2× = *resha'*, wickedness; 12× = *hata'*, sinful, sinners; 3× = *hote'*, participle of *hata'*; 1× = *hanep*, profane, irreligious, hence often heathen, apostate; 1× = *harash*, obscure, 'plowers' used figuratively for oppression by wicked (Ps. 128.3); 1× = *ra'*, evil, bad. *Rasha'* occurs 81× in the Psalms; 62 are translated as ἁμαρτωλός.

Psalter'.[1]

This fact should have considerable weight as we consider the
'sinner' of the New Testament. If the Gospel tradition was influenced
by the LXX's use of ἁμαρτωλός, the Psalms are likely to have played
the most important role. This is consistent with what is known about
the role of the Psalms in the religious life of Jews during this period.
The actual synagogue usage of Scripture for the pre-70 period is not
well attested; it seems certain however that the weekly reading would
have customarily come from the law and the prophets.[2] This is the
case in Lk. 4.16-20 in the reading of Isa. 61.1-2 at the commencement
of Jesus' ministry; and with Paul at the synagogue in Antioch Pisidia
in Acts 13.15. Paul went on, however, to expound the sermon and
there he quoted the Psalms three times.[3] *M. Shab.* 16.1 prohibited the
use of the Hagiographa in synagogue worship since it was thought to
detract from the study of the law; but such a prohibition would not
have been necessary if the Psalms had not been popular in the synagogue. Furthermore, the prominence of the Psalms in the liturgy of
the Temple and the feast days confirms that the Psalms were widely
known and used at this time.[4] The Hebrew Scripture reading from the
Hagiographa actually took preference over the Torah at the festival of
the Feast of Weeks. The Psalms are also the most quoted book in the
New Testament,[5] so there can be little doubt that the psalter figured
prominently in supplying the semantic understanding of the 'sinner' in
this period. As we consider the evidence for the 'sinner' in the
literature of late Second Temple Judaism, the Greek psalter should be

---

1.   T.W. Manson, *The Teachings of Jesus* (Cambridge: Cambridge University
Press, 1931), p. 324.
2.   On the use of the Psalms in synagogue worship see H. St John Thackeray,
The Septuagint in Jewish Worship: A Study in Origins (London: Oxford University
Press, 1921), pp. 67-76; and Jacob Mann, *The Bible as Read and Preached in the
Old Synagogue*, I (New York: Ktav, 1971), pp. xiii-xvii. See also Safrai, *The
Jewish People*, II, pp. 927-33.
3.   Acts 13.33, Ps. 2.7; Acts 13.35, Ps. 16.10; and perhaps Acts 13.22, Ps.
89.20.
4.   See especially the minor tractate of the Babylonian Talmud, *b. Sof.* 16 Rule
1-3 (Soncino Edition) for a list of the use of Psalms for the feast days of the Sabbath;
also *Pes. R.* 2 and *m. Tam.* 7.4.
5.   This fact is derived from the United Bible Society Greek New Testament
'Index of Quotations' (2nd edn, 1968), pp. 906-909.

weighted as an important source.

Who is the 'sinner' in the Greek Psalms? When we find the term 'sinner' in an ancient document can the historical referent ever be identified with any confidence? Many have tried to fix such an identity for the 'sinner'[1] in the Psalms and the varied results demonstrate the conjectural nature of the task.[2] The proposed answers cover a considerable range: Israel's national enemies,[3] the psalmist's personal enemies,[4] the 'Israelites who have gone astray',[5] or those both within and without Israel who have simply 'turned away from God'.[6] W.O.E. Oesterley, adopting a later post-exilic dating for the Psalms, believed the 'sinners' were the enemies of the *ḥasidim* of the Maccabean period.[7] He further concluded that since the 'sinners' in Pss. 86.14, 140.5 and 101.5 were 'haughty... proud' and had a 'high look and arrogant mind', they must have been the higher social stratum of society.[8] The dangers of such over-interpretation are self-evident.

A more effective approach will be to back away from such specific

---

1.   I will use the term 'sinner' here even though most modern English translations of the Psalms, esp. the RSV, will have the word 'wicked'. The LXX has ἁμαρτωλός in the texts quoted here.

2.   For treatments of the state of scholarship on this question see G.W. Anderson, 'Enemies and Evil-doers in the Book of Psalms', *BJRL* 48 (1965–66), pp. 18-29; also, more recently, Steven Croft, *The Identity of the Individual in the Psalms* (Sheffield: JSOT Press, 1987), pp. 15-48.

3.   H. Birkeland, *The Evildoers in the Book of Psalms* (Oslo: Dybwad, 1955), p. 93; Moses Buttenwieser, *The Psalms: Chronologically Treated with a New Translation* (New York: Ktav, 1969), pp. 368, 431.

4.   The view of Sigmund Mowinckel at one point (see Croft, *Identity*, pp. 15ff.).

5.   S.N. Rosenbaum, 'The Concept "Antagonist" in Hebrew Psalm Poetry: A Semantic Field Study' (PhD Thesis, Brandeis University; Ann Arbor: Xerox University Microfilms, 1974); quoted from Croft, *Identity*, p. 18. Gesenius says *rasha'* is rarely used of the Gentiles (*Gesenius' Hebrew and Chaldee Lexicon to the Old Testament Scriptures* [trans. Samuel P. Tregelles; Grand Rapids: Baker Book House, 1979], p. 781).

6.   Croft, *Identity*, p. 20, and A.A. Anderson, *The Book of Psalms*, I (London: Oliphants, 1972), p. 59.

7.   See W.O.E. Oesterley, *The Psalms* (London: SPCK, 1953), p. 59; but cf. Helmer Ringgren who represents the more recent view that the Psalms are earlier than the Maccabean period (*The Faith of the Psalmists* [London: SCM Press, 1963], pp. 37-38).

8.   Oesterley, *Psalms*, p. 160. Similarly S. Mowinckel, *Psalmstudien*, I (Amsterdam: Verlag P. Schippers, 1966; reprint of 1922 original), pp. 76-95.

proposals and examine the general features of the 'sinner' in our literature. One of the most telling basic observations about the 'sinners' in the Greek Psalms[1] is that they are a corporate entity. That is, when we speak about 'sinners' it is always in a plural, collective sense. Perhaps more than any other factor, this informs us of the kind of language with which we are dealing. The 'sinners' are a group who, in the mind of the author, are the very opposite of all that is good and acceptable.[2]

Some examples may demonstrate the point. In Ps. 10.3 (LXX 9.24) the 'sinner boasts in the desires of his heart'. The reference is singular (ὁ ἁμαρτωλός), but the psalm obviously describes the 'sinner' as a type. In Ps. 37.10-14 (LXX 36.10-14) we find,

> Yet a little while and the sinner will be no more; though you look well at his place, he will not be there. . . the sinner plots against the righteous, and gnashes his teeth at him. . . The sinners draw the sword and bend their bows, to bring down the poor and needy, to slay those who walk uprightly.

Again, the intent is not to identify an individual but to depict the nature of this group who are opposed to God's 'righteous'. The text moves from the singular (v. 10, ἁμαρτωλός/*rasha'*) to the plural (v. 14, ἁμαρτωλός/*resha'im*) without any real change in meaning. The singular *rasha'*/ἁμαρτωλός of the MT and LXX in Ps. 39.1 (LXX, 38.1) are translated in the RSV as plural, 'I will bridle my mouth, so long as the wicked *are* in my presence'. The language is singular but the intent is to express the 'sinners' as a plurality and the RSV rightly conveys the plural sense. The singular also occurs in the MT/LXX in Pss. 50.16 (LXX, 49.16); 55.3 (LXX, 54.4); 71.4 (LXX, 70.4) with the obvious meaning of the one who fits the type of a wicked one. Indeed, in the English text the word 'wicked' has lost all distinction between the singular and plural. So far as the Greek Psalms are concerned we

---

1.   The texts in Psalms where *rasha'* is translated by ἁμαρτωλός are: 3.7; 7.9; 9.16, 17; 10.3, 4, 15; 11.3, 7; 28.3; 32.10; 34.21; 36.11; 37.10, 12, 14, 16, 17, 20, 21, 32, 34, 40; 39.1; 50.16; 55.3; 58.3, 10; 68.2; 71.4; 73.3, 12; 75.8, 10; 82.2, 4; 91.8; 92.7; 94.3 (2×), 13; 97.10; 101.8; 106.18; 109.1, 6; 112.10 (2×); 119.53, 61, 95, 110, 119, 155; 129.4; 139.19; 140.4, 8; 141.10; 145.20; 146.9; 147.6.

2.   See Rengstorf, 'ἁμαρτωλός', *TDNT*, I, p. 320; the 'sinner' is the 'negation of right and order and custom to an inordinate degree'.

may not speak of the 'sinner' as a single person, he is a type for the 'wicked' as a group.

It is also instructive to examine the nature of the general information which the passages in the Greek Psalms convey about the 'sinner'. There are actually only two references in the whole of the Septuagint that identify the 'sinner' with a specific group. One occurs in Ps. 106.18 (LXX 105.18) where the company of Dathan and Abiram are referred to as ἁμαρτωλοί; the other is Isa. 14.5 where the king of Babylon is referred to indirectly as an ἁμαρτωλός. Otherwise, the level of information about the identity of the 'sinner' is quite general.

In several passages the 'sinners' are simply contrasted with the 'righteous' in order to demonstrate the different fate of each group (Pss. 7.9; 34.21; 68.2; 75.8; 91.8; 104.35). The use here is something like the *'ammei ha-aretz* as compared to the *talmidei hakamim*, i.e. a foil against which the good are favourably contrasted. The 'sinners' are also said to be in distress in this life (Pss. 32.10; 84.10; 112.10) and other passages consist of the 'righteous' calling for rescue from the 'sinners' (Pss. 36.11; 97.10).

The 'sinners' are vilified as men of 'violence' (Pss. 11.5-6; 58.2; 140.4), 'cruel and unjust' (Ps. 71.4) and 'workers of evil' (Pss. 28.3; 36.11-12; 92.7; 101.8; 141.5). Specific deeds for which they are condemned are befriending thieves and adulterers (Ps. 50.18) and slander (Ps. 50.19-20). In Psalm 119 the 'sinner' is the one who forsakes the law (Pss. 119.53, 109-10, 119, 155).

Among the most specific passages are those which identify the 'sinners' as Israel's national enemies (Pss. 9.15-16; 10.15-16; 94.3-5; 129.3-4) and those which condemn the 'sinners' as the oppressors of the poor and downtrodden (Pss. 10.2-3, 12-15; 37.14-16; 82.2-4; 94.1-7; 109.16; 146.9; 147.6). Similarly, the 'sinners' are those who have ill-gained prosperity at the expense of the meek who do not 'possess the land' (Pss. 37.7, 9-11, 22, 34; 73.3-12, 16-20).

The 'sinners' as Israel's national enemies and the oppressors of the poor are the most explicitly sociological identifications in the psalter. Still, all these passages reveal more about the ideological point of view of the writer than the historical or sociological identity of those designated 'sinners'.[1] Historical information may indeed underlie the de-

---

1. Birkeland, *Evildoers*, p. 17, saw a 'pattern' to the portrayal of the 'wicked' in the Psalms and noted that it develops with 'very few specific, individual features

scriptions but it would have been no more recoverable to the first-century reader of the Greek Psalms than it is to the modern reader. Thus far we have learned more about the ideology of the author of the Psalms than about the historical referents called 'sinners'.

Outside the canon there is a somewhat greater tendency to associate the 'sinner' with specific people or groups. 1 Maccabees is an example; there 'sinner' is used to refer to Antiochus Epiphanes (1 Macc. 1.10) and his people (1 Macc. 1.34; 2.44-48). We also have Tob. 13.6 where the term refers to the nation of Nineveh; and Wis. 19.13 where it refers to the Egyptians. Likewise, it would seem that many of the references to 'sinners' in the *Psalms of Solomon* have the immediate oppressors of Israel in view.[1] In the 'two ways of the righteous and the sinner' in the *Apocalypse of Weeks* in *1 Enoch* 91–107, one gets the distinct feeling that a specific group of people is in view. This group is vilified throughout for its oppression of the righteous (*1 En.* 95.7; 96.4; 97.8; 98.6-8; 99.6; 100.7) and finally condemned.

Other than these references, every mention of the ἁμαρτωλός in the Apocrypha[2] is of a general ideological nature, that is, part of a description of the struggle between absolute good (represented by God and the 'righteous') and absolute evil (represented by the 'sinners').[3] For example

> Good is the opposite of evil, and life the opposite of death; so the sinner is the opposite of the godly. . . From the beginning good things were created for good people, just as evil things for sinners' (Sir. 33.14, 39.25)

Additionally, what has been said of the 'sinner' in the Greek Psalms

being perceptible'.

1.   R.B. Wright, the translator of the *Psalms of Solomon* in Charlesworth, *OTP*, thinks *Pss. Sol.* 2.1 may refer to Pompey; see II, p. 651. Other passages also seem to have these oppressors in view, especially 15.9-11; 17.4-5, 21-25.

2.   There are 60 occurrences of ἁμαρτωλός in the Apocrypha; I find 7 more than those listed in *A Concordance to the Apocrypha/Deuterocanonical Books of the Revised Standard Version* (Grand Rapids: Eerdmans, 1983), p. 386; see also L.T. Whitelock, *An Analytical Concordance of the Books of the Apocrypha*, II (Washington, DC: University Press of America, 1978), pp. 310-11. 'Sinners' are found in Tobit (3×), *Wisdom of Solomon* (2×), Sirach (40×), 1 Maccabees (5×), 2 Maccabees (2×), *Prayer of Manasseh* (3×), 2 Esdras (5×).

3.   See these examples: Tob. 13.6; 4.17; *Wis.* 4.10; 19.13; Sir. 1.25; 2.12; 3.27; 5.6, 9; 8.10; 13.7; 19.22; 21.6; 41.5; 2 Macc. 12.23; *Pr. Man.* 5; 2 Esd. 15.22, 23; *et al.*

applies to these references: they are a corporate entity and they are not identified with specific individuals.[1] In the Pseudepigrapha many examples can be seen of the ideological usage of the term 'sinner'.[2] Among the pre-70 writings consider *Pss. Sol.* 13.6: 'For the destruction of the sinner is terrible; but nothing shall harm the righteous', and *Pss. Sol.* 14.1, 6,

> 1 The Lord is faithful to those who truly love him, to those who endure his discipline. . . 6 But not so are sinners and criminals, who love (to spend) the day in sharing their sin.[3]

Also *1 En.* 81.7-8,

> For the upright shall announce righteousness to the upright; and the righteous ones shall rejoice with the righteous ones and congratulate each other. But the sinners shall die together with the sinners; and the apostate shall sink together with the apostate.[4]

What we found to be true of the 'sinners' in the Psalms applies likewise to the Apocrypha and Pseudepigrapha: the usage is essentially ideological and corporate.

'Sinners' and the Theme of Judgment

The overriding theme in relation to the 'sinner' in the Psalms is that of condemnation. Indeed, almost half of the references to 'sinner' in the Greek Psalms refer explicitly to their destruction or damnation. Taken individually the passages are not remarkable, but when exam-

---

1.   The greatest use of ἁμαρτωλός is in Sirach, yet Büchler observed that in Sirach 'no definite action of a distinctive, punishable character is stated to indicate the nature of their [the sinners] transgression and its grade' (A. Büchler, 'Ben Sira's Conception of Sin and Atonement', *JQR* 13 [1923], p. 307).

2.   For a guide to the Greek Pseudepigrapha see A. Denis, *Concordance grecque des pseudépigraphes d'Ancien Testament* (Louvain-la-Neuve: Université Catholique de Louvain, 1987), pp. 134-35. There are 102 occurrences: *Psalms of Solomon* (35×), *Testament of Abraham* (14×), *3 Baruch* (1×), *Greek Apocalypse of Ezra* (10×), *Apocalypse of Sedrach* (10×), *Testament of Judah* (1×), *Testament of Benjamin* (1×), *Life of Adam and Eve* (1×), *1 Enoch* (27×), *Sibylline Oracles* (1×), *Jubilees* (1×). I have identified occurrences of 'sinner' (ET) in the following non-Greek Pseudepigrapha: *Apoc. Elij.* 1.11; 5.10, 27, 37; *2 En.* 10.4ff.; *Vis. Ezra* 8–11; 42; 60; *Ques. Ezra* 2; *4 Ezra* 16.53; *T. Isaac* 4.27-31.

3.   See also *Pss. Sol.* 15.1-12; 16.5; 17.4-5.

4.   See also *1 En.* 5.6; 22.1-14.

ined as a whole the theme of judgment clearly emerges. Some of these passages assign the 'sinner' to divine wrath in the severest apocalyptic language.

> On the sinner he will rain coals of fire and brimstone; a scorching wind shall be the portion of their cup. (Ps. 11.6)

> For in the hand of the Lord there is a cup, with foaming wine, well mixed; and he will pour a draught from it, and all the sinners of the earth shall drain it down to the dregs. . . (Ps. 75.8)

In these and many other passages the psalmist calls for the absolute destruction of the 'sinner', seemingly without the slightest desire that they be spared their plight.[1] The psalmist's cry is not simply for justice, although in some passages this is the point, but rather a demand for *judgment* upon the 'sinners'.

> As smoke is driven away, so drive them away; as wax melts before fire, let the sinner perish before God! (Ps. 68.2)

The language of 'sinners' in the psalter is the language of judgment, condemnation and utter destruction and this sense of judgment is thematically dominant.[2]

This pattern of the 'sinner' as the object of judgment is fully developed in the inter-testamental literature as well.[3] It is interesting to note that the earlier Pseudepigraphic literature[4] treats the 'sinner' in a manner almost identical to that of the Psalms. As in the Psalms, judgment is the dominant theme and the 'sinner' is not portrayed as one

---

1. See also Pss. 3.7; 7.9; 9.16, 17; 10.15; 11.6; 34.21; 37.10, 12-13, 20-22, 34; 50.22; 68.2; 75.8; 91.8; 92.7; 94.2, 3, 13; 101.8; 104.35; 119.55; 129.4; 141.5-7; 145.20; 146.9; 147.6.

2. Stephen Croft agrees that the whole concept of 'wicked/sinner' in the Psalms relates to their judgment before God (*Individual*, p. 20).

3. In an extensive topical analysis of the 'sinner' in the Apocrypha and Pseudepigrapha, E. Sjöberg observes with regard to the earlier literature, 'for the sinner the punishment of a righteous justice holds dominion, but for the pious it is the gracious mercy of God' (*Gott und die Sünder im palästinischen Judentum* [Stuttgart–Berlin: Kohlhammer, 1938], p. 200). See also P. Fiedler, *Jesus und die Sünder* (Frankfurt: Peter Lang, 1976), pp. 75-82.

4. That is, those pieces which are generally thought to pre-date the first century CE: *1 Enoch* and the *Psalms of Solomon*. The *Prayer of Manasseh* also originates from this period but it is an exception in its treatment of the 'sinner', as we shall see below.

for whom repentance and salvation are possible. This is absolutely clear in *1 Enoch*.[1] For example:

> Behold, he will arrive with ten million of the holy ones in order to execute judgment upon all. He will destroy the wicked ones and censure all flesh on account of everything that they have done, that which the sinners and the wicked ones committed against him. (1.9)

> For the upright shall announce righteousness to the upright; and the righteous ones shall rejoice with the righteous ones and congratulate each other. But the sinners shall die together with the sinners; and the apostate shall sink together with the apostate. (81.7-8)

Such a view is also characteristic of the so-called *Apocalypse of Weeks* of *1 Enoch* 91–107 where the 'sinners' are vilified throughout for their oppression of the righteous and are finally condemned.[2]

Perhaps the clearest example of this kind of thinking in early inter-testamental literature is in the *Psalms of Solomon*.[3] As has already been noted, the sense of identification of the 'sinner' in this book never seems to be far from an actual historical referent in the writer's world. There is more certainty and concreteness in this book's portrayal of the 'sinner' than in many other places in the inter-testamental literature. Nevertheless, the ideological concept of 'righteous' and 'sinner' as two sides of the ethical divide is very prevalent.[4] In *Pss. Sol.* 3.4-12 a series of three couplets occurs which clearly set out the writer's view of how humanity should be viewed.

---

1. Fragments of *1 Enoch* have been found at Qumran and its various segments date between 200 BCE and the early part of the first century CE; see Charlesworth, *OTP*, I, pp. 6-7; and further R.H. Charles, *Apocrypha and Pseudepigrapha of the Old Testament*, II (London: Oxford University Press, 1913), pp. 170-71. See further J.H. Charlesworth, 'The SNTS Pseudepigrapha Seminars at Tübingen and Paris on the Book of Enoch', *NTS* 25 (1979), pp. 315-23; esp. p. 322 on the relation of Enoch to Luke.

2. See esp. *1 En.* 95.7; 96.4; 97.8; 98.6-8; 99.6; 100.7. See also *2 En.* 10.4ff. and *Apoc. Elij.* 1.11; 5.10, 27 for a similar view of the judgment of the 'sinner'.

3. R.H. Charles dates *Psalms of Solomon* at middle of first century BCE (*APOT*, II, p. 625); R.B. Wright, the translator in Charlesworth, dates the bulk of the Psalms between 70–45 BCE (*OTP*, II, p. 461).

4. Sjöberg says of the 'sinner' in the *Psalms of Solomon*, 'Time and again the final punishment of the sinner is stressed. These will be wiped out but the godly will inherit the promised redemption of God' (*Gott und die Sünder*, p. 207).

The righteous stumbles and proves the Lord right;
he falls and watches for what God will do about him;
he looks to where his salvation comes from (3.5).
The sinner stumbles and curses his life, the day of his birth, and his
mother's pains (3.9).

The confidence of the righteous (comes) from God their saviour; sin after
sin does not visit the house of the righteous (3.6).
He [the sinner] adds sin upon sin in his life;
he falls—his fall is serious-and he will not get up (3.10).

The righteous constantly searches his house, to remove his unintentional
sins. He atones for (sins of) ignorance by fasting and humbling his soul,
and the Lord will cleanse every devout person and his house (3.7)
The destruction of the sinner is forever, and he will not be remembered
when (God) looks after the righteous. This is the share of sinners forever. . . (3.11).

This triplet shows that the twofold portrayal of the 'righteous' and
'sinner' was popular into the first century BCE and also that it was still
firmly tied to the concept of judgment of the 'sinner'. The treatment is
very similar to the treatment of the 'sinners' in the Psalms.[1]

As we have already seen, Sirach displays a similar usage of the
'righteous' and 'sinners' as two ideological categories. Just as is often
seen in the Psalms, Sirach's view of the world is one where there is no
middle ground between the two categories of good and evil and it is
the 'sinner' who represents evil. Sirach's attitude is perhaps best
summed up in this passage:

What fellowship has a wolf with a lamb? No more has a sinner with a
godly man. (Sir. 13.17)[2]

Thus, from the second century BCE to the turn of the era, strong literary evidence exists of a view of 'sinners' that is in basic harmony with
the ideological representation of the 'righteous' and the 'sinners' in the
Psalms. No restitution was contemplated for the 'sinner'; judgment
was the only prospect. Furthermore, this material is essentially ahis-
torical in its content; in the majority of cases it cannot be said to point

1.   As Charles has noted (*APOT*, II, p. 628).
2.   See also Sir. 12.4-7, 'The Most High himself hates sinners. . . ' See E.P.
Sanders, *Paul*, pp. 342-46, for a treatment of the wicked in Sirach, and A. Büchler,
'Sin and Atonement', pp. 305-35.

to specific persons in history but is primarily a reflection of the ideological and religious point of view of the author.

'Sinners' and Repentance

A person in a position to perform penance is in a very different situation from the 'sinner' for whom no such avenue is open; it marks the
divide between inclusion and exclusion from the people of God. It is
without question, however, that the 'sinner' of the Greek Psalms was
completely beyond the pale of such restoration:

> though the sinners sprout like grass and all evildoers flourish, they are
> doomed to destruction for ever. . . (Ps. 92.7)

> Let sinners be consumed from the earth, and let the wicked (ἄνομοι) be
> no more! Bless the Lord, O my soul! Praise the Lord! (Ps. 104.35)[1]

There is no hint of leniency nor reclamation for those who have been
assigned to this category and God is never seen to forgive the 'sinner'
in the Greek Psalms. When the Psalms do speak of forgiveness it is
not the notion of *resha'* ('wickedness') that is in view but *pesha'*
('transgression') and *ḥeṭ* ('sin').[2]

In the Apocrypha, Sirach is the only author who extensively deals
with the 'sinner' and the book is 'stamped throughout with the notion
of retribution for the sinner'.[3] While both Büchler and Sjöberg em-
phasize Sirach's offer of repentance to the sinner (e.g. Sir. 5.17;
17.24) and cite it as proof that the 'sinner' had a chance in Sirach's
theology,[4] the fact remains that the 'sinner' never does repent in Sirach. Rather than being the proof of the possibility of repentance for
'sinners', it is this very offer of repentance which makes the 'sinners''
condemnation so complete. It is precisely because God did not with-
hold an offer of forgiveness that the reader is able to understand the

---

1. See also Pss. 9.17; 11.6; 34.21; 37.10, 20, 22, 32; 58.6-9; 75.8; 91.8;
101.8; 119.155; 129.4; 141.5-7; 145.20; 147.6.
2. Psalm 51 immediately comes to mind. God forgives *pesha'* in Pss. 32.1;
51.5; Exod. 34.7; Num. 14.8; Job 7.21. He forgives *ḥeṭ* in Pss. 51.2 and 25.18.
So also in Lev. 6.1-6 (MT 5.20-26).
3. 'Das ganze Buch ist also vom Vergeltungsgedanken geprägt' (Sjöberg, *Gott
und die Sünder*, p. 209); see pp. 108-10 for his treatment of Sirach's use of 'sinner'.
4. Büchler, 'Sin and Atonement', p. 314; Sjöberg, *Gott un die Sünder*, pp.
208, 212.

full measure of guilt of the 'sinners' who ultimately reject every overture.

Consider also the psalm of Tob. 13.1-18. Here in v. 8 we find: 'Turn you sinners, and do what is right in his eyes, who knows whether he may not welcome you and show you mercy'. The text itself is the subject of some uncertainty; vv. 8-11 are a variant reading in Vaticanus and Alexandrinus to the generally superior text of Sinaiticus which omits the passage.[1] In any case, even taken as original, the passage is actually a prophetic call to repentance to the 'sinners' and thus, like Sirach, holds out little actual hope that the 'sinners' will respond positively. The Apocrypha confirms the same basic message of the Psalms: the 'sinner' is not the recipient of mercy.

In a similar way, the Hebrew *rasha'* itself rarely occurs, out of 253 instances in the Old Testament, in a penitential context, i.e. where the referent is spoken of in terms of repentance or restitution. A closer examination of two apparent exceptions reveals that they are not genuine cases of repentance at all. In Exod. 9.27 Pharaoh confesses that 'I and my people are wicked' (Heb. *resha'im*, LXX ἀσεβεῖς), but this repentance is clearly self-serving and Moses was not taken in. He replied to Pharaoh, 'But as for you and your servants, I know that you do not yet fear the Lord'. One understands immediately and with some irony that Pharaoh and his people are indeed 'wicked' in the normal sense of the word, that is, irredeemably condemned.

There is also the warning of the 'wicked' from their path of sin in Ezekiel, most poignantly in 33.11 where God says 'I have no pleasure in the death of the wicked, but that the wicked turn from his way and live . . .' (cf. also Ezra 18.21-23). However, the 'wicked' never actually repent in Ezekiel and are eventually destroyed (Ezra 9.5-8; 11.2-13; 21.1-5).[2]

Likewise, the Hebrew 'sinner' (*hata'*) is also usually an entirely pejorative designation. Only twice in its eighteen Old Testament occurrences is it used in the context of penitence.[3] So what is true of

---

1. See Zimmerman, *The Book of Tobit* (New York: Harper & Brothers, 1958), pp. 39-42, 127.

2. Notice, however, that this theme from Ezekiel is taken up and used as a call to repentance for the sinner in *1 Clem.* 10.2.

3. Pss. 25.8; 51.13. But cf. its negative connotation in Gen. 13.13; Num. 16.38; 32.14; 1 Sam. 15.18; Pss. 1.5; 104.35; Prov. 13.22; Isa. 13.9.

the Greek Psalms with regard to penitence for the 'sinner' is in basic agreement with the general notion of the 'wicked' and 'sinner' of the Hebrew text.[1]

What applies to the 'sinner' does not of course apply to all wrong-doers in the Old Testament. As many authors have shown, Judaism did have a theology of repentance for the wrongdoer which functioned alongside the standard cultic remedies for sin.[2] To say 'I am sorry' was never enough however. Maccoby describes the essence of the Jewish view of repentance: 'True repentance must comprise the gen-uine resolve to give up the repented sin'.[3] There is, for example, Lev. 6.1-7 where even the one who has sinned purposefully (including ly-

---

1. The attitude toward the 'sinner' in the Psalms seems to derive, at least in its mood, from the hard-line stance toward the law breaker found in Lev. 20.1-21. In that context the wrongdoer is to be put to death or 'cut off', the two evidently having the same meaning: 'Any man of the people of Israel, or of the strangers that sojourn in Israel, who gives any of his children to Molech shall be put to death. . . I myself will set my face against that man, and will cut him off from among his people. . . ' (vv. 1-3). Likewise, the penalty of death is fixed for those who consult mediums and wizards (vv. 6, 27), those who curse their father or mother (v. 9), commit adultery (v. 10), incest (vv. 11, 12, 17, 19-21), homosexual acts (v. 13), bestiality (vv. 15, 16), and the menstruant and her sexual partner. In a similar vein Num. 15.30-31 commands that those who do anything 'with a high hand', i.e. sin wittingly, whether he be an Israelite or otherwise, be 'cut off from among his people' (Hebrew, *hikaret*, niphal of *karat*) and 'his iniquity shall be upon him'. In neither of the above two passages is leniency or repentance contemplated. The destruction is unconditional and sure. To borrow G. Forkman's categories, the exclusion of the 'sinner' is 'definite' and 'total' (*The Limits of the Religious Community* [Lund: Gleerup, 1972], pp. 12-13).

2. This has been well demonstrated by the older apologists for Judaism; see C.G. Montefiore (Appendix III, 'On Repentance', *RLGT*, pp. 390-422) who says, 'The whole doctrine is genuinely and purely Hebraic. . . ' (p. 390). There is also the treatment of I. Abrahams, 'Publicans and Sinners', in *SPG*, pp. 54-61. Urbach sets out the rabbinic doctrine in 'The Power of Repentance', *Sages*, pp. 462-71; see also S. Baron, *A Social and Religious History of the Jews*, I (New York: Columbia University Press, 1957–76), pp. 294-95. More recently see Maccoby, 'Atonement and Repentance', *ERW*, pp. 89-92; and especially the section entitled 'The Consciousness of Sin and the Need of Forgiveness' by J.H. Charlesworth in his recent *Jesus within Judaism* (London: SPCK, 1989; first published by Doubleday, 1988), pp. 45-51. There he criticizes modern notions of early Judaism that depict it as being bereft of a theology of repentance.

3. Maccoby, *ERW*, p. 90.

ing, robbery, oppression of his neighbour) is permitted to make restitution and bring a guilt offering: 'and he shall be forgiven for *any of the things which one may do* and thereby become guilty'.[1] A similar statement of the possibility of repentance for wrongdoing is seen in Num. 5.5-7 where 'any of the sins that men commit by breaking faith with the Lord' are included, although the mention of restitution seems to indicate that wrong doing with respect to property is in view here. Even so, in Num. 5.11-29 the woman who fails the test of the waters of bitterness in regard to her fidelity to her husband is not stoned as was commanded in Leviticus 20. She simply becomes an 'execration' among her people and wastes away from the effect of the waters.

Nevertheless, the important point to be made here is that such repentance is never countenanced for the 'sinner' or the 'wicked'; they form an entirely discrete religious category, the necessary ideological counterpart of the 'righteous'. The fact that repentance was countenanced for the earnest wrongdoer sets the radically negative view of the 'sinner' in even greater relief.

Such ideological categories do not easily translate into concrete social settings, as has been evident from the lack of references to specific historic and social contexts in the texts about 'sinners' we have reviewed so far. The literature from Qumran demonstrates this same observation in a rather interesting way. In their theology the two spirits of 'truth' and 'falsehood', 'lightness' and 'darkness' function in much the same way as the 'righteous/sinner' language of the Psalms. In the Manual of Discipline the two groups are separated by an uncrossable moral divide: 'between the two categories he has set an eternal enmity'.[2] In practice however, the community could restore an offender to fellowship, even after purposeful breaking of the covenant.[3] It would seem that the necessity of promoting the interests of the sect in an actual social setting mandated a certain leniency, in spite of the rhetoric of ideology.

---

1. Also, Num. 5.5-7 and Deut. 30.1ff. express similar attitudes of the possibility for the transgressor to repent. See Forkman, *Limits*, pp. 16-27, for a review of expulsion in the Old Testament literature.

2. 1QS 4.16, 17. For the psalm-like condemnation of the wicked see also the Zadokite Document 2.2–3.11; 7.9.

3. 1QS 7.18-25. Similar provision is made in *t. Dem.* 2.8-9, the sectarian code of the Pharisees.

> Anyone who refuses to enter the (ideal) society of God and persists in
> walking in the stubbornness of his heart shall not be admitted to this com-
> munity of God's truth. . . unclean, unclean he remains so long as he re-
> jects the government of God. . . [however] only by a spirit of upright-
> ness and humility can his sin be atoned. . . then, indeed will he be ac-
> ceptable before God like an atonement-offering which meets with his
> pleasure, and then indeed will he be admitted to the covenant of the com-
> munity for ever.[1]

In practice, the theoretical enmity between the spirit of truth and the
spirit of falsehood was mitigated by social mechanisms that permitted
the rehabilitation of miscreants and the recruitment of new members.[2]
It is this type of social concern for restitution that is absent in the condemnation of the 'sinner' in the Psalms and shows the usage there to
be essentially ideological. In the Psalms it is not the ostracism of the
sectarian offender which is in view but the ideological condemnation
of the one who is God's enemy.

When we turn to the Pseudepigrapha the situation is quite different;
in this literature there are many expressions of entreaty for forgiveness for the 'sinner'. Thus, we must take exception to the assertion of
Sanders that the terminology of the 'wicked/sinners' is used 'with
complete consistency in the Gospels and in Jewish literature from Ben
Sira to the close of the Mishnah, a period of 400 years'.[3] This is sim-

---

1. 1QS 2.25–3.12. Any member who incurs expulsion may be readmitted after
two years repentant probation except one whose formal membership exceeded ten
years—he is forever banned (1QS 7.18-25).
2. A similar tendency is observable in later rabbinic literature. The loser in
halakhic disputes in the Mishnah is never called 'wicked'. The 'wicked' language
that is found is much less harsh than the Psalms; see *m. Ab.* 2.9 (cf. Ps. 37.21);
5.10-12; *m. Sanh.* 8.5; 10.3, 6. Not surprisingly, in the Babylonian Talmud the
references which deal with the 'righteous/wicked' are often based on quotes from the
Psalms, e.g. *b. Ber.* 7b, 8a, 10a, 61a-b; *b. Shab* 31b; *b. Erib.* 19a, 21a; *b. Ros.
Has.* 16b. Moreover, harsh ideological categories are at times mitigated by the
introduction of more categories than just the 'righteous' and 'wicked'. For three
categories: the 'righteous', the 'wicked' and the 'average', see *b. Ber.* 61a-b; *b.
Shab.* 152b; *b. Yom.* 75a-b; *b. Ros. Has.* 16b. Sometimes four: the 'perfectly
righteous', the 'not perfectly righteous', the 'not perfectly wicked', and the 'perfectly
wicked' (see *b. Ber.* 7a-b; and perhaps the four burial grounds in *b. Sanh.* 47a). The
purpose seems to be to bring language that does not readily lend itself to the
complexities of life's social realities into a more useful form.
3. E.P. Sanders, *Jesus and Judaism*, p. 179.

ply not so. There is a marked semantic shift in such terminology in the first century which shows how the 'sinner' has now become the object of God's mercy.

First, we observe that the Pseudepigrapha which are commonly thought to pre-date the destruction of Jerusalem share a viewpoint of the 'sinner' that is fundamentally the same as the Greek Psalms. The 'sinners' do not appear in a penitential context in *1 Enoch* or the *Psalms of Solomon*; the 'sinner' there is fully the object of condemnation and God's wrath.[1] In the two other major early Pseudepigraphic works, *Jubilees* (160–140 BCE) and *The Testaments of the Twelve Patriarchs* (c. 150 BCE) 'sinners' are not prominent.[2] Conversely, the Pseudepigrapha where the 'sinner' is spoken of in a penitential context (with the exception of the *Prayer of Manasseh*, as we shall see) tend to date from the post-destruction period.

The *Testament of Abraham* is an example where there are conventional Psalm-like expressions of the judgment of the 'sinner' (e.g. *T. Abr.* 13.3; 12) but also a new, more merciful view.[3] When the angel Michael consents to Abraham's wish to see all the inhabited world before he dies, the tour must be abbreviated when Abraham begins to consign all the 'sinners' he encounters to Hades. 'For behold', God says, 'Abraham has not sinned and he has no mercy on sinners' (*T. Abr.* 10.13). But God's view is found in v. 14:

> But I made the world, and I do not want to destroy any one of them; but I delay the death of the sinner until he should convert and live. Now conduct Abraham to the first gate of heaven, so that there he may see the

---

1. See *1 En.* 1.9; 5.6; 22.10-13; 81.7; 91.11; 94.5, 11; 95.2-3, 7; 96.1, 4; 97.7; 98.6, 10; 99.6; 100.2, 3, 9; 102.3, 5, 6; 103.5, 11, 15; 104.6, 7, 10; 106.18 (var.); *Pss. Sol.* 1.1; 2.1, 16, 34, 35; 3.9, 11, 12; 4.2, 8, 23; 12.6; 13.2, 5-8, 11; 14.6; 15.5, 8, 10-13; 16.2, 5; 17.5, 23, 25, 36.

2. The only references to the 'sinner' in the pre-destruction Pseudepigrapha are *T. Jud.* 25.5 and *T. Ben.* 4.2.

3. The book is difficult to date since there are no references to historical incidents. E.P. Sanders, however, doubts that the work could have been produced after 117 CE considering the state of upheaval in Judaism in Alexandria, its likely provenance, and dates it at 100 CE give or take twenty-five years. If the document is a Christian production, as M.R. James believed, it may actually be much later (Charlesworth, *OTP*, I, pp. 874-75).

judgments and recompenses and repent over the souls of the sinners
which he destroyed.[1]

Again we find in *T. Abr.* 11.11 that the destiny of the 'sinner' is a
cause for grief, not rejoicing.

> And when he [Adam] sees many souls entering through the broad gate,
> then he pulls the hair of his head and casts himself on the ground crying
> and wailing bitterly; for the broad gate is (the gate) of the sinners, which
> leads to destruction and to eternal punishment. And on account of this the
> first-formed Adam falls from his throne, crying and wailing over the de-
> struction of the sinners; for many are the ones who are destroyed, while
> few are the ones who are saved, righteous and undefiled.

This merciful attitude toward the 'sinner' is found in numerous other
places in the Pseudepigrapha: *T. Isaac* 4.27-31; *3 Bar.* 16.4-8; and
throughout the Ezra cycle: *Vis. Ezra* 8–11; *Ques. Ezra* 2-7 Recension
A; *Gk Apoc. Ezra* 1.10-12; 2.23; 5.1-6; 6.26ff.; *4 Ezra* 8.4-36, especially v. 31;[2] and the *Apoc. Sed.* 5.7.[3] None of these passages are
thought to pre-date the first century CE.[4]

Perhaps the most remarkable example of the 'sinner' being spoken
of in the context of repentance is the *Prayer of Manasseh*. This prayer
contains one of the earliest uses of 'sinner' in this way and may well
be the only pre-Christian example of the sort.[5] Charlesworth calls the

---

1.   Cf. Ezek. 33.11, 'I have no pleasure in the death of the wicked'. The LXX
translates *rasha'* as ἀσεβής in Alexandrinus but ἁμαρτωλός in Vaticanus.

2.   D. Boyarin has compared the elements of *4 Ezra* 7.102–8.36 to the *S^{e}lihot*
('forgiveness') liturgy of ancient Jewish practice ('Penitential Liturgy in *4 Ezra*', *JSJ*
1-3 [1972], pp. 30-34) but the *terminus ante quem* for such expressions would seem
to be *m. Ta'an.* 2.3 (cf. *b. Ros. Has.* 17b). His article certainly fails to demonstrate
any earlier genesis for the 'confession' element of the *S^{e}lihot* liturgy to which *4 Ezra*
8.31 seems to bear a resemblance. Even so, the liturgy itself does not use 'sinner'
language (see *ibid.*, p. 33).

3.   Perhaps also *LAE* 42.6 (Apocalypse) where Eve terms herself ἀνάξια καὶ
ἁμαρτωλή.

4.   See the discussions of dating by Charlesworth's contributors in *OTP*:
Testament of Abraham, I, p. 875; *Testament of Isaac*, I, pp. 903-904; *3 Baruch*, I,
p. 656; *Vision of Ezra*, I, p. 583; *Questions of Ezra*, I, p. 592; *Greek Apocalypse of
Ezra*, I, p. 563; *4 Ezra*, I, p. 520; *Apocalypse of Sedrach*, I, p. 606.

5.   Charlesworth and many scholars date the prayer in the 2nd–1st centuries
BCE, but a date sometime before the destruction is the earliest date which can be
relied upon, chiefly because of a lack of reference to or reflection of the destruction
(Charlesworth, *OTP*, II, p. 627). Ryle did not venture a date earlier than that by

prayer a 'virtually unparalleled confession of unworthiness and sinful-ness'.[1] In the prayer we find a moving account of a 'sinner', i.e. Manasseh, humbling himself and seeking restitution before God for his wrongdoing.[2] Interestingly, the 'sinner' is portrayed as both con-demned and redeemable in the prayer. The 'sinner' is found as the object of God's judgment and fury in v. 5:

> Because the grandeur of your magnificence cannot be endured, and none can endure or stand before your anger and your fury against sinners.

Then, in vv. 6 and 7a the conciliatory motif is introduced.

> But unending and immeasurable are your promised mercies; Because you are the Lord, long suffering, and merciful, and greatly compassionate; and you feel sorry over the evils of men.

Then vv. 7b and 8 brings the petition of Manasseh,

> 7b You, O Lord, according to the sweetness of your grace, promised forgiveness to those who repent of their sins, and in the multitude of your mercies appointed repentance as the salvation for sinners.[3] 8 You, there-fore, O Lord, God of the righteous ones, did not appoint grace for the righteous ones, such as Abraham, and Isaac and Jacob, those who did not sin against you; but you appointed grace for me, [I] who am a sinner.

It is unique that he specifically refers to himself with the word 'sinner'. More importantly, the prayer is significant because it was the wicked King Manasseh that offered it. He began to reign at twelve and we learn from 2 Kgs 21.1-9 that Manasseh:

> seduced them [the people of Israel] to do more evil than the nations had done whom the Lord destroyed before the people of Israel.

which the prayer must have been known in order to find its way into the Didascalia (3rd century CE), the earliest independent witness to the prayer (Charles, *APOT*, I, p. 614). See also the treatment of the prayer in Charlesworth's recent *Jesus within Judaism*, pp. 48-50.

1. Charlesworth, *Jesus within Judaism*, p. 48.
2. The general language of penitence in the prayer seems to derive from Exod. 34.6; Jon. 4.2; and especially Joel 2.12-13.
3. Verse 7b is not, however, in the earliest Greek manuscript, Alexandrinus. See H. Pfeiffer, *History of New Testament Times* (New York: Harper & Brothers, 1949), p. 458, and Charles, *APOT*, I, p. 621. Its earliest attestation is from the *Didascalia* in the Apostolic Constitutions and it is likely that v. 7b is a Christian interpolation. Verse 8 is not.

His list of misdeeds must surely place him among the worst offenders who ever ruled Israel. He:

> rebuilt the high places which Hezekiah his father had destroyed . . . erected altars for Baal. . . made an Asherah. . . worshipped the host of heaven and served them. . . built altars for all the host of heaven in the two courts of the house of the Lord. . . burned his son as an offering. . . practised soothsaying and augury and dealt with mediums and wizards. . . the graven image of Asherah that he had made he set in the house of which the Lord said to David and to Solomon his son, 'In this house, and in Jerusalem, which I have chosen out of all the tribes of Israel, I will put my name for ever. . . (2 Kgs 28.3-8).

And even though 2 Chronicles records that he humbled himself, requested and received God's favour (2 Chron. 33.10-13), a belief endured among the Jews into the post-70 period that he was so evil his prayer could not have been heartfelt.[1] In *2 Baruch* 64 the author catalogues Manasseh's sins (vv. 2, 3) indicating that he had driven the glory of the Most High itself from the sanctuary (v. 6) and then passes this judgment,

> Therefore, Manasseh was called the impious one in that time, and finally his habitation was in the fire. For although the Most High had heard his prayer, in the end he fell into the brazen horse and the brazen horse was melted. . . for he had not lived perfectly since he was not worthy. . . (vv. 7-9)

It would seem that Manasseh represents an archetypal 'sinner' in the classic sense of the Psalms. He fits the general description of one who is utterly condemned and, as *2 Baruch* and *m. Sanh.* 10.2 confirm, the possibility of repentance was deemed remote, if not impossible, for one such as he. Yet, here, quite apart from the usual habit of the earlier inter-testamental literature, the 'sinner' is portrayed as one to whom mercy and leniency should be extended.

The role of the 'sinner', beginning with the *Prayer* and continuing into the traditions of the later Pseudepigraphic literature, changes, quite remarkably, from a symbol for the utterly condemned to one to whom it is appropriate and desirable to show mercy. The literature of

---

1. *2 Bar.* 64.7–10; see A.F.J. Klijn's assessment of the dating of *2 Baruch* in Charlesworth, *OTP*, 1, pp. 616–17. Cf. also *m. Sanh.* 10.2, 'Three kings and four commoners have no share in the world to come. The three kings are Jeroboam and Ahab and Manasseh.'

the Christian community stands at the crux of this semantic shift. Whether the Gospel traditions were the cause of the shift is uncertain; but it seems clear that much of the later Pseudepigraphic material was influenced by this new role for the 'sinner'. The evidence of the *Prayer of Manasseh* would suggest that the view of the 'sinner' as a penitent was not unknown before the time of Jesus. Nevertheless, Jesus' call expressly to 'sinners' appears to be a considerable departure from the habit of his time. My conclusion is that the call to repentance was not new, but the call to repentance of the 'sinner' was.

'Righteous/Sinner' Language: Ideology, Metaphor and Symbol

We have seen that the words 'righteous' and 'sinner' are defined primarily in ideological terms in the literature of the late Second Temple period. Just as the 'righteous' represent those who do God's will, the 'sinners' are those who represent a whole complex of behaviour that is opposed to God and his ways. The literature we have examined does not condemn specific acts of wickedness so much as the idea of ungodly behaviour. The condemnation of the 'sinner' represents, more than anything else, an ideological point of view based on a conception of absolute right and wrong.

The ideological nature of such language is further demonstrated by the metaphorical and hyperbolic language in which the deeds of the 'sinner' are described. The 'sinner/s':

> bend the bow, they have fitted their arrow to the string, to shoot in the dark at the upright in heart. . . (Ps. 11.2).

> plots against the righteous, and gnashes his teeth at him; but the Lord laughs at him for he sees that his day is coming. The wicked draw their sword and bend their bows, to bring down the poor and needy, to slay those who walk uprightly (Ps. 37.12-14).

> pride is their necklace. . . eyes swell out with fatness. . . hearts overflow with follies. . . scoff and speak with malice. . . threaten oppression. . . set their mouths against the heavens. . . (Ps. 73.6-9).

This is not the language of sociology or history, but the rhetoric of ideology. Helmer Ringgren's observation about the opposition between the 'righteous' and the 'wicked' in the Psalms could not be more to the point:

> the opposition between the righteous and their enemies—whether they are
> called 'the wicked' or something else—is lifted up to the higher mytholog-
> ical or metaphysical level and related to the opposition between cosmos
> and chaos, or life and death, which. . . is so typical of the Israelitic view
> of life.[1]

A sociologically identifiable form of behaviour may actually underlie
the description of the 'sinner' as 'bending the bow. . . in the dark at
the upright in heart' but it cannot be recovered by us. The function
and purpose of such language is not the telling of history but the construction of an ideological perspective on the world: the 'righteous'
will overcome, the 'sinners' will be destroyed. It is perhaps one of the
fundamental axioms of a religious view of the world.

   In a similar sense the punishment of the 'sinner' is in the language
of metaphor.

> Arise, O Lord! Deliver me, O my God! For thou dost smite all my ene-
> mies on the cheek, thou dost break the teeth of the wicked (Ps. 3.7).

> The Lord has made himself known, he has executed judgment; the wicked
> are snared in the work of their own hands (Ps. 9.16).

> Break thou the arm of the wicked and evildoer (Ps. 10.15).

> But the wicked perish; the enemies of the Lord are like the glory of the
> pastures, they vanish—like smoke they vanish away (Ps. 37.20).

> For in the hand of the Lord there is a cup, with foaming wine, well mixed;
> and he will pour a draught from it, and all the wicked of the earth shall
> drain it down to the dregs. . . All the horns of the wicked he will cut off,
> but the horns of the righteous shall be exalted (Ps. 75.8-10).

   The probable effect of this language on the mind of the reader of
the Psalms in Greek would have been to evoke strong awareness of the
absolute evil of the 'sinner' and the certainty of his destruction. The
vivid metaphors and hyperbole serve to place the conflict between the
'righteous' and the 'sinners' in the highest possible contrast. The categories are mutually exclusive, there is no migration from one to the
other, just as good and evil are absolutely opposed. The opposition is
so sharp that the psalmist cannot conceive of any end for his opponent
other than condemnation.[2] The terms 'righteous' and 'sinner' express
the psalmist's view of the absoluteness of the moral order of the uni-

---

1.   Ringgren, *The Faith of the Psalmists*, p. 46.
2.   See Sjöberg, *Gott und die Sünder*, p. 207.

verse and are the means by which he organizes his world view. The term 'sinners' is merely a symbol for the enemies of God, the representatives of the condemned, the identification of whom makes possible the self-identification of the 'righteous'. In this way the psalmist provides a structure by which his or her own experiences can be interpreted. This structure, in turn, is adopted by the reader and can serve a similar function in a perhaps entirely different life context. 'Righteous/sinner' language 'works' for the reader in almost any situation, in almost any time. This fact accounts for the various identities proposed for the 'sinners' in the Psalms seen above. The vagueness of the content of the term is the reason it is universally applicable. One author has noted that some terms are of such a general nature that, upon scrutiny, 'they are found to have no clearly defined referent',[1] and this applies to 'sinners'. In a sense, it makes absolutely no difference who the historical referent of a Psalm was because the 'sinners' are, after all, exactly who the psalmist, or reader, *believes* them to be. They are the mental product of his world view. The 'sinners' actually exist only in the mind of the reader. The category contains only people who are assigned to it by the judgment of others.

For this reason it is best to speak of the 'sinners' not in terms of socially identifiable referents, but as a religious 'category'. A world view which contains conceptions of absolute right and wrong must have such a category. It is an essential element in a system of thought which distinguishes between good and evil; the 'sinners' are the necessary counterpart of the 'righteous'.

As we shall see in Part II, the basic 'categories' of the Gospel story function in a way similar to the ideological categories examined in this first part of our study. We have seen the difficulty in identifying the historical 'Pharisee', *'am ha-aretz* and 'sinner'. Yet the Gospel employs these categories to tell its story without any self-consciousness as to such difficulties. The 'Pharisees' are caricatured as the official Judaism that opposed the ministry of Jesus and the 'sinners' are the archetypal evildoers that become the beneficiaries of his call. Such religious 'categories' are the essential building blocks of the Gospel story.

---

1. G.B. Caird, *The Language and Imagery of the Bible* (London: Duckworth, 1980), p. 92.

PART II

Chapter 4

THE CALL OF LEVI

In Part II of this book selected portions of the Gospel of Luke will be examined with a view to achieving a better understanding of Luke's use of the 'sinners' theme. The material which relates to 'sinners' in Luke's Gospel is found in his central section, especially in chs. 5–19. It is here that the principal framework of controversy for the Galilean ministry is set out, and the chief players in the drama are the Pharisees and associates, the 'toll collectors and sinners', and Jesus. The passages which involve these characters are Lk. 5.27-32, 7.28-50, 15.1-32, 18.9-14 and 19.1-10; it is in these incidents and parables that Jesus' attitude toward 'sinners' is demonstrated and conflict with his contemporaries is aroused. Before turning to Luke 5 itself, an introductory section will deal with two issues which relate to the whole of Part II: the 'sinners' theme as it unfolds in the entirety of Luke and a consideration of Luke's portrayal of the Pharisees.

Introduction

The development of the story line in this central section of Luke depends on the growing controversy between Jesus and the Pharisees, with the 'sinners' being a key point of contention.[1] As we shall see, these 'sinners' provide the target group which Jesus attempts to reach and they are the source of conflict that demonstrates how Jesus differs from his fellow religionists. The 'sinners' are the principal device by which Luke demonstrates the extent and scope of Jesus' ministry; without 'sinners' the story would falter for want of a radical issue around which controversy can build.

Jesus similar declarations of purpose at Lk. 5.32 and 19.10 form an

---

1.   See J. Tyson, 'The Opposition to Jesus in the Gospel of Luke', *PRS* 5 (1978), p. 146.

inclusio describing the major theme which will dominate this section of the Gospel. When Levi abandons his toll table to follow Jesus (Lk. 5.28ff.), a banquet is convened to celebrate the event. The Pharisees object to the participation of Jesus and his disciples in this gathering saying, 'Why do you eat with toll collectors and sinners?' To this Jesus replies, 'I have not come to call the righteous, but the sinners to repentance'. The call of 'sinners' is thus established early on by Luke as one of Jesus' chief aims. An encounter with another 'sinner' and the accompanying charge of impropriety are also found in Lk. 19.1-10 in the story of Zacchaeus. Again, this scene culminates in a definitive statement of purpose by Jesus about the nature of his mission: 'For the Son of Man came to seek and to save the lost'. Robert Tannehill has noted the significance of this *inclusio*.

> Through repetition and significant placement the narrator emphasizes that these are important and comprehensive interpretations of the purpose of Jesus in God's plan.[1]

The inclusion of Levi among Jesus' followers in Luke 5 signals the inauguration of this mission to 'sinners' and the conversion of Zacchaeus serves as the vindication of this policy of inclusion pursued throughout the Galilean ministry.

The thematic unity of chs. 5–19 is further seen in the fact that all of Luke's Pharisee and 'sinner' material occurs in this section.[2] Five incidents in Lk. 5.17–6.11 introduce the theme of official opposition to Jesus in Luke. It begins at Lk. 5.17 with the objection by the 'Pharisees and teachers of the law' to the pronouncement of forgiveness for the paralytic; there is also the question on fasting (Lk. 5.33-39), the plucking of grain on the sabbath (Lk. 6.1-5) and the sabbath healing (Lk. 6.6-11). But the most significant incident in this small controversy section at Lk. 5.17–6.11 is the call of the 'sinner' Levi and the programmatic statement of purpose which accompanies the event. The 'sinner' theme is raised time and again (chs. 7, 15, 18) until, at the other end of the Galilean ministry, the conversion of the 'sinner' Zacchaeus closes the public ministry of Jesus and prepares the way for the Passion narrative. The 'sinner' motif is dropped after the Zacchaeus incident and at Lk. 19.39 the Pharisees make their final ap-

---

1. R. Tannehill, *The Narrative Unity of Luke–Acts* (Philadelphia: Fortress Press, 1986), pp. 107-108.
2. The only exception is the appearance of the toll collectors in Lk. 3.12.

pearance in the Gospel. Henceforth, the focus of controversy abruptly shifts to the setting of the Temple with 'the chief priests and scribes with the elders' (Lk. 20.1) now fulfilling the role of antagonists.[1]

Two factors combine to make the 'official' opposition encountered in Lk. 5.17ff. of special significance. First, prior to the commencement of his public ministry, Jesus is portrayed by Luke as having been raised in perfect orthodoxy. In Luke's special material Jesus had been circumcised (Lk. 2.21) and purified according to the Law of Moses at birth (Lk. 2.22). His parents were careful to 'do for him according to the custom of the law' (Lk. 2.27); and it was not until 'they had performed everything according to the law of the Lord' that they returned to Galilee (Lk. 2.39). Joseph and Mary attended Passover every year (Lk. 2.41) and Jesus himself demonstrated his love for the Temple (Lk. 2.49). Second, Jesus' special status as a prophet (Lk. 4.24) is repeatedly demonstrated from the commencement of public ministry at Lk. 3.21 to the beginning of our controversy section at Lk. 5.17. Various incidents attest to this status: the voice from heaven at his baptism (Lk. 3.22); his genealogy through David (Lk. 3.23ff.); his wilderness temptation (Lk. 4.1-13); and his initial rejection in Galilee from which he miraculously escapes harm (Lk. 4.16-30).

Having thus learned that Jesus was raised in orthodoxy and was the worker of great deeds, the official opposition encountered in Lk. 5.17ff stands in dramatic contrast to this positive portrait. As readers, we are surprised by this opposition because, in Luke's portrayal, it appears bigoted and unreasonable.[2] Notice, for example, that when Jesus casts out the unclean spirit in Capernaum on a sabbath (Lk. 4.31-37) there is no charge of impropriety raised by the onlookers, even though the act occurs in the synagogue and the authorities surely must have been present. The people are 'amazed' and the report of Jesus spreads far and wide. However, after the introduction of the opposition theme in Lk. 5.17ff. Jesus again heals on the sabbath; this time the man with the withered hand (Lk. 6.6-11). Here the scribes and Phari-

---

1. See also Lk. 20.19 and 22.2, 66, 'scribes and the chief priests'; Lk. 20.27, 'some Sadducees'; Lk. 22.52, 'chief priests and officers of the temple and elders'; see also Lk. 20.39, 46; 23.13.

2. The opposition is not completely unexpected. Conflict has also already been encountered from the devil (Lk. 4.1-12) and the people of Nazareth (Lk. 4.16-30); the foreshadowing of controversy can also be seen in Lk. 1.51-53 and 2.34.

sees 'watched him, to see whether he would heal on the sabbath', and were 'filled with fury' when he did so. The opposition theme has made a profound difference in Luke's interpretive presentation of two very similar incidents. The leaven of conflict has begun to work its effect on Luke's Gospel and to function as a catalyst for a deeper development of his story.

Luke's Pharisees

In order to appreciate the importance of the introduction of the Pharisees at the beginning of the central section of Luke, as well as for future reference in exegesis, it is necessary to give some attention to Luke's treatment of this group.[1] It is certainly true that the theme of conflict is one which is particularly susceptible to redaction in the Gospels,[2] and it is often said that Luke is less harsh on the Pharisees than the other Gospel writers. It would be more accurate to say that Luke is ambivalent in his treatment of the Pharisees and this fact is evidenced in an almost bewildering array of interpretations by scholars of Luke's attitude towards Pharisees.[3] Most frequently, far from being soft on his Pharisees, Luke portrays them as the very enemies of God's purpose. At other times, however, he presents them as the

1. For a general description of Luke's Pharisees see Tyson, 'Opposition to Jesus', pp. 144-50; also Tyson's article, 'Conflict as a Literary Theme in the Gospel of Luke', in *New Synoptic Studies* (ed. W.R. Farmer; Macon, GA: Mercer University Press, 1983), pp. 317-19. Numerous other recent authors have written on the subject, e.g. R.L. Brawley, *Luke–Acts and the Jews: Conflict, Apology and Conciliation* (Atlanta: Scholars Press, 1987), pp. 84-106; J.T. Carroll, 'Luke's Portrayal of the Pharisees', *CBQ* 50 (1988), pp. 604-21; E. Steele, 'Table-Fellowship with Pharisees: An Editorial Analysis of Luke 7.36-50, 11.37-54, and 14.1-24' (unpublished PhD dissertation; University of Notre Dame, 1981), pp. 146-49; J.A. Ziesler, 'Luke and the Pharisees', *NTS* 25 (1979), pp. 146-57.

2. See R. Bultmann, *History of the Synoptic Tradition* (Oxford: Basil Blackwell, 1972), pp. 52-53; see also J. Weber Jr, 'Jesus' Opponents in the Gospel of Mark', *JBR* 34 (1966), pp. 218-19.

3. Carroll calls Luke's treatment of the Pharisees 'puzzling' and 'complex' ('Luke's Portrayal', pp. 604, 607); Brawley notes the lack of consistency and 'ambiguities' in Luke on this subject (*Luke–Acts*, p. 85-86). Tyson says, 'Luke's attitude toward Pharisees and their allies appears to be ambivalent' ('Opposition to Jesus', p. 149).

'righteous'.[1] Moreover, the almost heroic representation of the Pharisees in Acts is often noted[2] and this only increases the enigmatic nature of Luke's attitude toward the Pharisees in his Gospel.[3]

How do Luke's Pharisees differ from those in the other Gospels? It would seem that Luke has adopted his basic body of conflict material about Pharisees from Mark (as does Matthew).[4] For example, the five conflict stories shown below derive from Mark and set the pattern for Luke's treatment of the same material.[5]

	Paralytic healed	Levi called	Question of fasting	Plucking of grain	Sabbath healing
Mk	2.1-2	2.13-17	2.18-22	2.23-28	3.1-6
Lk.	5.17-26	5.27-32	5.33-39	6.1-5	6.6-11
Mt.	9.1-8	9.9-13	9.14-17	12.1-8	12.9-14

Luke follows Mark's arrangement in general and also in placing this important series of conflict stories at the beginning of the Galilean ministry. Moreover, most of the traditions of conflict which appear in Mark are reproduced in one form or another in the triple tradition.[6]

1.   This is a little observed fact. See further below in Chapter 6, 'Implications for Luke's View of the Pharisees'.

2.   Brawley, *Luke–Acts*, pp. 88ff.; Ziesler, 'Luke and the Pharisees', pp. 146-48; Carroll, 'Luke's Portrayal', pp. 616ff. More recently B. Beck has proposed that even in Acts the Pharisees are a negative presence; see his *Christian Character in the Gospel of Luke* (London: Epworth Press, 1989), pp. 131ff.

3.   C.J. Hickling has said the treatment of the Pharisees in Acts 'is in contrast, both in content and in precision of historical concern' with the Gospel portrayal ('A Tract on Jesus and the Pharisees: A Conjecture on the Redaction of Luke 15 and 16', *HeyJ* 16 [1975], p. 265). His solution to this problem is the age of the material, the negative viewpoint of the Gospel being the latest material (p. 265).

4.   See J.C. Weber, 'Jesus' Opponents', pp. 214-22. In this study the thesis of Marcan priority is subscribed to, although it is not usually essential to the argumentation. In general, we follow the statement of W.R. Farmer that there is 'some sort of direct literary relationship between Matthew, Mark and Luke, and that the earliest of these was not Luke' ('Notes on a Literary and Form-critical Analysis of Some of the Synoptic Material Peculiar to Luke', *NTS* 8 [1961–62], p. 301. See further Farmer's *New Synoptic Studies* [Macon, GA: Mercer University Press, 1983]).

5.   Both Brawley, *Luke–Acts*, p. 85 and Carroll, 'Luke's Portrayal', p. 608, discuss the correspondence of Luke to Mark in this respect.

6.   Mk 2.1-12, 15-17, 23-28; 3.1-6, 20-27; 7.1-23 (Lk. 11.37-41); 8.11-13 (Lk. 11.29), 14-15 (Lk. 12.1); 10.2-10 (Lk. 16.18); 11.18-19; 12.13ff., and parallels. See C. Carlston, *The Parables of the Triple Tradition* (Philadelphia:

And even though Matthew and Luke add conflict material to their Gospels,[1] they adhere to the essential outlines of Mark's theme of controversy with the authorities in the non-Jerusalem portion of the ministry.

It is not the case, as some contend, that Luke is less harsh in his portrayal of the Pharisees than Matthew.[2] Both Matthew and Luke mention the Pharisees about the same number of times, yet all of Luke's material is organized in chs. 5–19, whereas Matthew's is much more diffuse (chs. 3–27). Thus, Luke displays a tighter and more directed presentation of his Pharisee material. Also, Luke often mentions the Pharisees where other Gospel writers do not specify them as Jesus' opponents.[3] An oft-cited 'exception' to Luke's uniformly negative view of the Pharisees is Lk. 13.31 where the Pharisees come to warn Jesus of Herod's plot to kill him. This is the single instance of a viewpoint in his Gospel similar to Luke's marked pro-Pharisee stance in Acts.[4] But the passage is incidental to the story line and anomalous to the general picture of Pharisees.[5]

Some examples of Luke's general portrayal of the Pharisees should serve to demonstrate his hostility. Other than Lk. 13.31 mentioned above, Luke is careful to avoid all positive references to the Pharisees. In the condemnatory material shared by Luke and Matthew (Luke 11 and Matthew 23), Matthew's Pharisees 'sit on Moses' seat' and Jesus' command is to do as they say but not as they do (Mt. 23.2-3). Even though Luke 11 contains most of the material in Matthew 23, he omits this information. It is significant in Luke 3 that the Pharisees do not come out for baptism by John as they do in Matthew's account of the incident (Mt. 3.7). For Luke this fact is later adduced as a fatal error

Fortress Press, 1975), pp. 10-11, 58-60.

1. Mt. 5.20; 15.3-6; 23.2-3, 5a, 7-12, 15-22, 24, 28; 27.62-66; Q: Mt. 15.12-13/Lk. 6.39; Mt. 23.4-5/Lk. 11.46; Mt. 23.13/Lk. 11.52; Mt. 23.23-36/Lk. 11.39-51; Lk. 5.17; 11.53; 13.31; 14.1ff.; 15.1; 16.14; 18.9ff.

2. As J.A. Ziesler argues, 'Luke and the Pharisees', *NTS* 25 (1979), pp. 146-57; also J. Dawsey, *The Lukan Voice* (Macon, GA: Mercer University Press, 1986), p. 126; Neusner, *Politics and Piety*, pp. 71-78; Brawley, *Luke–Acts*, pp. 86-88; Steele, 'Table-Fellowship with Pharisees', pp. 147-48.

3. E.g. at Lk. 5.21 and 6.7. See further H. Moxnes, *The Economy of the Kingdom* (Philadelphia: Fortress Press, 1988), p. 18.

4. Ziesler, 'Luke and the Pharisees', pp. 146-48.

5. Cf. Ziesler on Lk. 13.31, 'Luke and the Pharisees', p. 150.

for the Pharisees when he brings a passage, which in Mt. 21.32 is quite obscure, into a central place in the development of his story at Lk. 7.28ff. Luke tells his reader plainly that the Pharisees 'rejected the purpose of God' by ignoring the call of John the Baptist. Their failure to recognize the ministry of the Baptist is as clear a sign as Luke can give that the Pharisees are, in fact, the enemies of God's purpose.[1]

In another special logion Luke again skilfully implants the attitude he expects the reader to adopt with respect to the Pharisees by reporting these words of Jesus to the Pharisees (Lk. 16.15),

> You are those who justify yourselves before men, but God knows your hearts; for what is exalted among men is an abomination (βδέλυγμα) in the sight of God.

An 'abomination' (βδέλυγμα) is something which by its very presence before God provokes his wrath.[2] The underlying Hebrew (*to'ebah*) is often used in Proverbs in an ethical (that is non-cultic) sense just as it is intended here in Luke.[3] In Proverbs we learn that the conduct of the 'wicked' (*resha'im*) is *to'ebah* (LXX, βδέλυγμα).

> The way of the wicked is an abomination to the Lord (Prov. 15.9). . . . an unjust man is an abomination to the righteous (Prov. 29.27).[4]

The connection of the noun *to'ebah* with vain religious practice in Isa. 1.13 also seems appropriate for comparison to Lk. 16.15 in view of the indictment of the Pharisees for indulging in false piety.

> Bring no more vain offerings; incense is an abomination to me. New moon and sabbath and the calling of assemblies—I cannot endure iniquity and solemn assembly (Isa 1.13).

---

1.   So Carroll, 'Luke's Portrayal', p. 609; Tannehill, *Narrative Unity*, pp. 176-77.

2.   *BAG*, p. 137.

3.   BDB, p. 1073. Brawley (*Luke –Acts*, p. 86) makes the interesting observation on Lk. 16.14ff. that Luke calls Jesus' opponents φιλάργυροι, which appear in Greek literature as the negative counterpart to the philosophers (φιλόσοφος, e.g. Diogenes Laertius 6.56). On this basis he contends that Luke has used a Greek literary convention to portray Jesus' controversy with the Pharisees. But Brawley takes no notice of the powerful imagery of the term βδέλυγμα and its OT connotations. If Brawley is right, we have an interesting conflation of Greek literary convention and OT ideology.

4.   See also Prov. 6.16-19; 15.8, 26; 21.27; 24.9.

In another proverb we also find a condemnation of scoffing as an 'abomination' along the lines of the charge against the Pharisees of being scoffers (ἐξεμυκτήριζον αὐτόν, 'they scoffed at him') in Lk. 16.14.

> Every one who is arrogant is an abomination to the Lord; be assured, he will not go unpunished (Prov. 16.5).

The connection here in Luke with *to'ebah* could hardly form a more severe condemnation of the Pharisees. The OT understanding of the 'wicked' as an 'abomination' adds emphasis to Luke's portrayal of these Pharisaic leaders as scoffers and false religionists who are hateful to God. Luke alone uses the language of 'abomination' in reference to the Pharisees and it is characteristic of his tendency to portray the Pharisees as the extreme ideological enemies of God. Far from being soft on the Pharisees, Luke's treatment is more organized and negative than any of the other Synoptic evangelists.

To observe that Luke presents his Pharisees in a negative light still leaves open the important question of why he does so. In answering this question interpreters are often found looking down the proverbial well at their own reflection. Robert Brawley, for example, takes the position that Luke is soft on the Pharisees and that this shows the irenic purpose of Luke–Acts in establishing a basis for new inter-relationships between Jews and Gentiles in the Lucan community.[1] Halvor Moxnes, on the other hand, emphasizes that Luke is hard on his Pharisees.[2] This reinforces Moxnes's general thesis that the Pharisees are 'lovers of money' (Lk. 16.14) and the proper way to interpret Luke's treatment of them is as a critique of the economic structures of his day.

Interesting as this suggestion may be, it is not the most important aspect of Moxnes's approach. More significantly, Moxnes moves the consideration of Luke's Pharisees to the level of story and away from that of history. The question, says Moxnes, is not whether the Pharisees were really lovers of money, but 'what did Luke intend by this statement?'[3] At a cosmological level, he says,

> there is total disqualification of the Pharisees. Luke takes away from them

1. Brawley, *Luke–Acts*, pp. 1-5.
2. Moxnes, *Economy*, pp. 17-21.
3. Moxnes, *Economy*, pp. 5-6.

their right to God, to the law, and to the kingdom. . . The Pharisees in Luke's Gospel are not so much historical figures as stereotypes. His portrait of the Pharisees is designed to fit in to the overall theme of his Gospel. This is similar to the other Synoptic Gospels. Their interest is not so much to give a historically correct picture of various groups as to lump them together as opponents of Jesus. Their main characteristic is that they are described as <u>anti-types to Jesus and his disciples</u>.[1]

In a similar way John Carroll has criticized the lack of attention given in recent discussions to the role of Luke's Pharisees in 'plot development'.[2] Luke's treatment of the Pharisees is unique, says Carroll, in that he 'sketches a plausible evolution of hostility between Jesus and the Pharisees'.[3]

An appreciation of the Pharisees as a crucial element in the Lucan story brings the whole issue of religious categorization in this Gospel into focus. My own proposal for the reason for this Lucan hostility to Pharisees is that the Gospel story itself requires such a conflict. <u>No conflict, no Gospel story</u>. All other proposals must, in a sense, build on this fundamental observation. To speculate about the literary function of the Pharisees in his Gospel for the Lucan community or with respect to various social or economic factors is simply to build on this basic foundation. All Gospels, it would seem, must embody conflict and portray the struggle between an ideological good and evil; Luke's Pharisees, as we shall see, fulfil this role. The thesis offered here differs from those examined above in that the attempt made here is to push back to the most basic function of the Pharisees as a character group in the text. I turn now to the text of Luke to test my hypothesis.

Luke 5.17-26: The Setting

As we have already noted, at Lk. 5.17 controversy begins to play a

---

1. Moxnes, *Economy*, p. 152.
2. Carroll, 'Luke's Portrayal', pp. 606-607.
3. Carroll, 'Luke's Portrayal', p. 608. Carroll's answer as to the 'why' of this portrayal is that 'Luke uses Jesus' encounters with the Pharisees to portray opposing conceptions of the kingdom. And the Pharisees not only differ with Jesus on the nature and composition of God's *basileia* [the Pharisees have a restrictive, exclusivist understanding of the kingdom], but also, on the basis of this disagreement, they for the most part—in distinction from the people as a whole—in the end refuse participation in the kingdom defined by Jesus' (p. 616).

major part in the development of Luke's story. Verses 17-26 deal with the paralytic who is healed and forgiven in a dramatic scene at Capernaum. The significance of this controversy event centres around the theme of forgiveness of sins (v. 24) and thus forms a natural prologue to the relationship of Jesus to 'sinners' which is to follow.[1] This has also been presaged by the confession of sinfulness by Peter in Lk. 5.8 (ἀνὴρ ἁμαρτωλός εἰμι, κύριε). The confession there introduces the 'sinners' theme to the Gospel of Luke and first raises the prospect of forgiveness for the 'sinner'.[2]

The treatment of Lk. 5.17-26 need not be extensive here. Our interest is simply to see how vv. 17-26 form a preamble to the events and sayings of Lk. 5.27-32, where the core of the 'sinners' controversy material in this chapter is found. The Lucan setting of the healing of the paralytic is remarkable for several reasons. According to Luke there is an impressive audience gathered about Jesus from throughout Israel to witness what is about to occur:

καὶ ἦσαν καθήμενοι Φαρισαῖοι καὶ νομοδιδάσκαλοι οἳ ἦσαν ἐληλυθότες ἐκ πάσης κώμης τῆς Γαλιλαίας καὶ Ἰουδαίας καὶ Ἰερουσαλήμ. . .

In the preceding miracle of the cleansing of the leper in Lk. 5.12-16 the leper was charged by Jesus to tell no one of his healing except the priest. This next incident involving the paralytic, however, appears to be purposely staged by Luke as a crucial public event.[3] A setting in which such an important group of leading Jews has gathered is extraordinary.

It is perhaps understandable that in the history of the textual tradition a number of scribes removed the relative οἳ (v. 17b) or replaced it with δέ.[4] Thus, it becomes the sick who have come from all over the country and not the Pharisees and teachers of the law. Yet, the difficult reading is well attested and is most likely original.[5]

---

1. Tannehill, *Narrative Unity*, p. 104.

2. D. Hill, *The Gospel of Matthew* (Grand Rapids: Eerdmans, 1972), p. 173.

3. See the same tendency in Lk. 6.17 compared to Mt. 5.1.

4. ℵ*, 33 delete οἳ and D, it^{d,e}, syr^s replace it with δέ. See B. Metzger, *A Textual Commentary on the Greek New Testament* (London: United Bible Societies, 1975), p. 138; and further J.T. Sanders, *The Jews in Luke–Acts* (London: SCM Press, 1987), p. 170.

5. As Metzger judges (*Textual Commentary*, p. 138).

Compare this dramatic scenario to that of Mark where we learn only that Jesus was 'at home' and 'many were gathered together' (Mk 2.1) when the miracle occurred. In Mark it is only later in 2.6 and somewhat incidentally that he informs us that 'some of the scribes were sitting there'. The Marcan treatment is little concerned about dramatizing the setting and the identity of the opponents is vague. Likewise, Matthew knows nothing of this special Lucan information about the setting and Jesus has simply 'come to his own city' (Mt. 9.1) and 'some of the scribes' take issue with him (Mt. 9.3). Neither Mark nor Matthew sets the stage for an event of more than average importance. Overall, the dramatic function of the scene in Mark and Matthew is much weaker than in Luke and unlike them, Luke brings particular focus upon the conflict with the Pharisees. Luke's special treatment of the scene is all the more notable when it is recognized, as previously mentioned, that otherwise he follows Mark in the general arrangement of the material in chs. 5 and 6. There is little question that Luke has purposely set a dramatic stage for the important events to follow in 5.27-32.

Luke 5.27-28: The Call

> After this he went out, and saw a tax collector named Levi, sitting at the tax office; and he said to him, 'Follow me.' And he left everything, rose and followed him.

The events of 5.27-32 are of great importance to Luke's portrayal of the Gospel message in his book. In these few verses Luke sets out the basic themes of conflict, forgiveness and inclusion for 'sinners' which will dominate the work up to ch. 19. Luke introduces this important section about the call of Levi and the feast with 'tax collectors and others' prominently at the beginning of Jesus' ministry. The dramatic nature of the calling here in Luke can best be appreciated by reviewing briefly what has transpired in the material immediately prior to this passage. From the beginning of ch. 5 Luke reports a series of remarkable events that form a preface to the events in 5.27ff. There are crowds surging around Jesus to hear his teaching (5.1); Jesus goes to the lake shore and directs the miraculous draught of fish (5.4-7); Peter falls to his knees before Jesus proclaiming his sinfulness and he and his partners leave all to follow Jesus (5.8-11); prominent teachers gather from every corner of Palestine to hear Jesus (5.17); a paralytic is let down through the roof and Jesus first grants him forgiveness and then heals him on the spot (5.24); everyone is seized with amazement (ἔκστασις) saying, 'We have seen wondrous things today' (5.26).

Against this backdrop of highly-charged and extraordinary events we come, somewhat incongruously, to the report of Jesus' calling of Levi. At Jesus' command Levi does something remarkable indeed: καταλιπὼν πάντα ἀναστὰς ἠκολούθει αὐτῷ (cf. the less evocative ἀναστὰς ἠκολούθησεν αὐτῷ in the Synoptic parallels). The significance of the action implied in the phrase καταλιπὼν πάντα is reflected in a passage from *1 Clem.* 10.2, where Abraham:

> in the exercise of obedience, went out from his own country and from his kindred, and from his father's house, in order that, by forsaking (καταλιπών) a small territory, and a weak family, and an insignificant house, he might inherit the promises of God.

In Luke's telling, Levi did not simply rise and follow Jesus (Mk 2.14/Mt. 9.9) but he 'forsook everything' so that, as in *1 Clement*, he might follow the call.

The call of Levi involves no explicit miracle and is categorically unlike the events which lead up to it. Yet, for Luke it would seem that the fact of Jesus calling a toll collector[1] is so extraordinary that the event does not seem out of place among a series of miraculous events. It is actually a fitting climax to this list because the call itself is the miracle. Only the evocative power of the call can account for its inclusion and climactic position at this point in the narrative. Luke has purposely structured his reporting of these events to heighten the drama and impact of the relationship which Jesus bears to the 'toll collectors and sinners'.

From a historical perspective a wide variety of views have been

---

1. As is now recognized the τελώνης was a sub-contractor who collected tolls and not a member of the *societas publicanorum* who collected the Roman poll tax from house to house. Thus, τελώνης is rendered as 'toll collector' instead of 'tax collector'. See Donahue, 'Tax Collectors and Sinners', *CBQ* 23 (1971), pp. 45ff. See also Michel, 'τελώνης', *TDNT*, VIII, esp. pp. 96-98. J.D.M. Derrett also has an extensive section on toll collectors (*Law in the New Testament* [London: Darton, Longman & Todd, 1970], pp. 178-85). E. Badian's book *Publicans and Sinners: Private Enterprise in the Service of the Roman Republic* (Oxford: Basil Blackwell, 1972), is especially informative on the structure and social relevance of the Roman tax system.

proposed about the significance of Jesus' fellowship with toll collectors. The question of the actual offence involved in such an association will be explored at greater length below, but I will briefly note some of the interpretations here. Many scholars argue that associations with toll collectors were indeed 'characteristic' of Jesus' conduct.[1] In one treatment of the subject, Jesus' fellowship with the toll collectors is portrayed as having been so offensive that it was the chief cause of his death.[2] It is further argued that the charge of collaboration with Roman authorities and Jesus' association with them would have been a cause of extreme offence.[3] There are still others who feel the offence of Jesus' association with toll collectors is essentially a moral offence and not political at all.[4]

Quite in contrast to these views it has been argued recently that Jesus never actually had fellowship with toll collectors at all.[5] This argument is based on several observations: (1) the toll collectors do not occur outside the Synoptics; (2) the Synoptics preserve traditions that suggest Jesus had a negative view of toll collectors; (3) the references to his association with them are most often found on the lips of his critics; (4) only two passages actually report that he ate with them and these are judged to be artificial scenes; and (5) the identification of one of the twelve as a toll collector is problematic.[6] In his discussion of

---

1.   So Fiedler, *Jesus und Die Sünder*, pp. 119, 152. Most treatments of the subject simply assume fellowship with toll collectors to be an authentic characteristic behaviour for Jesus. For example, Jeremias, *NTT*, pp. 109ff., *Parables*, pp. 124ff., *JTTJ*, p. 267; as does Perrin, *Rediscovering*, p. 94; so also Michel, 'τελώνης', *TDNT*, VIII, pp. 103-105. Volkel declares, 'Der Umgang Jesu mit "Zöllnern und Sündern" zählt zum historisch gesicherten Bestand der synoptischen Evangelien' ('Freund der Zöllner und Sünder', *ZNW* 69 [1978], p. 1). J. Donahue, however, calls the association with toll collectors 'historical reminiscences' of Jesus' ministry, not necessarily 'historical representations' ('Tax Collectors and Sinners', *CBQ* 33 [1971], p. 60). Others dissenting from the standard view are W.O. Walker, 'Jesus and the Tax Collectors', *JBL* 97 (1978), pp. 221-38; and, more recently, R. Horsley; see below, this chapter.

2.   Perrin, *Rediscovering*, p. 103.

3.   Perrin, *Rediscovering*, p. 93; see also J. Gibson, 'Hoi Telonai kai Hai Pornai', *JTS* 32 (1981), p. 430.

4.   Jeremias, *NTT*, p. 111; also Michel, *TDNT*, VIII, pp. 101ff.

5.   Horsley, *Jesus and the Spiral of Violence*, pp. 212-17. A view earlier advanced by Walker, 'Jesus and the Tax Collectors', pp. 221-38.

6.   This is how Walker constructs his argument ('Jesus and the Tax Collectors',

the subject, Richard Horsley makes the observation that toll collectors probably did not make up a 'significant element'[1] in Jesus' following.

The common element of these various opinions is an overriding interest in dealing with the question on a historical level. It is necessary, however, to discern the difference between the 'historical' facts of Jesus' supposed association with 'sinners' and the ideological significance which those events assume in the Gospel text. It seems to me that the former does little to help us fully understand the latter. Whether Jesus numbered one, two or twenty toll collectors among his followers is beside the point; what matters is that this feature is used in the Gospel of Luke to indicate a radical departure from religious convention. Indeed, there is room to doubt that the befriending of toll collectors would have been seen at the time as a characteristic and symbolically profound feature of Jesus' ministry.[2] I would propose instead that, as time went by after Jesus' death, the lines of a clear ideological conflict over Jesus' treatment of 'sinners' emerged as a symbol for the purpose of his ministry. The lines of this ideological conflict were determined more by the need for such a conflict in the Gospel story than by an interest in an historical report of the composition of Jesus' coterie. If even one toll collector called himself Jesus' follower, this could account for the genesis of such a development. Donahue has noted, rightly I think,

> Though we may be dealing with historical reminiscences of the ministry of Jesus, it is not certain that we are dealing with historical representations.[3]

Even more to the point is the observation that Lk. 5.29 crystallizes

> into one symbolic moment what was actually a process. . . [which] from its very nature is not a historical report.[4]

Thus, in the development of the Gospel tradition a reminiscence of Jesus' tendency to associate with the dispossessed became invested with a symbolic importance that was probably not fully appreciated at the actual time the events occurred. The socially ambiguous behaviour of

---

pp. 237-38).

1. Horsley, *Jesus and the Spiral of Violence*, p. 21.
2. Cf. Hultgren, *Jesus and his Adversaries*, p. 111.
3. Donahue, 'Tax Collectors and Sinners', p. 61.
4. Bultmann, *HST*, p. 57.

Jesus toward outcasts became the basis for the emphasis we now see emerging with such force in Luke's Gospel. What is needed is the recognition that the boundaries between ideology and history become blurred when we speak of Jesus and the 'sinners', and that it is continually necessary to be aware of the difficulty in discerning between the two.

The real significance of the call of Levi and the 'many' who gathered at his house for a feast is not based on their specific social crimes but on their role as 'typical representatives' of the 'sinners'. To demonstrate this we can point to two instances involving toll collectors in Luke, the first in Luke 3, and the second the behaviour of Levi himself.

The first encounter with toll collectors in this Gospel occurs in the special material at Lk. 3.12 in connection with the ministry of the Baptist. In response to the preaching of John only Luke records that ἦλθον δὲ καὶ τελῶναι βαπτισθῆναι. While the RSV says 'tax collectors also came to be baptized', the sense is actually '*even* tax collectors came to be baptized'.[1] For Luke, toll collectors serve as archetypal 'sinners' beyond the pale of salvation and their response is reported to prove the power of John's preaching (as it will later for Jesus in Lk. 5.27). This event also sets the stage for further conflict over the inclusion of members of this hated group among Jesus' disciples.

Levi is another case in point of how the conduct of a toll collector has become cast in a typical mould. We note, first of all, that Levi acts decidedly unlike the way a real 'sinner' might be expected to act. He responds to Jesus without hesitation; in eagerness and gratitude he celebrates the willingness of the man of God to associate with him by a joyous feast where his fellow toll collectors demonstrate an identical attitude. It would seem that this toll collector and his associates are not really evil at all, but only in the sense required by the story where 'sinners' must be the respondents to Jesus. By means of a skilful literary reversal of roles the 'sinners' are subtly being portrayed as the

---

1.   The phrase δὲ καί, a Lucan favourite, carries this intensive function in the preceding v. 9 where it is used in a temporal sense, ἤδη δὲ καί; ἡ ἀξίνη . . . κεῖται, 'but even now the axe is laid'. Luke has a more obvious intensive usage in 18.11 in the parable of the Pharisee and the tax collector. The Pharisee gives thanks that he is not like others, ἢ καὶ οὗτος ὁ τελώνης, 'or even like this tax collector'. Cf. also Mt. 5.46.

'good guys'. This is one of the great ironies of the role of 'sinners' in the Gospels: they are the ones who do the right thing.

In human terms, of course, toll collectors are no more prone than other human beings to moral degeneration. In John's exhortation to the toll collectors we find no indication that their occupation was implicitly evil, only that they should be *honest* toll collectors (Lk. 3.13). And if Jesus had no fundamental objection to the payment of taxes ('Render to Caesar. . .' Lk. 20.25) he could not have objected to their collection.[1] Neither did Jesus call upon Zacchaeus to abandon his trade and break his contract with the government. Corruption was no doubt endemic in the profession[2] but there must have been both honest and dishonest toll collectors just as would be found in any profession. Conversely, neither should we accept the Gospel implication that toll collectors as a group were inclined to do right at Jesus' behest. As Ziesler has noted,

> we cannot identify Pharisees with the wrong attitude, any more than we can identify tax-collectors with the right one.[3]

In short, nothing relevant can be generally asserted about the morality of any such group, and this was fully confirmed in my assessment of other such notions as the *'ammei ha-aretz*, the 'despised trades' and the 'sinners' in Part I. Such supposedly concrete social categories have been seen to be completely without sociological substance. Likewise, toll collectors are symbolic 'sinners' in the Gospel drama of a Saviour who saves such people. The real enemies, at least in a material sense, are the Pharisaic antagonists. The 'sinners' are the victims, and even in some sense the 'heroes' of the story because they recognize and respond to God's servant. Levi's abandonment of his tax table has thus become a metaphor for the repentance of the unsavable, and any other conclusion simply misses the point of the narrative.

---

1.   H.C. Youtie, 'Publicans and Sinners', *Zeitscrift für Papyrologie und Epigraphik* 1 (1967), p. 4. See also Derrett, 'Render to Caesar', in *Law in the New Testament*, p. 315.

2.   Youtie, 'Publicans and Sinners', pp. 10-11. See further Badian, *Publicans and Sinners*, pp. 11-25, who demonstrates the necessary and efficient nature of the office of *publicani* in the Roman world in general.

3.   Ziesler, 'Luke and the Pharisees', p. 151; see also Youtie, 'Publicans and Sinners', pp. 18-19.

Luke 5.29-32: Levi's Banquet

And Levi made him a great feast in his house; and there was a large company of tax collectors and others sitting at table with them.

Other features of Luke's treatment of the setting of the feast also reveal his concern to heighten the drama of the calling of Levi and the subsequent meal given in Jesus' honour. Only Luke actually identifies Levi as a τελώνης (Lk. 5.27) whereas the others simply note that he was at a tax table (Mk 2.14/Mt. 9.9). In Luke's account the meal has become a δοχὴν μεγάλην, used elsewhere in the New Testament only in Luke's parable of the marriage feast (Lk. 14.7-14).[1] Mark and Matthew have Jesus simply 'at table in his/the house' when tax collectors and sinners come to join him, apparently without formal invitation (Mk 2.15/Mt. 9.10). Luke's affair is a planned event complete with guests and the incident is thus invested with a much greater importance. The fact that Luke unequivocally makes Levi the host of the feast establishes a link between the calling of the toll collector and the feast that is at least unclear in Mark and Matthew.[2] Finally, in Luke we have an ὄχλος πολύς as compared to the less dramatic πολλοί in reference to the number of 'tax collectors and sinners' (Mk 2.15/Mt. 9.10). It is clear that Luke has considerably enhanced the setting of the event and in so doing raises its significance to pivotal importance for his story.

Though Luke's treatment of the call and feast shows signs of being somewhat contrived, the incident is still useful for probing the nature of the offence created by this conduct of Jesus. We cannot help but wonder who would have been present at such a meal and why it could have caused such a fuss. The asking of such a question will help to clarify whether Luke's treatment of the scene has a plausible historical explanation or whether his treatment is largely a literary construction. What are the possible scenarios that might help to clarify the exact nature of the offence?

The narrative does not indicate whether this 'great feast' was spontaneous or planned. On the one hand, the event might be envisioned as

---

1. Also an LXX word for important feasts, cf. Gen. 26.30, Dan. 5.1. See J. Massyngbaerde Ford, *My Enemy is my Guest* (Maryknoll; Orbis Books, 1984), pp. 71-72.

2. J.M. Creed, *The Gospel according to St Luke* (London: Macmillan, 1950), p. 81.

a spontaneous response of celebration. Perhaps immediately following the toll collector's call a large and mixed crowd began to move toward Levi's house as they accompanied Jesus. As they approached the house however, only those who felt no particular scruples about entering a toll collector's residence would have gone in to take part in the feast. We can well imagine the general commotion and the haste of servants as the unplanned celebration gets under way. If this were the scenario, Luke's 'toll collectors and others' could have included a considerable range of people and the 'others/sinners' would simply be those who were not troubled about being seen in the company of a toll collector. That is a very loose criterion for inclusion as a 'sinner' and from this perspective those in attendance would not have been a particularly offensive crowd, morally, socially or religiously. Yet, the logic of the story demands an understanding of Jesus' fellowship with Levi and friends as a radical act, so Luke's intention in the scenario must have been somewhat different.

On the other hand, if the feast were a planned event by Levi he must have had something like a guest list or at least exercised some sort of control over who would be in attendance. If we adopt the view that the gathering would be one of genuine 'sinners' and that Levi, simply because he was a toll collector, had as his friends the very worst element of society (that is, other toll collectors, criminals, moral degenerates and despised tradesmen, etc.[1]), then this would have been a very unseemly gathering indeed. However, the idea of Levi sitting down intentionally to invite the very worst of society to this feast with the Teacher seems somewhat unlikely. A comment made some time ago still holds true.

> There never has been and there never can be a segregation of morally delinquent persons from others. Individual cases may be known, but different kinds of sinners are never found flocking together in such a way as to be openly discerned and labelled as such.[2]

The result is that in attempting to reconstruct the scene historically we find it almost impossible to imagine the actual circumstances that could give rise to offence. There is no reason to doubt that a similar event did actually occur which gave rise to the tradition. But whatever

---

1. As Ford does in speculating about the feast (*My Enemy is my Guest*, pp. 72-74).

2. Raney, 'Who Were the Sinners?', p. 580.

its original historical nature, it would seem that the incident has now crossed the divide from a simple event to a profound symbolic act in the Gospel narrative. As we saw earlier, event and ideological perspective meld to produce a convincing story.

The Pharisaic Question

> And the Pharisees and their scribes murmured against his disciples, saying, 'Why do you eat and drink with tax collectors and sinners?'

The Pharisees' question injects a new element of conflict into the developing drama. The purpose of the question at the level of story is perfectly clear: it produces the opportunity for Jesus to silence his antagonists and demonstrates the irresistible force of his mission in the face of a bigoted opposition. At the historical level, however, the question 'Why do you eat with toll collectors and sinners?' is one of the most enigmatic statements of Luke's Gospel. Of all the issues concerned with Jesus' association with 'sinners', the matter of table-fellowship is the most important and least understood. And since most of the 'sinners' material in Luke is connected with fellowship at table, the issue requires close attention.[1] The significance of this table-fellowship is often spoken of by scholars, yet the variety of explanations of its meaning (combined with the tendency of scholarship to rely on views from other sources) indicates that more analysis is needed to clarify the issues and alternatives.

While it may seem that it should be fairly simple to answer this question, the issue is compounded by a number of factors. The first factor is that, as we have seen, it is not completely clear with whom Jesus was eating. The 'toll collectors' are problematic enough but the 'sinners' are almost impossible to identify in any concrete social sense. This problem is, for all practical purposes, unsolvable and our lack of knowledge here handicaps the rest of the investigation. Nevertheless, the second factor must be addressed and that is the question of the basis of the offence of Jesus' dining habits; was the objection political, legal, moral, or religious in nature? Was it a combination of these, or is it simply a literary device with no historical foundation at all? Each

---

1.   The meal scenes in Luke are 7.36-50; 9.10-17; 10.38-42; 11.37-54; 14.1-24; 15.1-2; 19.1-10; 22.4-38; 24.29-32, 41-43. These encompass all our 'sinner' material. See I.H. Marshall, *Commentary on Luke* (Grand Rapids: Eerdmans, 1979), p. 219.

view has its proponents and each possibility must be examined in its turn.

Political Issues

What was the objection to Jesus eating with certain individuals? Perhaps the charge was political in nature, that is, Jesus' association with these individuals constituted a breach of fidelity to his nationality as a Jew.[1] Two points can be made in this connection. First, the charge that Jesus' activity with respect to toll collectors was traitorous has had wide influence. This view has been challenged however, by more recent assertions that the collaboration charge is unjustified since Herod Antipas's connection with the Romans was only indirect in Galilee in the time of Jesus and thus the charge would not be particularly appropriate in that province.[2] It can at least be maintained that the 'quisling' charge for a toll collector in Galilee would not necessarily have been as serious as some have suggested.

But the political dimension of the question can be shown to be inadequate on grounds other than this, and this leads to our second point. The charge in Lk. 5.30 is not that Jesus consorts or makes alliance with these people but that he *eats* with them. Moreover, the Pharisees do not seem to object to Jesus' companions until he eats with them. This is the chief reason for discarding the political factor as a plausible explanation of the offence. If the make-up of Jesus' following implied that he was involved in traitorous activity why was this charge not openly brought, as it was at his trial (Lk. 23.2, where, we note, he was acquitted of the charge, Lk. 23.13-16)? 'Why do you betray your nation?' is a much more effective charge than 'Why do you eat. . . ?' It is possible, of course, that this was the actual concern and the church changed it to the more innocuous and vague 'why do you eat. . . ?' in order to deflect the accusation and protect the memory of

---

1.   Perrin has been the chief proponent of this view (*Rediscovering*, p. 103): 'now they [the Jewish authorities] could face a popular resentment with the overwhelming retort that the fellow, for all his personal attractiveness and superficial popularity, was worse than a Quisling'. The view has been often repeated, for example, in E.P. Sanders, *Jesus and Judaism*, p. 178.

2.   This view has been fully set out by Donahue, 'Tax Collectors and Sinners', pp. 45ff.; it has also been put forward by F. Herrenbrück, 'Zum Vorwurf der Kollaboration des Zollners mit Rom', *ZNW* 78 (1987), pp. 186-99. See also Wengst, *Pax Romana*, p. 59.

Jesus from the charge of being a traitor. But this did not prevent the charge from being raised in connection with the Passion narrative. If this is the case then the church intentionally trivialized and hid the true criticism in an essentially non-political accusation. This is all highly speculative, indeed the most speculative of all the alternatives. Furthermore, if the true offence was treason it would have been in the interest of the church to answer the charge—not cover it up. When these factors are combined with the weakness of the political collaboration charge as a whole, it would seem that the political factor does not provide a very satisfactory understanding of the charge in Luke 5.30.

Legal Issues

Should this problem be approached from the perspective of a legal dispute? Was the issue a question of biblical or rabbinic injunction and were Jesus' actions thus considered an attack on the law? Perhaps as no other, it is Jeremias who has influenced the discussion of Jesus and the 'sinners' with regard to his habits of table-fellowship. Although Jeremias has always argued that the legal issues surrounding ritual purity had nothing to do with the objection to Jesus' fellowship at table with 'sinners', the view has persisted and is often found in recent writings. The reason for this, I believe, is the confusion that surrounds Jesus' relationship to the Pharisees. Their beliefs about ritual purity and food, as well as the basic biblical requirements about such matters are not well understood and the basic issues must be discussed here.

At the most basic level the question is: Was Jesus breaking a law by eating with 'sinners'? There are a number of legal matters that could perhaps have been at issue. First, it might be suspected that some help could be gathered from the literature that deals with Jewish prohibitions against table-fellowship in the ancient world. There is nothing in the Mosaic code with respect to table-fellowship with wayward Jews or even with Gentiles;[1] nevertheless the Jews had a reputation for being unsociable at table.[2] But it is vital to point out that this had solely to do with table-fellowship *with Gentiles*. In all of Philip Esler's re-

---

1.   See Esler, *Community and Gospel*, p. 84.
2.   Esler, *Community and Gospel*, pp. 78-84, for a full treatment of the ancient sources about table-fellowship among Jews.

cent book where he argues that legitimization of table-fellowship be-tween Jew and Gentile is the 'central arch' of Luke's purpose in Luke–Acts,[1] the 'sinner' material we are treating here in Luke's Gospel is never mentioned by Esler. The reason is that in our passage it is Jews eating with Jews that is at issue and, as such, it has no connection with the issues which confronted the church with regard to Jew/Gentile re-lations.[2] Jews eating with Jews stands apart as a completely different problem. Could this perhaps explain why the debate about table-fel-lowship in Acts 10.28; 11.2 and Gal. 2.11ff. never cites the custom of Jesus as precedent for how the church should solve this important is-sue?[3] As a legal matter, the concerns of Jew/Gentile table-fellowship appear to have no relationship to our 'sinner' material in the Synop-tics.

Could there have been issues relating to tithing and the matter of 'demai' produce as a potential source of legal conflict between Jesus and his contemporaries? As I noted in my treatment of tithing in Chapter 2, tithing was a biblical injunction and a great many oral traditions had developed in this area by the time of Jesus.[4] But these injunctions had also become widely ignored and non-observance was exacerbated by many social and economic factors. Still, in a situation such as the one described in Lk. 5.30, Jesus would have no doubt been in danger of eating untithed food. The heave-offering of the first tithe was considered sacred, that is, unlawful for any but the priest to eat, and it is possible that Jesus would have been liable to the charge of eating that which the Torah prohibited to anyone but the priesthood. This is the meaning of the vow to be taken after tithing in Deut. 26.13.

> When you have finished paying all the tithe of your produce in the third year, which is the year of tithing, giving it to the Levite, the sojourner, the fatherless, and the widow. . . then you shall say before the Lord your

1. Esler, *Community and Gospel*, p. 72.
2. As Borg has noted, 'table-fellowship with Gentiles was not a feature of the ministry of Jesus' (*Conflict, Holiness and Politics*, p. 84). R. Guelich has further observed, 'Neither "toll collectors" nor "sinners" functioned in the early church as a synonym for Gentiles' (*Mark* [Dallas: Word Books, 1989], p. 103).
3. See the excellent treatment of the issues at stake in Gal. 2 in J.D.G. Dunn, 'The Incident at Antioch (Gal. 2.11-18)', *JSNT* 18 (1983), pp. 3-57.
4. See above, Chapter 2 for basic material on tithes. See also Safrai, *The Jewish People*, II, pp. 818ff.

God, 'I have removed the sacred portion out of my house. . . according
to all thy commandment which thou hast commanded me; I have not transgressed any of thy commandments, neither have I forgotten them'.

As can be seen in the eating of other offerings reserved only for the
priests, the penalty was to be 'cut off' or put to death at the hands of
heaven.[1] But this must have been a very common transgression among
a people who ignored tithing in general, and the unwitting nature of
the offence may have further mitigated the culpability. In any case,
there was no 'human' punishment connected with the transgression. If
this offence had underlain the Pharisaic charge why was the charge
not brought and the biblical punishment invoked? Why raise a vague
question when a concrete charge complete with biblical remedy is
available? Evidently this was not the meaning of the charge, 'Why do
you eat. . . ?' On the whole, the generally low level of observance of
the tithing laws during this period makes the whole question an unlikely source of conflict and legal prescriptions with regard to tithing
are unlikely to be the issue at stake in Lk. 5.30.

What about the suggestion that Jesus was breaking the law by incurring ritual impurity in his contact with these 'tax collectors and sinners'?[2] The answer is that he undoubtedly *was* incurring ritual impurity. But this violated no law unless he attempted to enter the Temple
in such a state. Even then it would be strictly a matter of personal
conscience, for generally no one but the individual knows his/her own
state of purity. That is why it was necessary to declare everyone in
Jerusalem to be in a state of ritual purity during the time of the festivals.[3] There was simply no way to police 'purity' and this was the
only way to protect the sanctity of the Temple. Furthermore, Sanders
has surely laid to rest any false conceptions that ritual impurity implied sinfulness or that it was at all uncommon.[4] Most people had
corpse-uncleanness most of the time. To have contracted ritual impurity simply meant one could not enter the Temple and apart from

---

1.   Lev. 7.19-21; 22.9-15. Cf. *b. Sanh.* 90b.

2.   As many hold, e.g. Tyson, 'Conflict as a Literary Theme', p. 318; Marshall,
Luke, p. 219; J. Weber, 'Jesus' Opponents', p. 215; R. Pesch, 'Das
Zollnergastmahl (Mk 2.15-17)', in *Mélanges Bibliques* (ed. A. Deschamps and
André de Halleux; Gembloux: Duculot, 1970), p. 78.

3.   *b. Bez.* 11b; see also *b. Hag.* 26a; *m. Hag.* 3.6.

4.   See the discussion in E.P. Sanders, *Jesus and Judaism*, pp. 182-84.

this it did not limit 'ordinary associations, except for very short periods of time'.[1] Furthermore, the Galilean context of the event made such considerations even less pressing since Galileans were, obviously, physically far removed from the Temple.

It should also be unnecessary to demonstrate that Jesus' conduct had anything to do with breaking the Pharisaic ideal for table-fellowship, that is, eating all food in a state of ritual purity as does the priesthood. No one would expect a non-Pharisee to observe these rules, especially in Lk. 5.30 where it is the disciples' behaviour that is questioned by the Pharisees. Galilean fishermen would have been unlikely in any case to be concerned about observance on such a level. If the Pharisees were charging Jesus with consorting with non-Pharisees then few in Israel would have been guiltless of the charge. In conclusion, there seems to be no significant question of law at stake in the Pharisaic criticism in Lk. 5.30 and we must look elsewhere for its significance.

Moral Issues
Perhaps the offence of Jesus' table-fellowship with 'sinners' was based on moral considerations. It has in fact been maintained that the basis of offence was 'exclusively moral'[2] yet our problem is still not easily solved. The taking of offence is almost always, even in modern times, a somewhat impenetrable and irrational process.[3] It is a consummately 'human' phenomenon and does not lend itself easily to analysis. Still, we must enquire whether the offence implied in the Pharisaic question, 'Why do you eat. . . ?' was based on moral grounds. Was it the perceived immorality of Jesus' hosts that caused consternation? Was it that it 'looked bad' for a would-be rabbi to consort with such people? Or was it that such fellowship held out the possibility of becoming morally tainted, in which case the Pharisaic question was an expression of concern for the reputation and moral standing of Jesus and his disciples? Or is the offence based on the perceived immorality of Jesus

---

1. E.P. Sanders, *Jesus and Judaism*, p. 182.
2. Jeremias, *NTT*, p. 111.
3. This is particularly true, I suggest, with respect to religious sensibilities. We cannot help but think of Salmon Rushdie's *Satanic Verses* which has caused such a profound offence among Muslims around the world. While Rushdie must have been aware, being a Muslim himself, that his book would cause some offence, could he have guessed at its depth or violence? How can one predict an umbrage that seems to nurse its own indignation?

in associating with wicked people?

J.D.M. Derrett devotes considerable space to this last position in his *Law in the New Testament*.[1] Derrett, who claims to understand the 'ancient oriental mind', says that it was considered wicked to eat the food of a person whose earnings were tainted, as in the case of the toll collector.

> And eating with tainted people, simply swallowing their food, accepting non-charitable presents from them, seems to inflict *ipso facto* a taint indistinguishable from that borne by the unrighteous themselves.[2]

But other than his insight into the disposition of the oriental mind, he can produce no evidence to support this argument. Indeed, how can he, it being difficult to know how any ancient person might have reacted to any circumstance. Derrett's argument has its appeal to modern interpreters, but it has no historical basis. And while any of the above suggestions may have played a part in the offence caused by Jesus, we should not think that we have settled the issue. Few point out the fact that the text itself does not tell us what the offence is, it simply presents it as a fact of the story. From the point of view of the text, the offence is nothing more than evidence of the religious prejudice of these Pharisees who oppose all that Jesus does. It is simply a 'fact' of the text.

Jeremias has advanced a more pointed suggestion that has become the basis for much of modern theological thinking about Jesus and the 'sinners'.

> That he called them [the despised and lost], and not the righteous, was

---

1. Derrett, *Law in the New Testament*, in his section on Zacchaeus, pp. 278-85.

2. Derrett, *Law in the New Testament*, pp. 281-83; see also p. 131. Derrett's comments do bring to mind the case of *Joseph and Aseneth*. Joseph, who would not eat at the table of the Egyptians as a matter of course (*Jos. Asen.* 7.1), also refused the kiss of greeting from Aseneth. Joseph says, 'It is not fitting for a man who worships God, who will bless with his mouth the living God and eat blessed bread of life and drink a blessed cup of immortality and anoint himself with blessed ointment of incorruptibility to kiss a strange woman who will bless with her mouth dead and dumb idols and eat from their table bread of strangulation and drink from their libation of a cup of insidiousness and anoint herself with ointment of destruction' (*Jos. Asen.* 8.5). The issue here is the association of Aseneth with idol worship and the food offered to idols. But there is no indication in our text that any such practice is at issue in Luke.

apparently the dissolution of all ethics; it seemed as if moral conduct meant nothing in God's eyes. The world around Jesus based man's relationship with God on his moral conduct. Because the gospel did not do that, it shook religion to its foundations.[1]

In response to this I will argue that few Jews would have failed to see the need for a shepherd of Israel to seek the 'lost' and wayward. As has already been shown, it is erroneous to view the Judaism of Jesus' day as being unable to appreciate the necessity of calling the wayward to repentance. The depiction of Judaism as a religion with no conception of mercy toward the 'lost', and a religion where their ostracism is the 'supreme religious duty'[2] for Jews should be dismissed from the discussion.

The stated purpose of Jesus' fellowship with 'sinners' was always that they should repent (5.32); this is Luke's theme throughout the 'sinner' material (cf. 15.6, 19.10). Few could have objected to Jesus' attempt to reform the irreformable. Would not the response of any reasonable Jew to the conversion of Zacchaeus, as Sanders has so pointedly noted, have been relief and joy?[3] How could anyone object to a toll collector reforming his ways? The absence of the issue outside the Gospels shows that the objection to reaching out to the wayward was not a substantive one; why else would the subject have dropped completely out of consideration in the rest of the New Testament?[4] Thus, it is best to discard Jeremias's way of viewing the moral dilemma engendered by this fellowship. The calling of the 'lost' can in no way be construed as the 'dissolution of ethics'. On the contrary, it was the affirmation of all that Judaism taught about the importance of moral conduct and few would have failed to perceive this.

1. Jeremias, *NTT*, p. 119; see also B. Meyer, *Aims*, p. 160; Perrin, *Rediscovering*, p. 103.

2. Jeremias, *NTT*, p. 118; cf. also J. Riches, *Jesus and the Transformation of Judaism* (London: Darton, Longman & Todd, 1980), p. 99; Perrin, *Rediscovering*, p. 103; Hultgren, *Jesus and his Adversaries*, pp. 86-87.

3. Cf. the story of Rabbi Aqiba who reclaims the son of an oppressive tax collector, see Abrahams, 'Publicans', p. 55. See further E.P. Sanders, 'Jesus and the Sinners', *JSNT* 19 (1983), p. 23.

4. This is why E.P. Sanders must say that there was something unacceptable about the *kind* of repentance Jesus required (*Jesus and Judaism*, p. 207). See further, N.H. Young, '"Jesus and the Sinners": Some Queries', *JSNT* 24 (1985), pp. 73-75.

We shall return to this subject when we consider a new possible solution for the offence caused by Jesus' statement in Lk. 5.32.

Religious Symbolism

Another way Jesus' table-fellowship has been understood is in terms of its religious symbolism. The fellowship of Jesus with 'sinners' has been said to represent their inclusion in the Kingdom of God.[1] It is well attested in ancient literature that eating with someone was considered an intimate act of fellowship to be reserved only for the like-minded;[2] this view is also seen in the Mishnah.

> But if three have eaten at one table and have spoken over it words of the Law, it is as if they had eaten from the table of God for it is written, 'And he said unto me, This is the table that is before the Lord'.[3]

In the special material in Lk. 13.26 the villagers in the parable of the narrow door are said by Jesus to argue for their acceptance by the householder with the comment, 'We ate and drank in your presence. . .' Still, caution is necessary to avoid assigning too much significance to table-fellowship between Jews. One has asserted, for example, that every meal established 'an ontological union' between the participants.[4] But perhaps the best representation of the significance attached to this issue by many biblical scholars is the view of Jeremias.

> The oriental, to whom symbolic action means more than it does to us, would immediately understand the acceptance of the outcasts into table-fellowship with Jesus as an offer of salvation to guilty sinners and as the assurance of forgiveness.[5]

---

1. Again, it was Perrin who led the way for this view, *Rediscovering*, pp. 106-108; see also Strack–Billerbeck, III, p. 1146. D. Smith reviews Perrin's position and others ('The Historical Jesus at Table', in *The Society of Biblical Literature: 1989 Seminar Papers* [Atlanta: Scholars Press, 1989], pp. 466-67).

2. E.g. Ps. 100.5 (LXX); Prov. 23.1ff.; Lk. 14.15; Acts 10.28; 11.2; Gal. 2.12ff.; 1 Cor. 5.11; 8.10; Didache 9.5. Also see *3 Macc.* 3.4; *Jub.* 22.16; *Jos. Asen.* 7.1; Tob. 1.11; Sir. 31.12-32; Jdt. 12.2; *T. Levi* 14.5-6; *b. Sanh.* 23a; *b. Ber.* 43b.

3. *M. Ab.* 3.3; the scripture quoted in the mishnah is Ezek. 41.22.

4. Ford, *My Enemy is my Guest*, p. 71.

5. J. Jeremias, *Eucharistic Words of Jesus* (London: SCM Press, 1966), p. 204. See also B. Meyer, *Aims*, p. 160; Bornkamm, *Jesus of Nazareth*, p. 81.

The significance is taken a step further by Norman Perrin who finds in Jesus' table-fellowship a symbolic action so offensive as to have driven the authorities to 'desperate measures'.[1] According to Perrin, this ultimately is the fatal offence and this table-fellowship is 'the central feature of the ministry of Jesus; an anticipatory sitting at table in the Kingdom of God'.[2]

In Marcus Borg's reconstruction, Jesus' table-fellowship was perceived by the Pharisees as a challenge to the 'internal movement of reform which was intended to make Israel a holy community of priests'.[3] Borg calls this struggle a 'hermeneutical battle with historical-political dimensions'.[4] Borg may be right, but two points should give us pause. The first is that none of this is evident from the text. Borg simply presses his assessment of the social-political Pharisaic agenda back upon Jesus' table-fellowship and it has now become an 'historical-political hermeneutical battle'. Second, in view of the fact that the text does not tell us *why* the Pharisees were offended, it would seem a perilous undertaking to describe with such certainty what the Pharisaic perceptions of Jesus' table-fellowship were. Even if Jesus' table-fellowship had been intended by him to be a parabolic act of inclusion at the messianic banquet, and had been understood as such by his disciples, it seems difficult to imagine that outsiders to his circle could have clearly comprehended the significance of such an esoteric doctrine by simply observing Jesus eating a meal.

Here the matter of separating 'what happened' from what it later came to signify is very important. The significance of these events at the time they occurred does not necessarily conform with the role they now play in the Gospel story itself. In order for the Pharisees to have taken offence at Jesus' table-fellowship we must assume they *properly* understood Jesus' actions as a parabolic event.[5] In other

---

1.   Perrin, *Rediscovering*, p. 103.
2.   Perrin, *Rediscovering*, p. 107.
3.   Borg, *Conflict, Holiness and Politics*, p. 84.
4.   Borg, *Conflict, Holiness and Politics*, p. 143.
5.   One of the most thoroughly theological expositions of Jesus' table-fellowship is that offered by Otfried Hofius, *Jesu Tischgemeinschaft mit den Sündern* (Stuttgart: Calwer Verlag, 1967), pp. 18-19. He describes the significance of Jesus' table-fellowship as twofold. 1. It is the granting and appropriation of forgiveness of God for the 'sinner'. 2. It is the forerunner of the eschatological meal in the Kingdom of God. He goes on to say later that the Pharisees and scribes would 'doubtless have

words, Jesus and the Pharisees must all share the same perception of the event, the same story-universe so to speak. This is something that can happen with ease in a literary context but does not often happen in an actual social context. Dennis Smith has recently drawn attention to the possible difference between a meal in its historic setting and the use of that meal in a literary context to accomplish a literary goal.[1] It is obvious that the two do not always match.

The tendency of ideology to overtake an act and invest it with symbolic significance can be seen in the treatment of Jesus' table-fellowship from a theological perspective by Otfried Hofius. In his brief book he draws upon two references from the Pseudepigrapha to demonstrate early Christian understanding of the significance of Jesus' table-fellowship with outcasts.

> Then shall I arise in gladness and I shall bless the Most High for his marvels, (because God has taken a body, eats with human beings, and saves human beings).

That portion in brackets is a Christian interpolation to the *T. Sim.* 6.7. This interpolation, observes Hofius, points not to the atoning death or resurrection of Jesus but to the great fact of his table-fellowship with human beings. The wonder for the author of this interpolation was that in Jesus of Nazareth, as Hofius puts it, 'the holy God himself has set a table with lost men and precisely so that he might prove himself the rescuer of these men. That is the wonder that inspires worship!'[2] The value of Hofius's observation is that it demonstrates how the issue became theologized at an early date. The symbolic importance of this fellowship grew because of the astonishing implication that it was God himself who had been sitting at table with the disciples. In other

understood' this significance (p. 21). But what is instructive is that Hofius can only make this statement after he has spent several pages himself explaining what Jesus' fellowship with 'sinners' meant. This is Fiedler's criticism of Hofius; see *Jesus und die Sünder*, pp. 150-51.

1. D. Smith, 'The Historical Jesus at Table', pp. 467-68. He points to the Greek literary genre of the *symposium* as an example of how meals are often used in ancient Greek literature for the presentation of a hero type. See further Smith's article, 'Table-Fellowship as a Literary Motif in the Gospel of Luke', *JBL* 106 (1987), pp. 613-38. The interpretation of Luke's meal settings as examples of the Hellenistic symposium genre is the subject of Eli Steele's dissertation, 'Table-Fellowship with Pharisees'; pp. 55ff., esp. 86, 145-46.

2. Hofius, *Tischgemeinschaft*, p. 7.

words, the importance became commensurate with the development of the christology of the church.

To conclude this section, the problem of the cause of the offence at the level of history remains. If such a question was indeed asked by the Pharisees it may have simply been attributable to Pharisaic idiosyncrasy, or perhaps even a combination of the factors so far discussed: moral, legal, political and theological. The motive of the question, 'Why do you eat with toll collectors and sinners?' will have to remain an open question.

The function of table-fellowship in the Lucan narrative probably cannot be fully appreciated at a single level, historical or literary. At the historical level it must have carried some significance at the time it occurred, otherwise it is difficult to account for the origin of the triple Gospel tradition of fellowship with 'sinners'. But the precise nature of that meaning has been subsumed by a treatment of this tradition in the Gospels which transformed simple events into a powerful symbolic statement of Jesus' mission. The opposition engendered by this fellowship may have worked at the historical level for the early church to explain Jesus' conflict with the religious authorities and, at least with respect to Mark (Mk 3.6), his death. But its higher, religious purpose was to show the superiority of Jesus' mission in that he sought and rescued the very worst of society. Over the years, as the actual cause for offence faded in memory, the conflict came to represent an ideological confrontation between Jesus and his adversaries; a key parable in the struggle of Jesus against evil.

Jesus' Reply

> And Jesus answered them, 'Those who are well have no need of a physician, but those who are sick; I have not come to call the righteous but sinners to repentance'.

We come now to the saying which is the culmination of the events of ch. 5. More than any other saying, this one provides a window into the purpose and mission of Jesus for Luke's story. It stands at the start of the Galilean mission and sets the tone of conflict right through to ch. 19 and the companion logion, 'The Son of Man came to seek and to save the lost'. As will be seen, it not only tells us how Jesus differs from his contemporaries but also provides the *raison d'etre* for his whole mission.

Lk. 5.29-32 form a tripartite controversy dialogue which is common to Gospel literature and involves a revolutionary action, a protest, and the silencing of that protest by a pronouncement.[1] Jesus' fellowship with the 'sinners' (revolutionary action) provokes a challenge from the Pharisees (protest) and Jesus silences them with his pronouncement. This tripartite form involves viewing the 'sinner' from three different perspectives. First, there is that of the narrator who tells us that Jesus sat at table with a large company of 'toll collectors and others'; next there is the negative perspective of the Pharisees, 'Why do you eat with toll collectors and sinners?'; and finally there is Jesus' perspective that these 'sinners' are the ones to whom he must issue his call.

This issue of perspectives can be seen in Luke's treatment of v. 29. Luke will not call those with whom Jesus gathers 'sinners', preferring the less forceful 'toll collectors and others'. It is surprising that he passes up the opportunity to repeat the parallel Marcan phrase 'toll collectors and sinners' considering that 'sinners' is a favourite term and he does not shrink from the couplet elsewhere (Lk. 5.30, 7.34, 15.1). But to use it here would involve Luke in an inconsistency, for it would be an affirmation of the Pharisaic charge. To Luke they are not 'sinners'[2] in the sense the charge implies. Mark possesses no such subtlety and calls them 'sinners' himself; thus Mk 2.15, 16, 17 are all seen from one perspective. Luke shows his skill as a writer in his more sensitive understanding of the perspectives involved and thus leaves open the possibility of a more nuanced interpretation of the incident.

Understanding this flexibility in the term 'sinner' is important because the term's meaning is always determined by the lips on which it is found. Failure to clearly identify this aspect of the 'sinner' issue has contributed to the confusion in the literature on this subject. One writer has defined the Old Testament 'sinner' as one who lives in 'conscious or witting opposition to the divine will' and equates the New Testament 'sinner' with the Old Testament one.[3] I hope the case

---

1. See Daube, *The New Testament and Rabbinic Judaism*, pp. 171-75; Hultgren, *Jesus and his Adversaries*, pp. 53-58; and Fiedler, *Jesus und die Sünder*, p. 121.

2. Note the correspondent absence of καὶ ἁμαρτωλῶν in the Pharisaic question in v. 30 in manuscripts C and D; also ἀσεβεῖς for ἁμαρτωλούς in א in v. 32.

3. Rengstorf, 'ἁμαρτωλός', *TDNT*, I, p. 327.

has been made that this definition of 'sinner' is erroneous, but the telling point is found in the next sentence where the same author makes the following remark:

> For the Pharisee, however, an ἁμαρτωλός is one who does not subject himself to the Pharisaic ordinances, i.e., the so-called *'am ha-ares*. He is not a sinner because he violates the Law, but because he does not endorse the Pharisaic interpretation.[1]

Are the 'sinners' those of the first definition or the non-Pharisees of the second? The answer is that it is all merely a matter of perspective and not a matter of history at all.

How does all of this affect the interpretation of Jesus' famous logion? Conventional understanding of the couplet in 5.31 and 32 has focused on how Jesus' call to the lost was a radical departure from convention and constituted a grave offence to the religious authorities. On one level, I have argued that the calling of 'sinners' was indeed radical since it was a term that heretofore had applied only to the irredeemably lost. This Gospel habit of portraying the 'sinner' as one deserving of mercy does mark a turning point in the history of the usage of the term. Yet, this should not obscure the fact that the logion itself is perfectly orthodox in its attitude that a religious figure should seek the reformation of the lost and as such it was not a radical departure from Jewish thinking.[2] On the contrary, Jesus' stated intention of seeking the lost would have been understood by all as perfectly justifiable conduct for a spiritual shepherd in Israel (cf. Lk. 15.1-7).

Consider, for example, the probable relation of the prophecy of Ezekiel's indictment of the shepherds of Israel (Ezek. 34.4ff.) to Luke 5.[3]

> The weak you have not strengthened, the sick you have not healed, the

---

1. Rengstorf, 'ἁμαρτωλός'.

2. E.P. Sanders has described Judaism as holding a 'universal view that forgiveness is always available to those who return to the way of the Lord' ('Jesus and the Sinners', pp. 21-22). See also N. Young, '"Jesus and the Sinners": Some Queries', pp. 73-75.

3. The connection of Ezek. 34 to this theme in Luke has been well noted by commentators. For example, W. Grundmann, *Das Evangelium nach Lukas* (Berlin: Evangelische Verlagsanstalt, 1969), p. 307; J. Fitzmyer, *The Gospel according to Luke* (New York: Doubleday, 1985), pp. 1221-22; Marshall, *Luke*, pp. 138-39, 601, 698; Hofius, *Tischgemeinschaft*, pp. 24-25.

crippled you have not bound up, the strayed you have not brought back, the lost you have not sought, and with force and harshness you have ruled them (v. 4).

This portion of ch. 34 is an indictment of the failed leadership of Israel's 'shepherds' and the resulting scattering of the flock under their care (v. 5).[1] Because of this God will rescue the sheep from the shepherds' mouths (34.10) and undertake their care himself. Ezek. 34.16 expresses how God will perform the role of shepherd as it should properly be done.

Although there is some verbal correspondence between the Lucan vorlage, Mk 2.17, and Ezekiel at this point it is not necessary to posit direct dependence in order to appreciate the similarity in concept.[2] The logic is the same; the proper role of the shepherd is to tend to the needy in his flock and the proper role of the physician is to tend to the sick. Lk. 5.31 functions as a negative appraisal of the leaders in much the same way as Ezek. 34.4; it is the sick and lost to whom the shepherd must attend. Both should be understood as a criticism of failed spiritual leadership and not a call to a new philosophy of ministry. Neither logion is introducing anything new or revolutionary for all can see the sense of the illustration: a good shepherd cares for his feeble sheep and a doctor cares for the ill.[3]

Against this backdrop we have the second half of the saying which spells out how the job should be done. Again, Ezekiel:

> I will seek the lost, and I will bring back the strayed, and I will bind up the crippled, and I will strengthen the weak, and the fat and the strong I will watch over; I will feed them in justice (34.16).

God says 'I will seek the lost because my shepherds have not'. Likewise, Jesus is to call the 'sinners' not the 'righteous' who have no need. The point is, these Pharisees, the spiritual leaders of Israel for the purpose of the story, have ignored their vital responsibility. The

---

1.   W. Zimmerli, *Ezekiel*, II (Philadelphia: Fortress Press, 1979), p. 214.

2.   Cf. Mark, οὐ χρείαν ἔχουσιν οἱ ἰσχύοντες ἰατροῦ ἀλλ' οἱ κακῶς ἔχοντες, to LXX, Ezek. 34.4, τὸ ἠσθενηκὸς οὐκ ἐνισχύσατε καὶ τὸ κακῶς ἔχον οὐκ ἐσωματοποιήσατε.

3.   *Contra* Montefiore, *RLGT*, p. 222: 'That a teacher should go about and associate with such persons and attempt to help "cure" them. . . was, I imagine, an unheard of procedure. . . That the physician of the soul should seek out the "sick" was a new phenomenon.'

sense of Jesus' saying is: '*I* will do the job correctly, *I* will call sinners because *you* have not!' Jesus does not introduce a new concept of ministry but simply indicts the Pharisees for a failed responsibility.

The *Prayer of Manasseh* contains a verse that expresses a similar sentiment. As has been noted, this prayer is one of the earliest examples of 'sinner' language being used in a positive context of repentance. As such, it has considerable significance for Luke 5.

> You therefore, O Lord, God of the righteous ones, did not appoint grace for the righteous ones, such as Abraham, and Isaac and Jacob, those who did not sin against you; but you appointed grace for me, [I] who am a sinner (*Pr. Man.* 8).

In a way very similar to Lk. 5.31-32 this saying is bifurcate and begins with a statement that the 'righteous' have no need of grace. The logic is clear: righteous people have no need of rescue. The saying implies that few would suggest the need of grace for Abraham and his sons; it is the '*sinner*' who requires rescue. Likewise, Jesus' saying is free of irony; it is to be understood in a perfectly straightforward fashion.[1] The reasonable and proper thing to do is to seek the lost; thus, 'I came not to call the righteous but the sinners to repentance'. The similarity between the Gospel saying and the *Prayer of Manasseh* is so striking that Jesus' statement may well be dependent on the *Prayer*.

Conclusion

It has been argued here that Luke has purposely heightened the drama of the call of Levi to focus attention on the controversy with the Pharisees and thus bring the 'righteous/sinner' issue into a sharp ideological focus. The resulting theme of conflict is fundamental to his story line. A summary of the findings would include these points:

1. The events, such as the call of Levi and the feast receive a unique treatment from Luke which heightens their significance in the story compared to the other Gospel writers.

---

1. Cf. Lk. 15.1-7 where I also contend there is no irony in the use of 'righteous'. With respect to Lk. 5.32, C.H. Dodd calls the use of 'righteous' by Jesus 'bitter irony' (*The Parables of the Kingdom* [London: Nisbet, 1935], p. 118; also in *The Founder of Christianity* [New York: Collier Books, 1970], p. 44).

2. On a historical level, at the time of their occurrence they could not have communicated unambiguously the ideological categories they later came to signify. The margin between historic event and symbolic act has become blurred.

3. The question of the historical offence of Jesus eating with 'sinners' cannot be forced to decision at this point, it is simply a 'fact' of the text.

4. The calling of the 'sinners' instead of the 'righteous' should not be understood as a radically new philosophy of ministry but as a perfectly sensible and proper task for a Jewish teacher. The 'righteous' are not excluded, the 'sinners' are included.

Luke's use of the term 'sinner' cannot be understood in terms of concrete sociological categories but is, by nature, a question of religious ideology and it is on this level that our passage reveals its most profound meaning. Moreover, Luke has organized the players in his drama into discrete religious categories which function as essential elements in the structure of the story. Thus far, it would appear the 'sinners' are one of Luke's most important tools for organizing and giving shape to his Gospel message.

Chapter 5

THE STORY OF THE SINFUL WOMAN

We now turn to Lk. 7.28-50, the second significant passage in the Gospel of Luke which deals with 'sinners'. The pericope consists of two distinct yet related segments: Lk. 7.28-35, the proverb of the children playing in the market, and Lk. 7.36-50, the story of the sinful woman. Both segments contain considerable difficulties in terms of structure and interpretation, particularly vv. 36-50, and my analysis will touch on some (but certainly not all) of these matters. The main objectives of this chapter will be: (1) to analyse the use of the 'sinner' motif by Luke in these two segments, (2) to investigate the thematic continuity between Lk. 7.28-35 and 36-50, and (3) to relate the treatment here to the 'sinner' material already discussed to this point.

Luke 7 in Relation to the Previous Material in Luke

The material in Luke 7 now affords the opportunity to compare and assess Luke's interest in the 'sinner' in relation to what we have observed in Luke 5. The parable of the children playing in the market (Q material) and the story of the sinful woman (special Lucan material) show a clear relationship to themes already broached by Luke. In particular, this is evident in the way Lk. 7.28-50 looks back to two important incidents already reported in the Gospel and then goes on to develop their importance.

The first concerns the toll collectors, Pharisees and John the Baptist in Lk. 7.28-35. We recall that in the Q material at Lk. 3.7-9 (Mt. 3.7-10) Luke pointedly omitted the Pharisees from among those who came out to be baptized by John. I have maintained that this demonstrated the tendency of Luke's Pharisees to reject completely John and Jesus and so foreshadowed conflict to come.[1] At the same time, the toll col-

1. See the article by J. Kilgallen which focuses on the relationship of Lk. 7.36-

lectors were presented as the worst of the archetypal 'sinners' ('*even*
the toll collectors came out to be baptized', Lk. 3.12) and their response to John served, literarily, as a testimony to John's ministry.
Not only was this an indicator of the direction and purpose of John's
ministry (the worst will be called to repentance) but it was also a fore-
cast of conflict with regard to 'sinners' in Jesus' ministry.

In a similar way, these three character groups are also the topic of
Lk. 7.28-35. In the midst of a discourse by Jesus endorsing John's
ministry (vv. 24-29) Luke rather awkwardly inserts an editorial
comment on the people's reaction.[1] They have just been told the 'least
in the kingdom' will be greater than John, who is himself the first
among men (7.28).

> When they heard this all the people and the tax collectors justified God,
> having been baptized with the baptism of John; but the Pharisees and the
> lawyers rejected the purpose of God for themselves, not having been bap-
> tized by him (7.29).

This comment harks back to the incident in Lk. 3.7-9 both in terms of
the positive response of the toll collectors, who are now the 'least in
the kingdom', and also in terms of the negative response of the Pharisees. The difference here in Lk. 7.29 is that the Pharisees are now
clearly identified as being in the wrong about John's baptism. This
editorial comment appears to be related to material also present in
Matthew (Mt. 21.31b-32) which is addressed to the 'chief priests and
elders'. In Luke the tradition is turned against the Pharisees and thus
makes explicit that which was implicit in Lk. 3.7-9: the Pharisees, by
their absence from the group to be baptized by John, never accepted
John and thus showed themselves to be the enemies of God's purpose.
The 'sinners' recognized John as God's servant but the Pharisees did
not. For Luke's story the Pharisees' failure to respond to John confirms their status as the ideological enemies of God and his purposes.
Luke's religious categories are absolute; the complete failure of the
Pharisees is purposely played against the willing response of the
'sinners' in order to portray the ideological conflict in the most vivid
terms possible. There is no ambiguity for Luke, or his sympathetic

---

50 to Lk. 7.28-35 ('John the Baptist, the Sinful Woman, and the Pharisee', *JBL* 104
[1985], pp. 675-79).

1.   As Kilgallen has noted ('John the Baptist', p. 677).

reader, as to who is on the side of right and who is on the side of wrong.

The second important echo from earlier in the Gospel takes the form of the complaint about Jesus' habits of table-fellowship. In Chapter 4 we considered in some detail the implications of the complaint, 'Why do you eat with toll collectors and others?' Now, in Lk. 7.31-35 and 36-50 the complaint resurfaces in two different forms. I will first consider Lk. 7.31-35 since it forms an important prologue to the story of the sinful woman forgiven (7.36-50).

Luke 7.28-35: The Parable of the Children in the Market

As was the case in Luke 5, the charge against Jesus of consorting with 'toll collectors and sinners' now also plays an important role in ch. 7 of Luke. It will be argued here that the complaint in Lk. 7.34 of Jesus' association with 'sinners' serves a pivotal function in connecting the parable of the children in the market and the story of the sinful woman. The first parable informs the reader as to how to evaluate the charge, that is, it is capricious and unfounded. The story of the sinful woman then proves that Jesus' association with 'sinners' serves a positive function by producing repentance. Thus, all of Lk. 7.28-32 and 7.36-50 pivots around the central charge in Lk. 7.33-35 and the purpose of this material is to vindicate the policy of inclusiveness toward 'sinners' pursued by Jesus. It further demonstrates that Jesus is not himself dissolute but fulfilling his proper role as seeker of the lost (Lk. 5.31-32).

The complaint about Jesus eating and drinking with 'sinners' (Lk. 7.34) is prefaced by a proverb in which 'this generation' is compared to children sitting in the market place calling to one another:

> We piped to you and you did not dance
> we wailed, and you did not weep.

There are three options for the interpretation of the parable. The first two involve allegorizing the characters in the couplet and assigning the roles to groups and individuals in the Gospel story. First, the market scene could be interpreted with Jesus and John as the 'we' and the people or religious leaders as the ones called upon to dance and weep.[1]

---

1. So Fitzmyer, *Luke*, p. 679; A.R.C. Leaney, *The Gospel according to St*

Or, the order could be reversed, the 'men of this generation', again, either the people or the authorities, call to Jesus and John to do their bidding but the men of God will not comply.[1]

The third option is the one adopted here. The saying was a proverb, probably already known in a popular form,[2] which should be understood without recourse to allegory. The children in the parable cannot agree and each group petulantly insists on its own way. Play is rather comically paralysed by the selfishness of all concerned. The two groups call to one another (ἀλλήλοις, cf. Matthew's less reciprocal τοῖς ἑτέροις), alternately suggesting different games; first piping for a mock wedding and then weeping as in a funeral. A simple parallelism is the interpretive key to the caricatured complaint repeated by Jesus after the proverb.

> For John the Baptist has come eating no bread and drinking no wine; and you say, 'He has a demon'. The son of man has come eating and drinking; and you say, 'Behold, a glutton and a drunkard, a friend of tax collectors and sinners!' Yet wisdom is justified by all her children (vv. 33-34).

Jesus repeats the complaints as though they were the taunts of selfish children who cannot agree on the game they want to play. We should recognize the element of chiding humour in the proverb and thus in Jesus' commentary. In this way Jesus upbraids his opponents as petulant, dissatisfied children for it seems nothing can please them.[3] Their childish inconsistency demonstrates their attitude toward both John and Jesus for they found the asceticism of John distasteful and the liberties of Jesus condemnable. How to please such a lot as this! There is then a parallelism between the images of the proverb and the way Jesus describes his opponents; the proverb is meant only to describe the general attitude of dissatisfaction and indecision among all the 'men of this generation'.[4]

Luke (London: A. & C. Black, 1958), p. 145; H. Schürmann, *Das Lukasevangelium* (Freiburg: Herder, 1984), pp. 423-25.

1. Creed, *Luke*, p. 108; so also Marshall, *Luke*, p. 300.
2. Cf. Herodotus 1.141; Aesop's *Fables* 27. Bultmann also believes it circulated independently (*HST*, p. 199); see also Grundmann, *Lukas*, p. 167.
3. See J. Jónsson, *Humour and Irony in the New Testament* (Leiden: Brill, 1985), pp. 154, 169; so also Dodd, *Parables*, pp. 28-29.
4. For this interpretation see Grundmann, *Lukas*, p. 167: 'Der Vergleichspunkt

The parable is applied by Luke in 7.33-34 and so the objections repeated by Jesus appear as petulant 'complaints' rather than serious 'charges' in the sense of a legal challenge. The latter would be too serious a label and the taunts have none of the character of a serious assault. The text thus implies that these complaints should be taken no more seriously than those of such children. In response to John's ministry, great as he was among men, these 'children' could do no more than dismissively announce, δαιμόνιον ἔχει. What is more, in relation to Jesus himself their assessment is equally errant and unperceptive: ἰδοὺ ἄνθρωπος φάγος καὶ οἰνοπότης, φίλος τελωνῶν καὶ ἁμαρτωλῶν. The charges are simply the product of a childish impudence and Jesus' repetition of them is an exasperated caricature of the opposition which 'this generation' seemed to show to every overture from John and himself.

The point is, of course, that John had no demon and Jesus himself was no friend of 'tax collectors and sinners' in the sense that he shared in their dissipation, for that presumably is the way the slander was intended. Yes, John abstained from food and drink and yes, Jesus associated with less desirable people but it is the failure of his contemporaries to comprehend the purpose and intent of these actions that stirred the rebuke. In short, Jesus dismisses the whole business with another proverb: 'Yet wisdom is justified by all her children'. Jesus was prepared to let his actions about eating and drinking speak for themselves. The sense of this proverb is 'observe my table-fellowship and make your own judgments'. But Fitzmyer, for example, again allegorizes the parable and takes the 'children' of 7.35 to be Jesus and John who are justified by the generally positive response of the people (7.29).[1] But allegorizing misses the point of the story; the question at issue is specifically the complaint about Jesus' table-fellowship and whether it is justified or not. Lk. 7.35 refers to this and not to the

---

liegt nicht darin, dass Jesus und die Täufer als eine Gruppe einer anderen Gruppe gegenübergestellt werden order im Volke zwei Gruppen unterschieden werden, sodern in der Unentschlossenheit der spielenden Kinder, die nicht wissen, was sie eigentlich wollen'. So also F. Mussner, 'Der nicht erkannte Kairos (Mt. 11.16-19 = Lk. 7.31-35)', *Bib* 40 (1959), pp. 600ff. Dodd (*Parables*) says 'any attempt to work it out by way of an allegorical equivalence of terms breaks down' (p. 28).

1. Fitzmyer, *Luke*, p. 679; similarly Marshall, *Luke*, pp. 298, 301; see also F.W. Danker, *Jesus and the New Age* (Philadelphia: Fortress Press, 1988), pp. 168-69.

larger issue of accepting or rejecting Jesus and John. In this case
Matthew's ἀπὸ τῶν ἔργων αὐτῆς is perhaps a bit less confusing than
Luke's ἀπὸ πάντων τῶν τέκνων αὐτῆς. It is Jesus' 'works', his
fellowship with 'sinners', that speaks for itself. Verses 36-50 are
introduced as a prime example of *how* wisdom is justified by her
'children'. The wisdom of Jesus' actions towards 'sinners' is justified
by his works, which we now see in the following Lucan pericope.

Luke 7.36-50: The Story of the Sinful Woman

The story of the sinful woman forgiven is known to us only from
Luke and thus will prove to be particularly important for understanding the special way that Luke views the whole issue of Jesus' fellowship with 'sinners'. The purpose of the story appears to be threefold.
First, it is advanced by Luke as a prime example, 'Exhibit A' if you
will, of the alleged offensive behaviour of 7.34 and as such it acts as
the refutation of the complaints about Jesus' table-fellowship. But the
story goes on to develop other Lucan themes as well. Thus, 7.36-50
also acts as an exposé of the 'typical' Pharisaic attitude and gives Luke
another effective opportunity to press home the negative ideological
portrayal of the opponents of Jesus in contrast to the 'sinner'. Third,
the story is an eloquent statement of the conception of forgiveness
which Luke will now begin to develop more fully in his 'sinner' material.

The connection of the story of the sinful woman with 7.31-35 is
clear and immediate. The story appears to be a way to demonstrate
and confirm, by means of a specific example, the ludicrousness of the
complaints about Jesus' table-fellowship.

Literarily, the close relationship between these two stories is seen in
the way Luke makes the transition in story and scene with as little interruption as possible. A lively sense of immediacy has already been
established throughout the report of Jesus' comments in Lk. 7.31-35,
particularly with respect to the use of the verbs of vv. 33 and 34.
There is the second person plural, καὶ λέγετε. . . (cf. Mt. 11.18, 19,
λέγουσιν) and the perfect tense of ἐλήλυθεν (cf. Matthew's aorist
ἦλθεν). One gets the impression from Luke that these charges are cir-
culating now, John is still at large and Jesus is actively encountering
opposition at this time.

The transition of scene at v. 36 to the story of the sinful woman continues the sense of immediacy:

> One of the Pharisees asked him to eat with him, and he went into the
> Pharisee's house, and took his place at table.

There are none of the characteristic temporal phrases that Luke often
uses to move into a new pericope,[1] nor is any change of location
noted. From the reader's perspective the incident follows immediately
after the preceding exchange without interruption and it seems that
Luke intentionally includes this special material here in answer to the
foregoing complaints.

The scene of the incident is in the house of Simon the Pharisee
where Jesus is invited to eat. It is a passage that bears a resemblance to
the anointing of Jesus in the three other Gospels (Mt. 26.6-13; Mk
14.3-9; Jn 12.1-8).[2] On the whole, however, the differences are such
that the Lucan passage should, for the purposes of interpretation, be
treated as an independent tradition. Luke differs in placement in time
(before travel narrative in Luke vs. Passion narrative in others), location (Luke, unspecified vs. Bethany for Matthew, Mark and John), the
host (Luke's Pharisee Simon vs. Simon the leper in others), cause of
controversy (in Luke the woman is a 'sinner' while none of the other
Gospels refer to her moral status: in them the issue is the cost of the
ointment), the opponents (Simon in Luke vs. Jesus' own disciples), and
Jesus' response to the remonstrants (Luke has the two debtors;
Matthew, Mark and John have the anointing as preparation for death).

For our analysis, the most significant point is that immediately following the complaint that Jesus eats with 'sinners' he is found at table,
not with a 'sinner', but in the house of a Pharisee. This is not, as some
have suggested, a demonstration of Jesus' beneficence to all levels of
society.[3] Nor is it a sign of 'greater friendliness towards the Pharisees

---

1. Cf. Lk. 5.17, 27; 6.1, 6, 12, 17; 7.1, 11, and so forth.

2. On the question of the dependency of Luke on the other Gospels for this
material see the discussion by G. Bouwman, 'La pécheresse hospitalière (Lc., VII,
36-50)', *ETL* 45 (1969), pp. 172-74; and A. Legault, 'An Application of the Form-
Critique Method to the Anointings in Galilee (Lk. 7.36-50) and Bethany (Mt. 26.6-
13; Mk. 4.3-9; John 12.1-8)', *CBQ* 16 (1954), pp. 131-45. See especially Steele's
survey of scholarly opinion on this matter ('Jesus' Table-Fellowship with
Pharisees', pp. 5-12).

3. Danker, *Jesus and the New Age*, p. 169.

on the part of Luke',[1] but actually just the opposite. With Luke's fine sense for reversal and irony, the setting shows that Jesus encounters the greatest impiety when he eats at the table of the so-called 'righteous'. The setting serves as another thrust in Luke's indictment against the righteousness of the Pharisees and further refutes the complaint of 7.34. The story works here precisely because it is at a Pharisee's table that the incident occurs. In this way the false piety of the Pharisee and the genuine repentance of the woman can be shown in close contrast. True repentance is found face to face in the same room with false piety and the impact for the reader is dramatic.

Having already been informed by Luke of the intransigent attitude of the Pharisees (Lk. 5.21, 30; 6.2, 7; 7.29) we are not surprised now to find a specific Pharisee portrayed in unflattering terms. Luke has established a negative motif with regard to Pharisees and this story represents a 'type-scene' where that motif can be repeated and developed.[2]

The 'sinner' motif is somewhat different here from that which we have previously encountered in Luke. The 'sinners' are not being used as a vague foil in a wide-ranging statement as in Lk. 5.32. Here it is a specific case with specific individuals, yet features of the ideological 'sinner' remain. In keeping with the usual treatment of the 'sinner' the details of the story are rather vague. The sinful woman is a decidedly 'flat' character. We are not told what the woman's crime was although we perhaps assume the worst because of her deep personal distress.[3]

---

1. Ziesler, 'Luke and the Pharisees', p. 150; Steele, 'Jesus' Table-Fellowship with Pharisees', p. 147.

2. Tannehill, *Narrative Unity*, p. 105. Luke's characteristic of setting important scenes at table has been the focus of attention in recent research. I do not follow Steele ('Jesus' Table-Fellowship with Pharisees', pp. 92, 131), however, in assuming that the idea of having dinner with a Pharisee was inherently impossible for Jesus. Steele says, 'Jesus should have been regarded as unacceptable for fellowship based on his contact with tax collectors and sinners, as well as for his lack of regard for other features of the Pharisaic agenda' (p. 3). On this basis he asserts that the setting here is freely created by Luke (p. 86). I agree the setting here is artificial, but not that it is historically impossible.

3. Derrett (*Law in the New Testament*, pp. 167-68) thinks the woman is a prostitute; so also H. Leroy, 'Vergebung und Gemeinde nach Lukas 7.36-50', in *Wort Gottes in der Zeit: Festschrift für K.H. Schelkle* (ed. Helmut Feld and Josef Nolte; Patmos: Verlag Düsseldorf, 1973), p. 92. But the text does not tell us so, nor is Jesus ever charged with associating with prostitutes. K. Corley argues in a recent

Her offence and identity are left vague and we know nothing of her acquaintance with Jesus, although, in terms of the story, something had obviously already transpired between them. Creed has rightly described the story as 'impressive in its total effect, and in detail lacking in verisimilitude'.[1] The text is unselfconscious about the curious circumstances of the scene, such as how the woman came to be admitted to the house in such a disruptive manner. Even though it was not unknown for pious Jews to open their houses to the unfortunate,[2] the host is clearly uncongenial in this case. Because of this lack of specificity the woman is able to serve as a typical representative of her sinful kind. Even if an actual incident underlies the story, Luke's portrayal is full of ideological import.

The character portraits are developed with great skill by Luke. The picture of the woman standing over Jesus' feet weeping and uncovering her head to wipe the tears away is poignant. To have entered such company, loosed her hair and wept would have been a disgrace to a woman. Yet she seems oblivious to all in her grief and gratitude to Jesus. She kisses his feet as a gesture of profound thankfulness.[3] One can imagine the embarrassed silence and shock of the host and other guests at this emotional display by a woman with such a reputation. Yet, the reader cannot fail to be touched by her contrition and joy mingled together; the scene is genuinely moving.

However, we are not left long to the beauty of the moment. The reader is brought up short by the thoughts of Simon at v. 39,

> If this man were a prophet, he would have known who and what sort of woman this is who is touching him, for she is a sinner.

article that the slur of 'prostitute' was often used with regard to women of questionable character, particularly in the context of banquets. Corley suggests that it was Luke's intention to give such an impression, but on the whole Corley doubts that the charge was well-founded with regard to Jesus' female followers; see 'Women in the Context of Greco-Roman Meals', in *Society of Biblical Literature: 1989 Seminar Papers* (Atlanta: Scholars Press, 1989), pp. 520-21.

1. Creed, *Luke*, p. 109.

2. See J. Koenig, *New Testament Hospitality* (Philadelphia: Fortress Press, 1985), pp. 16-17.

3. Jeremias contends that ἀγαπάω in 7.42 means 'give thanks' since there is no equivalent word in either Hebrew or Aramaic (*Parables*, pp. 126-27); see also Fitzmyer, *Luke*, p. 690 n. 43.

In this single sentence, Luke has again cast his Pharisee in the role of the enemy of right thinking.[1] Since no one can know what a Pharisee is thinking (cf. 7.49), we see Luke at his editorial best here. The Pharisee's thoughts are revealed to us to typify the ultimate in insensitivity to the plight of the 'sinner'. Luke, Jesus and the reader can see that what has happened in the woman's life is a desirable thing, but not Simon and his guests. Simon is seen to be completely impervious to the moving demonstration of repentance and turns the scene into an opportunity to criticize Jesus. The contrast between the sinful woman and Simon is a profoundly ideological one: the true and godly sentiment of repentance encounters the ultimate in self-righteousness, each personified in its own character in the story.

An important reversal of the reader's attitude in favour of the 'sinner' is achieved by Jesus' response to Simon's coldness. Through his rebuke of Simon in the parable of the debtors and his words to the woman, Jesus shows that it is the sinful woman who has God's favour and not the respected Pharisee.[2] Jesus intimates that the attentions of the sinful woman are more acceptable to him than the hospitality, such as it was, of Simon's table.[3] The situation is now fully reversed and the 'sinner' has become the 'heroine' and the Pharisee the 'villain'. Thus, the complaint of Jesus' table-fellowship with 'sinners' is fully answered by the story. The reader understands the true nature of that table-fellowship and the complaint is seen to be ill-conceived and unfair. The Pharisee comes out of the story exactly like the portrait of the children playing in the market place: uncomprehending and self-centred.

In the remainder of the story the theme of forgiveness for the 'sinner' comes to the fore and it is here that we now find Luke's special emphasis emerging. The point of the overall story is clear: the intimate fellowship of the 'sinner' with Jesus results in penitence and forgiveness. Nevertheless, the structure of 7.36-50 is complex and not without bearing on the interpretation of the text.[4] There appear to be

1. See Leroy, 'Vergebung und Gemeinde nach Lukas 7.36-50', p. 92; also Kilgallen, 'John the Baptist', p. 678.
2. Tannehill, *Narrative Unity*, p. 117.
3. Marshall, *Luke*, p. 310.
4. See Fitzmyer, *Luke*, pp. 684-88 and Marshall, *Luke*, pp. 305-306 for an overview of the various options on the tradition form of the text.

four parts to this portion of the text:[1] (1) the narrative of the incident of the sinful woman in Simon's house (vv. 36-39); (2) the parable of the two debtors (vv. 40-43); (3) Jesus' application of the parable to Simon and the woman (vv. 44-47) which is capped by the ambiguous saying at v. 47; and (4) the authority of Jesus to forgive sins: this completes the circuit back to the narrative flow of the story (vv. 48-50).

It has been suggested that the main problem of interpretation is that the narrative (vv. 36-39) describes love as the condition of forgiveness while the parable (vv. 40-43) describes love as the consequence of forgiveness.[2] Lk. 7.47 seems to embody this confusion. Indeed, the two halves of v. 47 do seem to form an unlikely couplet, but the answer lies in the relationship of the narrative (vv. 36-39) to the parable (vv. 40-43). The narrative focuses on the penitential behaviour of the sinful woman. As has been noted, we are not told what is the actual cause of her behaviour (grief over sin? or perhaps joy over forgiveness of sin?). Nevertheless, it seems fair to assume that it is repentance that is demonstrated by her actions,[3] but as readers we simply assume that she intends to renounce the offending behaviour that first brought her to grief. This is an unspoken assumption which the reader brings, but there is no textual indicator for it. The parable, on the other hand, shifts the focus to the creditor who graciously forgives the debtors. The emphasis shifts from repentance to forgiveness, two closely related but still distinct phenomena. This is how the narrative and the parable differ.

Lk. 7.47 is the key to bringing these two themes together and it demonstrates Luke's (or his tradition's) special interest in repentance and forgiveness for the 'sinner'.

(a) Therefore, I tell you, her sins, which are many, are forgiven, (b) for she loved much; (c) but he who is forgiven little, loves little.

The saying in v. 47 attempts to synthesize the two disparate perspec-

---

1.   So J. Dupont, 'Le Pharisien et la pécheresse (Lc 7.36-50)', *Communautés et Liturgies* 4 (1980), pp. 262-63.

2.   As in Creed, *Luke*, p. 110; see further Kilgallen, 'John the Baptist', pp. 675-79. Dupont sensibly describes the relationship between repentance and forgiveness in this passage: 'il y a simplement interdépendance' ('Le Pharisien', p. 260).

3.   So Leroy, 'Vergebung und Gemeinde nach Lukas 7.36-50', p. 92; J. Navonne, 'The Lucan Banquet Community', *Bible Today* 50 (1970), p. 158.

tives of the narrative and the parable.[1] Verse 47a, b refer to the repentance theme of the narrative at vv. 36-39. The saying 'for she
loved much' (RSV; Greek, ὅτι ἠγάπησεν πολύ) refers to the sinful
woman's actions and should be understood not as the basis of forgiveness, but as the evidence of forgiveness. The ὅτι, argues M. Zerwick,
conveys an evidential sense and the context of 47c confirms that this is
the proper understanding, although the text on its own is ambiguous.[2]
Verse 47c, on the other hand, refers to the parable[3] and serves to
connect the narrative to the parable. The gracious forgiveness which
is the point of the parable is connected to the penitent behaviour of the
sinful woman.

For all the difficulty of the structure of 7.47, the point is simple
enough: 'That her sins are forgiven is evident in the fact that she acts
as she does, that is, in a penitent and grateful manner. But the one who
has experienced little of this gracious forgiveness lacks this attitude.'
Repentance and forgiveness have become the great equalizers for the
'sinner' and have restored her to God's favour. The situation in Simon's house has now been turned completely on its head and the necessary reversal to 'save' the 'sinner' has been achieved by Luke.

Conclusion

After Jesus has finished upbraiding his host he turns his attention to
the woman.

> And he said to her, 'Your sins are forgiven'. Then those who were at
> table with him began to say among themselves, 'Who is this, who even
> forgives sins?' And he said to the woman, 'Your faith has saved you, go
> in peace'.

We are now able to see the connecting ties of Luke's development of
the 'sinner' theme. The initial allusion to forgiveness for the 'sinner'
was found in Peter's confession (Lk. 5.7) and although no direct mention of forgiveness was made, Jesus' response was positive ('Do not be

---

1.   See G. Braumann, 'Die Schuldner und die Sünderin: Luk. VII. 36-50', *NTS*
10 (1964), pp. 488-89; Marshall, *Luke*, p. 305; Creed, *Luke*, p. 110.
2.   So M. Zerwick argues convincingly in *Biblical Greek* (Rome: Scripta
Pontificii Instituti Biblici, 1963), p. 144-45; Fitzmyer, *Luke*, p. 687; so also
Kilgallen, 'John the Baptist', p. 675.
3.   Fitzmyer, *Luke*, p. 684.

afraid; henceforth you will be catching men'). Next, in the healing of
the paralytic (Lk. 5.17-26) Jesus responded to the man as he was let
down through the roof in words almost identical to those in Lk. 7.48,
'Man, your sins are forgiven you'. In both places (Lk. 5.20; 7.48) this
is followed by a remonstration by the Pharisees about Jesus' words
(cf. 'Who is this who speaks blasphemies? Who can forgive sins but
God only?', Lk. 5.21, and 'Who is this who even forgives sins?', Lk.
7.49).

This was followed by the call of Levi and the 'policy statement' of
Lk. 5.32 about the calling of 'sinners' to 'repentance' as the focus of
Jesus' call. Now, here in Luke 7, forgiveness has been added for the
first time to the formula and dramatically demonstrated for a specific
'sinner'. In this way Luke brings the themes of forgiveness and the
'sinners' into tighter connection. The ideological concept of the
'sinner' has now become fully wed to this emphasis on forgiveness and
they combine to portray the purpose of Jesus' ministry.

While Luke has now concretized the 'sinners' theme in the characters of the sinful woman and Simon, these two are still clearly meant
to represent the two extreme ends of the ideological spectrum for
Luke. The sinful woman is the representative of the repentant 'sinner',
and Simon is the prototypical blind religionist. Luke's overall ideological cast to the issue remains unchanged, except that now the 'sinner'
has been shown to be the proper object of forgiveness, and this forgiveness is advanced as the solution for the 'sinner's' plight.

Chapter 6

THE GOSPEL FOR THE LOST ?

In this section I deal primarily with the contribution of ch. 15 to the 'sinner' theme in Luke. First, however, we must glance backward to the material in chs. 8–14 to determine its relationship to ch. 15 and to our subject in general. Attention will then be given to the structure of ch. 15 and the clues such an analysis provides for its interpretation. Next, a proposal will be made about what ch. 15 teaches about the 'sinner' and the Pharisaic objection to Jesus' association with them. Finally, the implications of ch. 15 for Luke's portrayal of his Pharisees will be briefly explored.

Luke 8–14

The theme of forgiveness has already been traced through the first seven chapters of Luke and it was observed that the references to forgiveness and repentance at Lk. 5.20 and Lk. 5.32 are finally combined in Lk. 7.34-50 with the ideological concept of the 'sinner'. There I maintained that the association of the 'sinner' with 'forgiveness' was an important development for Luke which culminated in the saying at Lk. 7.48 where Jesus declares to the sinful woman, 'Your sins are forgiven you'.

Immediately following this, in Lk. 8.1, Luke's story enters a new phase. Our literary marker is a standard Lucan phrase which serves as a pause in his report and also sets the stage for further progress in the story: 'Soon afterward he went on through cities and villages, preaching and bringing the good news of the kingdom of God'.[1]

The portrayal of Jesus as one who not only calls to repentance but pronounces forgiveness in Luke 7 is now picked up in the story by means of a number of statements which show that Jesus is indeed an

---

1.   Cf. Lk. 4.43; 9.6; 20.1; see also Tannehill, *Narrative Unity*, pp. 81, 189.

extraordinary figure. The question of Lk. 7.49, 'Who is this, who even forgives sins?' (cf. Lk. 5.21) is echoed in Lk. 8.25 by Jesus' disciples: 'Who then is this, that he commands even wind and water, and they obey him?' This shows how Luke is now concerned to raise the question of Jesus' identity and accentuate his special status. Mighty deeds attest this status: the storm stilled (Lk. 8.24), the woman with the flow of blood (Lk. 8.46ff.), the raising of Jairus's daughter (Lk. 8.54ff.), the feeding of the five thousand (Lk. 9.10ff.). In addition, Peter's confession of Jesus as the 'Christ of God' and Jesus' reply ('The Son of Man must suffer many things. . .', Lk. 9.18ff.) serve further to unveil Jesus as a transcendent figure. The Transfiguration and God's voice are the ultimate testimony: 'This is my Son, my Chosen; listen to him' (Lk. 9.35).[1]

Two special Lucan editorial comments are particularly revealing about the author's concern to reinforce the significance of Jesus' identity. The story of the unclean spirit which is cast out of the boy (Lk. 9.37-43) is triple tradition material. Jesus succeeds in casting out the demon where the disciples failed and Luke appends a comment which, perhaps by its very ambiguity, appears to be a christological signpost for Luke: ἐξεπλήσσοντο δὲ πάντες ἐπὶ τῇ μεγαλειότητι τοῦ θεοῦ. Could it be that Luke has purposely left his reader to wonder about the full import of this comment?

Compare this also to Luke's treatment of the closing scene of the healing of the Gerasene demoniac (Lk. 8.38-39; cf. Mt. 8.28-34; Mk 5.1-20). In Mark and Luke the healed demoniac begs to follow Jesus. Mark reports Jesus' words as follows:

> Ὕπαγε εἰς τὸν οἶκόν του πρὸς τοὺς σούς καὶ ἀπάγγειλον αὐτοῖς ὅ σα ὁ κύριός σοι πεποίηκεν καὶ ἠλέησέν σε. καὶ ἀπῆλθεν καὶ ἤρξατο κηρύσσειν ἐν τῇ Δεκαπόλει ὅσα ἐποίησεν αὐτῷ ὁ Ἰησοῦς. καὶ πάντες ἐθαύμαζον (Mk 5.19).

Mark's treatment does give an impression of an intentional parallelism between the activity of Jesus and the 'Lord'. But he uses κύριος[2] rather than θεός and focuses on the third person aspect of the work that was done, 'how he has had mercy on you'. Compare this to Luke's bolder assessment of the scene.

---

1. See also Lk. 10.9, 22; 11.32; 12.8, 40 for other events that display Jesus' special status.

2. But preserved in D is σοὶ ὁ θεός.

'Υπόστρεφε εἰς τὸν οἶκόν σου καὶ διηγοῦ ὅσα σοι ἐποίησεν ὁ θεός.
καὶ ἀπῆλθεν καθ' ὅλην τὴν πόλιν κηρύσσων ὅσα ἐποίησεν αὐτῷ
ὁ Ἰησοῦς (Lk. 8.39).

Like Mark, Luke does not shy from using a parallelism that implies a
strong connection indeed between θεός and Ἰησοῦς. We note
however, that he does use the less ambiguous θεός and not κύριος.
Furthermore, Luke places ὁ θεός and ὁ Ἰησοῦς at the end of 8.39a
and 39b respectively, strengthening the implied parallelism between
the terms.[1] This passage would not be without its effect on Luke's
reader. The cumulative effect of all this is to heighten the reader's
appreciation of the extraordinary status of Jesus and, ultimately, to
heighten the significance of the fellowship between Jesus and 'sinners'.

It is one thing to call 'sinners' to repentance (Lk. 5.32) but quite
another thing to pronounce forgiveness for them as Jesus does in Lk.
5.24 and 7.49. The elevation of Jesus' identity to a level beyond the
ordinary implies that forgiveness for 'sinners' is somehow related to
the identity of Jesus himself. The act of pronouncing forgiveness is
validated in the story by Jesus' developing exalted identity, and so the
association of Jesus with 'sinners' takes on a new and profound
significance. Furthermore, as will be seen below, Jesus' views towards
the 'sinners' are intended by Luke to be seen as representative of
God's views of the 'sinners'. In Luke's presentation, the *acts* of Jesus
(Lk. 15.1-2) represent the will and attitude of God himself[2] (15.7,
'there will be more joy in heaven over one sinner who repents than
over ninety-nine righteous persons who need no repentance'; so also
15.10, 24, 32). The identity of Jesus and his relationship to 'sinners' in
the Gospel have assumed major importance for Luke.[3]

---

1.   So Blass–Debrunner, *A Greek Grammar of the New Testament and Other
Early Christian Literature* (trans. R. Funk; Chicago: The University of Chicago
Press, 1961), p. 249, par. 473; and A.T. Robertson, *A Grammar of the Greek New
Testament* (Nashville: Broadman Press, 1934), p. 417.

2.   Jeremias, *Parables*, p. 132; F. Schnider, *Die velorenen Söhne: Strukturana-
lytische und historisch-kritische Untersuchungen zu Lk 15* (Göttingen: Vandenhoeck
& Ruprecht, 1977), p. 70; P. Mourlon-Beernaert, 'The Lost Sheep: Four
Approaches', *TD* 29 (1981), pp. 144-45.

3.   As Schnider has noted (*Die verlorenen Söhne*), 'Die Jesuserzählung von Lk
15 bringt damit den Anspruch Jesu zum Ausdruck, dass er in seinem Verhalten zum
Menschen das Verhalten Gottes zum Menschen erschliesst' (p. 70). He goes on to
point out the 'christological' significance of this development, especially with regard

Before turning to the material of ch. 15 itself, it must also be observed how two aspects of the material of chs. 13 and 14 contribute to our understanding of Luke's 'sinner' material. The first concerns the brief pericope of special Lucan material at Lk. 13.1-5.[1] The comment of Jesus reported by Luke in 13.3 is unique in the Gospel tradition: οὐχί, λέγω ὑμῖν, ἀλλ' ἐὰν μὴ μετανοῆτε πάντες ὁμοίως ἀπολεῖσθε (that is, as did the sinners). It is Luke alone who universalizes (λέγω ὑμῖν) the category of the 'sinner' to include all people.[2] This call to 'repent' includes the disciples, the multitudes, indeed, everyone who escaped these disasters: *they* are now the ἁμαρτωλοί/ὀφειλέται. Luke begins also to draw his Gospel audience, by way of association with Jesus' audience, into the category of the 'sinner': you will all likewise perish unless you repent. The reader, by extension, also feels a sense of inclusion in Jesus' general appraisal of the human condition and the call to 'sinners' is assuming a subtly kerygmatic force.[3]

The premise of the pericope is that the fate that befell these 'sinners' was their just and proper reward. Jesus does not say they were undeserving of their end,[4] but rather δοκεῖτε ὅτι οἱ Γαλιλαῖοι οὗτοι ἁμαρτωλοὶ παρὰ πάντας τοὺς Γαλιλαίους ἐγένοντο, ὅτι ταῦτα πεπόνθασιν;[5] they were simply *no worse* 'sinners' and suffered, only

to Lk. 15 (pp. 70-71).

1. The connection of Lk. 13.1-9 and Lk. 15.1-32 has been noted by W.R. Farmer, 'Notes on a Literary and Form-critical Analysis of Some of the Synoptic Material Peculiar to Luke', *NTS* 8 (1961–62), pp. 301-16. They share the 'same formal structure' (p. 306) and common content on the issue of repentance for the sinner (pp. 313ff.).

2. The editorial introduction to the logion (Παρῆσαν δέ τινες ἐν αὐτῷ τῷ καιρῷ, Lk. 13.1) also shows that the words of Jesus are addressed to a general audience. Jesus had been teaching not only the disciples (Lk. 12.1, 22, 32, 41-42) but the multitudes as well (Lk. 12.1, 13, 54).

3. Cf. also Acts 3.26.

4. As F.W. Young notes ('Luke 13.1-9', *Int* 31 [1977], p. 60).

5. The use of the preposition παρά to express comparison in place of ἤ or the genitive is found elsewhere in Lk. (3.4, 13; but also Rom. 14.5; Heb. 2.7-9); see Blass–Debrunner, *A Greek Grammar*, p. 99, par. 185 and pp. 127-28, par. 245. See Jeremias, *Parables*, p. 112, who says that is an attempt to translate the Aramaic *min*, there being no comparative or superlative in Aramaic grammar. Cf. Lk. 18.14a, παρὰ ἐκεῖνον.

incidentally, the fate reserved for all 'sinners'.[1] Then comes the crucial widening of the lesson of their death: λέγω ὑμῖν, ἀλλ' ἐὰν μὴ μετανοῆτε πάντες ὁμοίως ἀπολεῖσθε. The reader cannot distance him or herself from these events by saying, 'violence and death have overtaken those who are deserving sinners while we are secure'.[2] Now πάντες are ἁμαρτωλοί.

This constitutes a subtle but very important development in Luke's rhetoric of salvation. It is unremarkable in the story at 13.1-5 that a 'sinner' should repent or even die for his sinfulness; this is completely expected. Nor is it unusual that a universal call to repentance be extended (cf. Mt. 3.11; 4.17; 21.32; Mk 1.4, 14; 6.12). But here Luke provides a rationale for repentance that is nowhere else clearly stated in the Gospels: it is because *all* are 'sinners' that *all* must repent.[3] This is in contrast to the usual rationale that it is the advent of the Kingdom which is the reason for repentance (Mt. 3.2, 11-12; 4.17; Mk 1.14-15).[4] Furthermore, the assumption that the reader is now to be included in this religious category is a key step in Luke's apologetic purpose.

This identification of the reader with the 'sinner' is termed a 'development' because all of the imagery of the 'sinner' so far in Luke has been negative. The 'toll collectors and sinners' of Levi's banquet (5.29) are not people with whom a reader would readily identify. We indeed sympathize with their plight as victimized outsiders and perhaps applaud their success in obtaining access to Jesus, but we do not see ourselves in their shoes. In a number of other places in Luke

---

1. F.W. Young says, 'He singles out for particular disclaimer one possible interpretation: that individuals more sinful than others have received just reward for their sins' ('Luke 13.1-9', p. 61).

2. F.W. Young, 'Luke 13.1-9', p. 62. See also G. Schwarz, 'Lukas XIII.1-5', *NovT* 11 (1969), p. 126.

3. So H. Conzelmann, *The Theology of St Luke* (trans. G. Buswell; Philadelphia: Fortress Press, 1961), p. 227. Carlston (*Parables of the Triple Tradition*) has noted in regard to Luke's repentance theme that 'Jesus is now thought of not primarily as the one who invites even the outcast to the Messianic banquet but as the one who demands that sinners repent. This change is, naturally, conformable to Luke's special understanding of repentance and sin. Repentance is no longer a general term for the movement of a whole people back to God. It is now a specific term for a once-for-all individual conversion, which must be supplemented by good works' (p. 60).

4. Again, see Conzelmann, *The Theology of St Luke*, p. 227 n. 2.

ἁμαρτωλοί is nothing more than a term of derision: Lk. 6.32-34, 'even sinners do the same' (cf. Mt. 5.46-47; 18.17; 21.31-32); so also Lk. 24.6-7, 'the Son of Man must be delivered into the hands of sinful men' (cf. Mk 14.41; Mt. 26.45). The same could be said of the sinful woman in 7.36-50 who is called an ἁμαρτωλός by Luke (v. 37), Simon (v. 39) and even Jesus (vv. 47-48). Certainly also here at 13.2 and 4 'sinners' is a pejorative term with which one would not readily identify oneself.

Yet this is consonant with Luke's tendency to accentuate themes of reversal. It is reversal that will now dominate Luke's attention up until ch. 15. This is the theme of the teaching on the narrow door in 13.22-30; many will seek to enter the door of salvation (13.23-24) but few will be successful. It is precisely those who might be expected to find a way in (13.26, 'we ate and drank in your presence, and you taught in our streets') who are themselves rejected (13.27, 'depart from me all you workers of iniquity!'). The principle is summed up in the saying, 'And behold, some are last who will be first, and some are first who will be last' (13.30). In the parable of the marriage feast, reversal is seen in the logion at 14.11: 'For everyone who exalts himself will be humbled, and he who humbles himself will be exalted'. So also in the climax of the parable of the great banquet: 'For I tell you, none of those men who were invited shall taste my banquet' (14.24).[1]

These reversal stories serve to confirm the total reversal of conventional thinking that has just been advanced in 13.1-5. This produces a most unexpected result: now it is the 'sinner' and not the 'righteous' to whom salvation has come. This is the legitimization and redemption, as it were, of the 'sinner' imagery. Such a process demands radical themes of reversal and Luke has obliged.

Two views of the 'sinner' are now beginning to meld into one. The 'sinner' is no longer just a member of a hated social group (e.g. 5.29; 7.36-50) or one of the damned (e.g. 6.32-34; 10.13-15; 13.2, 4), but has become one who has an inherent need for God (13.3, 5). Luke's apparent purpose is to convince his audience that all are 'sinners' in need of forgiveness and to establish repentance as the only remedy for that condition. The partly sociological, partly ideological 'sinner' of

---

1. The reversal theme continues to be prominent also after Lk. 15: 16.15, 19-31; 17.33; 18.9-14, esp. v. 14; 18.25.

the Gospel tradition has become a vehicle for a universal call to repentance, a call which includes the Gospel audience.

The Structure of Luke 15

The analysis of ch. 15 will require a somewhat different approach from that of chs. 5 and 7. For our purposes here in Luke 15 it is the general structure of the chapter which will prove to be of interest to the inquiry. More specifically, we are interested in the common thematic elements of the three parables and the setting in which Luke places them. As a result, the concern here is not with the parables as individual entities, nor in the details of the parables as such, but in the way the chapter functions as a whole.[1]

Structurally, ch. 15 is composed of an introductory setting (vv. 1-3) and a trilogy of parables, two short and one longer (vv. 4-7, 8-10, 11-32).[2] Here, as in chs. 5 and 7, a concrete social setting is interpreted ideologically for the reader. But in the case of ch. 15 the relationship between the acts of Jesus and their ideological interpretation is especially dramatic. The setting is brief and to the point (vv. 1-3), and the interpretive portion (vv. 4-32) is extensive. Thus, structurally, the three parables provide the reader with a way to understand the ideological significance of the setting in which they occur, that is, Jesus' association with 'sinners'.

The Setting: Lk. 15.1-3

> Now the tax collectors and sinners were all drawing near to hear him. And the Pharisees and the scribes murmured, saying, 'This man receives sinners and eats with them'. So he told them this parable. . .

This setting is the key to the interpretation of the three parables.[3] Luke's Pharisees again raise the now familiar question about Jesus' association with 'sinners'. The three parables are a comment on that controversy and can only be properly understood in that context. Luke's setting means that all of ch. 15 is focused on the issue of the

---

1.   See Schnider for a good treatment of how the component parts of ch. 15 work together as a unity (*Die verlorenen Söhne*, pp. 67-71).

2.   See Farmer, 'Form-critical Analysis', especially pp. 305ff.

3.   So L. Ramarosan, 'Le coeur du troisième évangile: Lc 15', *Bib* 60 (1979), p. 350; see also Tannehill, *Narrative Unity*, p. 106.

errant Pharisaic attitude and is thus to be understood as controversy material.[1] The purpose of the parables is to justify Jesus' behaviour against the Pharisaic charge ('This man receives sinners and eats with them') and press home a counter-criticism against the Pharisees themselves.

In the brief scenario at vv. 1-2 we find the usual lack of concrete information and details we have come to expect when dealing with 'sinner' material. There is no location or chronology given for the setting. The language is clearly hyperbolic; all (πάντες) the 'toll collectors and sinners' gather about Jesus.[2] This hyperbole is characteristic of Luke in his narrative asides ('all' his adversaries were put to shame and 'all' the people rejoiced [Lk. 13.17], 'all' were astonished [Lk. 9.43]).[3] This tendency to exaggerate for the sake of emphasis shows, especially with respect to Lk. 15.1-2, that we are dealing with a 'type-scene'[4] which should not be taken as a specific incident in Jesus' life.[5] This is confirmed by the abruptness of the turn in the narrative from the parable of the salt at 14.34-35 to the new scene at 15.1-2. Without any transitional phrases or preparation Luke simply enters in upon the new scene. The new setting lacks the features of a specific event and there is an artificial feeling to the scene. Luke's editorial hand is clearly evident in producing an appropriate setting for the three parables of Jesus.[6]

The relation of setting to parable is interesting here. Like the scenario at 5.28-32, the setting is masterfully arranged for the teaching that is to follow.[7] In the case of ch. 15 the setting and parables com-

1. So Hickling, 'A Tract on Jesus and the Pharisees', pp. 254-55; Jeremias, *Parables*, pp. 124, 131.

2. Cf. Grundmann who takes the πάντες as meaning 'throughout Palestine' (*Lukas*, p. 305), but in either case it is hyperbole.

3. See also Lk. 9.6; 7.17; 6.17-19; 5.26; 4.17 and further J. Jeremias, 'Tradition und Redaktion in Lukas 15', *ZNW* 62 (1971), p. 185. He also notes the similarity to the hyperbole we have already noted in Lk. 5.17.

4. Tannehill, *Narrative Unity*, p. 106.

5. Marshall, *Luke*, p. 599; Grundmann, *Lukas*, p. 305.

6. Bultmann, *HST*, p. 193, 334-35; Brawley, 'The Pharisees in Luke/Acts', pp. 66-68; Jeremias, 'Tradition und Redaktion', pp. 185, 189. But cf. the view of Farmer who holds Lk. 15.1-2 to be pre-Lucan ('Form-critical Analysis', p. 302).

7. Jeremias notes the structural similarity between Lk. 5.29ff. and Lk. 15.1ff. ('Tradition und Redaktion', pp. 186-88), as does Fiedler, *Jesus und die Sünder*, p. 148.

plement one another extremely well.[1] These parables about the 'lost'
being found are matched literarily to a concrete circumstance of Jesus'
ministry and their didactic force is remarkable. The supposedly concrete rejection of 'sinners' by the Pharisees gives the opportunity for a
trilogy of parables to demonstrate the error of exactly such an attitude.

The Three Parables

The setting and the parables are two halves of an interpretive whole;
this can be seen in the common structure and content of the three
parables. The parables stand together as an answer to 15.1-2. By
repetition and development of the theme of seeking the 'lost' they represent a cumulative response to the Pharisaic charge: 'This man receives sinners. . .'

The parallel structure of the first two parables can be seen in the
fact that they share certain common elements: (1) the identification of
the main character (vv. 4, 8); (2) the description of the loss and the
resulting search (vv. 4, 8); (3) the finding of the lost object (vv. 5,
9); (4) the calling of friends in an invitation to rejoice over the discovery (vv. 6, 9); and (5) the culmination with the saying that explains there is rejoicing in heaven ἐπὶ ἑνὶ ἁμαρτωλῷ μετανοοῦντι
(vv. 7, 10).

The parable of the lost coin follows the order of events of the parable of the lost sheep exactly, and differs structurally only in that it
lacks certain descriptive elements present in the first parable. Most
notably, the parable of the lost coin lacks the comparative element in
the final saying. In the first parable there is more joy in heaven over
the repentant 'sinner' than those who need no repentance; also, the
verb of v. 7 is in the future tense (ἔσται) giving it more of an apocalyptic feel (cf. the present γίνεται at v. 10).[2] The second parable
simply reinforces the point of the first by an alternate example. The
force of repetition adds weight and clarity to the point at issue. Except
for minor differences both parables appear to have an identical intent
in illustrating the principle of rejoicing over a lost 'sinner'. They

---

1. J.D.M. Derrett says, 'the appropriateness of the parable to its setting is
extraordinary' ('Fresh Light on the Lost Sheep and the Lost Coin', *NTS* 26 [1980],
p. 46).
2. Jeremias, *Parables*, p. 136.

respond directly to the charge of v. 2 and illustrate Jesus' opinion on the matter.

The third parable, the lost son, corresponds generally in structure to the first two and expands and reaffirms the same message. The salient structural divisions are: (1) the identification of the main character (ἄνθρωπός τις εἶχεν δύο υἱούς, v. 11); (2) the description of the loss of the 'object'—in this case the son and his living (καὶ ἐκεῖ διεσκόρπισεν τὴν οὐσίαν αὐτοῦ ζῶν ἀσώτως, v. 13) and the resulting 'search' (εἰς ἑαυτὸν δὲ ἐλθὼν ἔφη..., v. 17); (3) the son is 'found' by his father (ὁ πατήρ... ἐπέπεσεν ἐπὶ τὸν τράχηλον αὐτοῦ καὶ κατεφίλησεν αὐτόν, v. 20); and (4) the father calls his servant and reports the recovery of his son and orders rejoicing (φέρετε τὸν μόσχον τὸν σιτευτόν... ὅτι οὗτος ὁ υἱός μου νεκρὸς ἦν καὶ ἀνέζησεν ... καὶ ἤρξαντο εὐφραίνεσθαι, vv. 23-24).

The significant additions to the third parable are the insight into the physical and then psychological struggle of the son (vv. 13-20a), the father's reaction to his son's return (vv. 20b, 22-24), the son's confession (v. 21), and the elder son's reaction (vv. 25-30). These additions serve the function of explaining why the Pharisaic criticism of 15.2 is amiss. The 'sinner' actually suffers and struggles to come to terms with his moral failure (vv. 13-20). The father is relieved, not offended, when the son returns (vv. 20b, 22-24). The sinful son is repentant and thus deserving of mercy (v. 21), unlike the passivity of the lost sheep and coin in the first two parables. Finally, by way of the analogy between the Pharisees and the elder son, the latter's reaction shows all the lack of concern for the wayward that is meant to characterize the Pharisaic attitude.

Verses 25-32 are an integral component to ch. 15 as a whole.[1] The extended description of the dissatisfaction of the older son at the treatment of the younger is an essay on the failure of the Pharisees to seek the lost.[2] By showing the objections of the elder son to be unreasonable the third parable closes the circle that was opened by the reported

---

1. So argues Jeremias, *Parables*, pp. 128ff. and Bultmann, *HST*, p. 196. But cf. J.T. Sanders, 'Tradition and Redaction in Luke XV.11-32', *NTS* 15 (1968–69), pp. 433-34, who argues that since the parable is 'zweigipfelig', or has a double climax, this indicates that 25-32 is a later addition to the parable. See also Jeremias, *Parables,* p. 131 and 'Tradition und Redaktion', p. 181.

2. Verses 11-32 'reinforce and bring to a climax' the previous material in the chapter; see E.E. Ellis, *Gospel of Luke* (London: Nelson, 1966), p. 197.

criticism of vv. 1-2, then set up and developed in vv. 3-7 and 8-10, and resolved now, in vv. 11-32 by showing the criticism to be invalid (ὁ ἀδελφός σου οὗτος νεκρὸς ἦν καὶ ἔζησεν, καὶ ἀπολωλὼς καὶ εὑρέθη, v. 32).[1] This circle accomplishes two purposes. It answers the Pharisaic criticism of v. 2 but then goes on the attack by elucidating the Pharisees' failure to fulfil their duty to reach out to 'sinners'.[2] The whole structure of ch. 15 works together toward this end: first to refute the criticism against Jesus and then to indict the Pharisees for a failed responsibility.

When the parables of Luke 15 are considered separately they each bring forth great themes in their own right. The compassion of the shepherd who searches for the lost sheep, the portrait of the forgiving father, the lost son and his repentance are all profoundly moving. But the function of these parables must be viewed in counterpoint to the setting in which Luke places them. Their purpose is to add weight and drama to the argument that the charge of vv. 1-2 is ill conceived. Yes, Luke 15 is about the grace of God, but it also serves an important function as a critique of the errant attitude of the Pharisees and their failed responsibility for seeking the 'lost'.[3]

Seeking the 'Lost': A New Gospel?

I have argued that the three parables of ch. 15 are a response to the Pharisaic attitude to 'sinners', but what is it about that attitude that is being criticized? It is at this point that much of the traditional interpretation of Luke 15 has gone off-track. By emphasizing the content of the parables themselves rather than the way they work together in juxtaposition to the setting, many have transformed the forgiveness of the father and the seeking of the lost into a 'gospel' which the histori-

---

1. See Schnider, *Die verlorenen Söhne:* 'Anfang und Ende entsprechen sich also' (p. 67, see also p. 69).

2. As J.T. Sanders has put it, 'The parable of the Prodigal Son thus serves the function of moving the discussion from a defence of Jesus' associations with the "lost" to an attack on the attitudes and dealings of the Pharisees themselves. . . the line between the first and second parts of the parable of the Prodigal Son is the line between defence and offence' ('Tradition and Redaction', p. 438.).

3. Jeremias put the matter correctly: 'The parable of the Prodigal Son is therefore not primarily a proclamation of the Good News to the poor, but a vindication of the Good News in reply to its critics' (*Parables*, p. 131).

cal Pharisees could not accept.[1] Although Jeremias understands the controversy nature of the chapter, he still makes this mistake. Since many seem to refer to Jeremias on this matter I shall look at his comments. For him the parable of the lost son was 'addressed to men who were like the elder brother, men who were offended at the gospel'.[2] Jesus hopes to move them to abandon their 'resistance to the gospel' and wants them to experience the joy that the 'Good News' brings.[3] Examples could be multiplied from many corners of NT scholarship that accept this basic point of view about Jesus' relations with the 'sinners'. In this view Jesus 'was extending his redemptive activity of healing and forgiveness to the needy'.[4] We are to appreciate the 'startling nature' of Jesus' proclamation of forgiveness to the 'lost'[5] and the father in the third parable has 'overstepped the bounds of conventional religion'[6] by accepting his son back. There is nothing at all uncommon about this scholarly view.[7]

But what does it mean when one says the Pharisees were 'offended' by the gospel? Such language rests on the assumption that the 'historical' Pharisees and scribes could not countenance any attitude of seeking the 'lost' or forgiving them once they were 'found'. Thus they were 'offended' by even the suggestion of seeking those outside their own circle. The very selection of language in which the issue is presented by Jeremias demands the moral censure of the Pharisees for rejecting the 'gospel'. Such language is common to the tradition of

---

1. Thus Ramarosan, who calls ch. 15 'le coeur du troisième évangile' is somewhat off the mark. So also Jülicher who calls it a 'little gospel within the Gospel'. If true at all it can only be so in a limited and secondary sense ('Le coeur du troisième évangile; Lc 15', pp. 358-60 and Ramarosan quoting Jülicher, p. 356).

2. Jeremias, *Parables*, p. 131.

3. Jeremias, *Parables*, p. 132.

4. R. Guelich, *Mark 1–8.26* (Dallas: Word Books, 1989), p. 106.

5. Perrin, *Rediscovering*, p. 94; so also D. Dormeyer, 'Revolutionär muss es für die jüdische Gesselschaft klingen. . . ', and seeking the lost is a 'Neuordung' ('Textpragmatische Analyse und Unterrichtsplannung zum Gleichnis vom verloren Schaf, Lk. 15.1-7', *Die evangelische Erzieher* 27 [1975], p. 353).

6. Perrin, *Rediscovering*, p. 97.

7. For example, see also Hickling, 'A Tract on Jesus', p. 259; Bornkamm, *Jesus*, pp. 78-79. In reference to Lk. 15, B. Meyer says 'exclusion to the morally evil from the social life of the morally good. . . was a principle deeply rooted in the imposing religious and moral tradition of the nation' (*Aims*, p. 160, but see pp. 159-61).

interpretation of Luke 15 but it shows an unwillingness to address the material objectively.

At the historical level there is no evidence to suggest that such a view of the 'lost' was characteristic of rabbinic notions, early or late, about the forgiveness of sins.[1] Furthermore, it is misleading to cite the occasional rabbinic reference to joy over the downfall of the godless as representative of the rabbinic doctrine on the whole.[2] Such rabbinic references should be taken in the same way that the Psalms speak about the 'righteous' and the 'wicked', that is, as the ideological extremes in a religious system of thought. There may have been individuals and groups who felt this way in Jesus' day, and certainly in the post-destruction period at least some of the rabbis recorded harsh feelings of this sort about the *'am ha-aretz*. But to characterize 'Judaism' as a whole in such a light is unjustified. Jeremias has made the classic error of reading Luke's caricatured portrayal of the Pharisees as history.

But even at the level of the text there is little evidence for such a view of the Pharisaic doctrine toward the 'lost'. There is no evidence in the Gospel of Luke that the Pharisees thought people could not obtain forgiveness for their sins. They objected to Jesus' suggestion that *he* could forgive sins (Lk. 5.24; 7.49) but they are plainly said to believe that God does indeed forgive sins (Lk. 5.21). It is incorrect to assert, from the perspective of the Gospel of Luke itself, that the Pharisees were being criticized by Jesus for not believing in forgiveness for those who needed it. Jeremias and others consign the Pharisees to a judgment which Luke did not intend.

---

1.   See the previous discussion in Chapter 3, 'Sinners and Repentance'. Note also the excellent treatment of the rabbinic doctrine by Abrahams (*SPG*, pp. 139-49); and also Maccoby's treatment of *m. Yom.* 8.9 (*ERW*, pp. 89-92). E. P. Sanders's treatment of the subject is caustic but effective in countering Christian characterizations of Judaism as a religion without forgiveness (*Jesus and Judaism*, pp. 200-204). Charlesworth says the idea that humans could seek forgiveness from God 'must no longer be attributed in the history of ideas to the creative genius of Paul' (*Jesus within Judaism*, p. 50). Rather, this was already part of the 'deep and penetrating advances of Jewish theology' in Jesus' day (*Jesus within Judaism*, p. 50).

2.   As does Marshall, *Luke*, p. 602. Abrahams's description of such highly derisive rabbinic texts about the godless as 'theoretical metaphysics rather than practical religious teaching' is probably the correct approach (*SPG*, p. 143).

The proper treatment of this material is aided by a backward glance at the material in ch. 5. The interpretation of ch. 15 is based on the same rationale as that which applied to the saying at Lk. 5.31, 'Those who are well have no need of a physician, but those who are sick'. This was a simple, universally understood maxim whose logical force applied also to Jesus' outreach to 'sinners'. It was precisely because the Pharisees knew this maxim to be true that Jesus' logion was a fitting critique. He calls them, not forward to a new teaching, but back to an old one. The rationale of the parables of the lost sheep, coin and son is the same as that of Luke 5. Of course a shepherd will seek the 'lost' sheep and the housewife the 'lost' coin. Any father who loves his son will welcome him back. It is the universal good sense of these illustrations that make them such a powerful refutation to what is now exposed as a foolish criticism of Jesus' association with 'sinners'. Just as no one could deny that only sick people need physicians (Lk. 5.31) neither could any one deny the simple, obvious truths of these parables. To suggest that the Pharisees (historical or literary) believed otherwise is to make them the defenders of ludicrous and nonsensical beliefs. And while Luke does not like the Pharisees, I do not believe this is what he intends.

The point can be demonstrated outside the text of Luke as well. It is not surprising that the long shadow of Ezekiel 34 is also invoked with respect to Luke 15.[1] God expects his shepherds to seek the lost and the depiction of the Jewish people as lost sheep is a common theme.[2] In ancient tradition Moses was the first to show his fitness to lead the people of God by seeking a lost goat from the flock of Jethro. After Moses pursues the wayward animal and carries him on his shoulder back to the flock God says to Moses,

> You have had sufficient love to lead a flock of flesh and blood, and so will you with your life, lead my flock Israel.[3]

This advances on the irrefutable logic that if restoring lost livestock

1. 'That [Ezek. 34]. . . lies behind this chapter is not doubted' (Derrett, 'Fresh Light', p. 37). See also Marshall, *Luke*, p. 601; Grundmann, *Lukas*, p. 307. Others have suggested Jer. 31.10-20 as the background of the lost/found theme (G. Quell, 'πατήρ', *TDNT*, V, p. 973; Grundmann, *Lukas*, pp. 304-305).

2. So Derrett, 'Fresh Light', p. 37.

3. *Exod. R.* 2.68b; see Derrett, 'Fresh Light', pp. 43-44; also Jónsson, *Humour and Irony*, p. 120.

was a universal responsibility,[1] how much more so the restoration of the lost sheep of God's own people (cf. Lk. 14.5)?

As in Lk. 5.31-32 the point of the parables of ch. 15 is primarily that the Pharisees have failed in their fundamental duty to seek the 'lost'. If Jesus offends the Pharisees it is not because he offers forgiveness to 'sinners' but because his actions and parables indict the Pharisees for a failed responsibility. They are not fulfilling their role as shepherds because they are not calling 'sinners' to repentance and thus, by extension, to forgiveness as well. The whole point of ch. 15 is to commend Jesus for doing what everyone knows a shepherd should do and to criticize the 'Pharisees' for failing to do the same.

Implications for Luke's View of the Pharisees

We have observed that the view Luke adopts toward his Pharisees is usually a negative one.[2] There is, however, a common feature of the material at Lk. 5.28-32 and here in Luke 15 which must qualify that assessment to some extent. In Lk. 5.32 I argued that there was no irony in the statement, 'I have not come to call the righteous, but sinners to repentance'. Just as those who are well have no need of a physician, so the 'righteous' have no need of rescue. The same argument applies in ch. 15 to the 'righteous' in vv. 7 and 10. The parable of the lost sheep is simple; it is about leaving those who are safe to seek those who are in danger and the resulting joy when the lost are restored to the fold.

λέγω ὑμῖν, ὅτι οὕτως χαρὰ ἐν τῷ οὐρανῷ ἔσται ἐπὶ ἑνὶ ἁμαρτωλῷ μετανοοῦντι ἢ ἐπὶ ἐνενήκοντα ἐννέα δικαίοις οἵτινες οὐ χρείαν ἔχουσιν μετανοίας.

It is not that the ninety-nine are no occasion for joy, but the joy over finding the lost one *exceeds* that which is felt for the ninety-nine. The conjunction ἢ can mean either 'compared with' or, in an exclusive sense, 'in contrast to'; context is the decisive factor as to which way to interpret it.[3] But the latter sense is unlikely, particularly since it would demand the δικαίοις be understood as fully ironic and this does not fit the overall context of the parable. In this parable Jesus clearly

1. Exod. 23.4; Derrett, 'Fresh Light', pp. 38-40.
2. See above Chapter 4.
3. Blass–Debrunner, *A Greek Grammar*, p. 128, par. 245.

thinks some indeed are 'righteous' in the sense of being in the fold[1] and this includes, by analogy, the Pharisees. The 'sinner' with whom Jesus associates is the lost sheep and those within the fold, the ninety-nine, ought to rejoice instead of grumbling.

To admit that Jesus may have thought some were righteous has always been hard for interpreters of the tradition.[2] Even Jeremias, who does not find irony in the term 'righteous', modifies the force of Lk. 15.7 by translating v. 7b, 'than over ninety-nine respectable persons [δικαίοις], *who have not committed any gross sin'* (my italics).[3] But if the ninety-nine, the nine coins, and the elder son are not the Pharisees allegorically they at least represent them analogically.[4] They remain 'in the fold' and in none of the parables is it suggested that they are wicked. In fact, for the purposes of the parable, the Pharisees are the 'righteous'! One would not guess, on the basis of these parables, that the Pharisees are represented elsewhere in the Gospel of Luke as the enemies of God.

Those 'in the fold', that is, the Pharisees, are criticized only for their inability to rejoice over the 'found' and, by extension, their failure to seek them themselves. This is mild compared to Luke's handling of the Pharisees in other places in his Gospel. Nor does Luke 15 contain the harsh themes of reversal we have noted in the parable of the banquet (Lk. 14.15-24) and the marriage feast (Lk. 14.7-14), which are both given while at table with a Pharisee. The severe tone of the Pharisaic objection in Lk. 15.2 is similar to that found elsewhere in Luke and in those places it has signalled the introduction of harsh controversy.[5] But the contents of ch. 15 do not follow this gen-

---

1. So Conzelmann, *The Theology of St Luke*, p. 227 n. 2. Also Arndt, *The Gospel According to St Luke*, p. 248: the 99 'have not fallen; they are in safety; God is well pleased with them'. See also Leaney, *Luke*, p. 219.

2. That is, those who understand 'righteous' as ironic. Dodd (*Parables of the Kingdom*) asks, 'did Jesus really teach that there were righteous persons who needed no repentance?' (p. 119). Jónsson says (*Humour and Irony*), 'v. 7 is definitely ironical, as Jesus does not mean to say that there really exist people who are not in need of repentance' (p. 121). For other examples, see also D. Fletcher, 'The Riddle of the Unjust Steward: Is Irony the Key?', *JBL* 82 (1963), pp. 27-28, and Borg, *Conflict, Holiness and Politics*, p. 95, esp. n. 72.

3. Jeremias, *Parables*, p. 135.

4. Hickling, 'A Tract on Jesus', p. 255.

5. See Lk. 7.34-50; 5.29–6.11; often signalled by the verbs γογγύζω (Lk.

eral pattern and are remarkably 'soft' on the Pharisees. It shows us
that the categories we have observed cannot be pressed in all cases.

Conclusion: The Legitimization of the 'Sinner'

At another level, the overall effect of ch. 15 is to confirm the legitimization of the 'sinner' in the view of the reader. When we read
'sinner' in vv. 7 and 10 the meaning from the point of view of Luke
is, 'those who want to repent and return to God should do so'. Not
only is the seeking of the 'sinner' viewed as right and proper, but to
be a repentant 'sinner' is a positive thing. The lost son of 15.11-32 is a
positive figure in that he 'comes to himself' and turns from his folly.
He is morally culpable yet his plight is presented to the reader in sympathetic terms. We have been privy to his falling into need and being
moved to repentance and we understand the psychology of his repentance (vv. 17-19). In this way the 'sinner' is legitimized in our thinking and the barriers to identifying with him or her are being dismantled.

Luke's intentional development of a sympathetic view of the 'sinner'
is unique among the Gospels. No other canonical Gospel shows such
an interest in developing the role of the 'sinner' into one with whom
the reader can not only sympathize, but ultimately identify. It is but a
short step from understanding the plight of the lost son to recognizing
elements of our own experience in his struggles. Luke's 'sinner' has
evolved from a despised element of society (Lk. 3.12; 5.28; 6.32ff.) to
a sympathetic figure with whom the reader is encouraged to identify
(Lk. 7.36-50; 13.1-5; 15.1-32).

5.30) and διαγογγύζω (Lk. 15.2; 19.7).

Chapter 7

THE PHARISEE AND THE TOLL COLLECTOR

We have already looked at two stories in Luke's 'sinner' material based upon events in Jesus' ministry (Lk. 5.28ff.; 7.36ff.). In ch. 15 we saw our theme demonstrated by means of three parables introduced by a brief but telling life situation (Lk. 15.1-2). We now turn to the second segment of material in Luke which deals with the 'sinner' motif in parable form: the Pharisee and the toll collector. I shall first briefly discuss the relationship of Lk. 16.1–18.8 to our parable. Next follows a discussion of how the structure of Lk. 18.9-14 contributes to our understanding of the parable. Finally, I deal with the content of the pericope itself and offer some suggestions on how it should be interpreted.

Luke 16–18

The parable of the rich man and Lazarus (Lk. 16.19-31) reinforces the themes of reversal and exclusion from the kingdom which have been set forth by Luke already in chs. 13 and 14. The rich man has lived sumptuously but is delivered to torment in Hades at his death. The destitute Lazarus, on the other hand, is carried to the bosom of Abraham. While the reason for the condemnation of the rich man is not explicitly stated, we assume that his chief sin was that of self-indulgence and failing to care for the less fortunate (vv. 19-21). This is only an assumption, however, and v. 25 would seem to indicate that his crime was nothing more than being fortunate in his earthly life (cf. 6.24, 'Woe to you that are rich, for you have received your consolation').[1] But in v. 30 the rich man exclaims in regard to his still-

---

1. For a treatment of the issue of the 'rich' as it relates to Luke's 'sinner' material see W.P. Loewe, 'Towards an Interpretation of Lk. 19.1-10', *CBQ* 36 (1974), pp. 322-23.

living relatives, 'No, father Abraham; but if someone goes to them from the dead, they will repent'. Now we have learned indirectly that no matter what specific form the rich man's sins took, his true downfall was his own failure to 'repent'. He is a 'sinner', but not of the heroic kind.

Where ch. 15 viewed the 'sinner' from the point of view of God, whose concern was their restoration to the flock, this parable shows the point of view of the obdurate 'sinner' himself. The 'sinner', now represented by the rich man, fails to take the opportunity for restoration into the fold and suffers regret and 'anguish' in the flames of Hades. His fate calls to mind the statement of 13.3, 'unless you repent you will all likewise perish'. In the rich man's plaintive cry ('Father Abraham, have mercy on me') we hear an echo of those in 13.25-28 who were shocked to find themselves excluded from the kingdom of God:

> There you will weep and gnash your teeth, when you see Abraham and Isaac and Jacob and all the prophets in the kingdom of God and you yourselves thrust out.

Luke has now added the negative element of warning to the positive element of God's desire for the restoration of the lost in ch. 15. By extension, the reader's desire to be counted among those safe in the fold is augmented by the fear of sharing the fate of those who fail to 'repent'.

Chapter 17 reinforces a similar line of thinking. In 17.3-4 the efficacy of 'repentance' is emphasized, and even though the need should recur seven times in one day, 'you must forgive him'. Above all for Luke, repentance works. But, more pointedly, the threat of judgment for the recalcitrant 'sinner' is very much in view in 17.22-37 when the Second Advent is described in terms of the fire and sulphur which rained on Sodom (v. 30): 'So will it be on the day when the Son of Man is revealed'. Even though this pericope is not primarily about repentance, and 'sinner' language is not used, its implication for the unrepentant can scarcely fail to have its effect.

The Parable

The primary interpretive question which will concern us in this chapter is how to understand the portrayal of the Pharisee and toll collector in the parable. Most interpreters of Lk. 18.9-14 have tended to view the parable as one which is based on a representation of the actual practice of Pharisaism in Jesus' day. According to this interpretation, the point of the parable was to criticize the flawed piety of Pharisaism, represented by the Pharisee, and to show how true piety functions, as seen in the actions of the humble toll collector. While I.H. Marshall concedes that the portrait of the Pharisee is 'slightly overdrawn' it is nevertheless 'drawn from life. . . Jesus is attacking the Pharisaic religion as it was, not an exaggeration of it'.[1] For Fitzmyer, the Pharisee is 'a type or representative of faithful Jewish observers of Mosaic regulations' and Luke 'scarcely caricatures the Pharisaic type'.[2] The important implication of this interpretation is that Jesus brings a new way of approach to God in contrast to the flawed status quo represented by Pharisaism.

Jewish interpreters have understandably been less enthusiastic about the summarily negative representation of Judaism implied in this interpretation of the Pharisee in Luke 18. C.G. Montefiore, for example, has called the Pharisee a 'caricature' and noted:

> Objection can only be raised when the parable is said to illustrate, not the dangers and perversions of the Rabbinic religion, but the Rabbinic religion itself—as if the Pharisee of the parable were the average Pharisee. . . and worse still, as if this odious Pharisee represented not the perversion, but the type and even the ideal—as if he was the very man whom the Rabbis would wish to be and were.[3]

More recently, other commentators have expressed a similar view that the Pharisee of this parable is a 'caricature'.[4] This interpretation is, in

---

1. Marshall, *Luke*, pp. 677-80.
2. Fitzmyer, *Luke*, pp. 1186-87; also Creed, *Luke*, p. 202. See also L. Schottroff (see n. 4 below), p. 451 and Fiedler, *Jesus und die Sünder*, p. 230, who discuss others who share this basic view, most notably, Jeremias, Linnemann, Haenchen, Perrin and other commentators.
3. Montefiore, *RLGT*, p. 396. Similarly Abrahams, *SPG*, pp. 58-59, 139-49.
4. Most notably, Luise Schottroff, in an article entitled 'Die Erzählung vom Pharisäer und Zöllner as Beispeil für die Theologische Kunst des Uberredens' in *Neues Testament und Christliche Existenz: Festschrift für Herbert Braun* (ed. Hans Dieter Betz and Luise Schottroff; Tübingen: Mohr [Paul Siebeck], 1973), pp. 439-61. See also Fiedler's treatment of Schottroff (*Jesus und die Sünder*, pp. 228-33). Besides Schottroff, Charlesworth calls the Pharisee a 'sad caricature' (*Jesus within Judaism*, p. 46); D. Tiede says the parable presses the contrast 'probably to the point

my view, the correct one and is fully consistent with the way I have suggested that Luke uses his Pharisees for the purposes of telling his Gospel story. The 'historical' Pharisees have not been in evidence so far in the Gospel of Luke and this remains true with regard to this parable.

It will be shown here in two sections how the parable of the Pharisee and the toll collector confirms, on the whole, the features of Luke's ideological treatment of his 'sinner' material. The Pharisee in this parable is indeed archetypal, but in a more benign fashion than, say, Lk. 5.30 or 7.29. There the Pharisees opposed Jesus in a dark and malevolent way. Here, the Pharisee is still a negative figure, but in a more boorish, almost buffoonish sort of way. I will first undertake an analysis of the structure of Lk. 18.9-14 in order to show its underlying ideological basis. Second, a treatment of the content of the pericope itself will serve to further confirm this interpretation.

The Structure of Lk. 18.9-14

The structure of the parable of the Pharisee and the toll collector has many similarities to the 'sinner' material I have already analysed. The pericope contains: a Lucan introduction (v. 9), the parable itself (vv. 10-14a) and the concluding logion (v. 14b).[1] The most salient feature is the way in which Luke has set the parable (vv. 10-14a) in the context of a life situation connected with the controversy between Jesus and the Pharisees (v. 9).[2] Just as 15.1-2 provided the hermeneutical key to the remainder of ch. 15, so also the introductory setting of this parable provides, from a literary perspective, the interpretive framework in which the parable must be understood. Commentators have long noted the apparent seams between vv. 9 and 10 and again, possibly, between 14a and 14b. But from the point of view of Luke's Gospel we must view the pericope as a whole. Our interest lies not in de-constructing the narrative into form-critical segments but in assessing the impact of the whole to Luke's developing story. Note,

---

of caricature' (*Luke* [Minneapolis, MN: Augsburg, 1988], p. 307).

1. Bultmann, *HST*, pp. 192-93, 334-35, 178-89; Fitzmyer, p. 1183. See also F. Schnider, 'Ausschliessen und ausgeschlossen werden: Beobachtungen zur struktur des Gleichnisses vom Pharisaer und Zollner Lk 18.10-14a', *BZ* 24 (1980), pp. 42-56; Grundmann, *Lukas*, p. 349.

2. Fiedler classes it with Lk. 15.1-2 as a 'typical Lucan introduction' (*Jesus und die Sünder*, p. 148).

for example, how v. 14b is imported verbatim from Lk. 14.11 in the parable of the marriage feast. If, form-critically, the verse is an importation here in 18.14b, what remains more important is that it 'fits' here simply because Luke put it here.[1] The predisposition to highlight the supposed disunity of the composition can obscure the more important aspect of the reiteration of Lk. 14.11 at 18.14b: that is, that the repetition of the reversal theme has become an important connecting sinew of Luke's story development.

The introduction of the parable by v. 9 has implications for the type of material with which we are dealing. The Lucan setting is artificial and there is no more reason to expect to find 'historical' information in 18.9 than we found in 15.1-2. Indeed, identifying τοὺς πεποιθότας ἐφ' ἑαυτοῖς could not, on any account, be considered a 'historical' endeavour. The identification is an ideologically determined assessment of the intended target audience (εἶπεν δὲ καὶ πρός. . .). So, whereas it was deemed appropriate to trace possible historical connections about 'sinners' and 'Pharisees' in Luke 5 due to the nature of that narrative material, it is the nature of the narrative here that makes such investigations unnecessary. As with the setting at 15.1-2, there is simply not enough connection to a concrete setting to make such a procedure necessary or fruitful.

One of the features of the ideological treatment of Jesus' controversy with the Pharisees and 'sinners' has been the tendency to portray the division in dualistic terms. The Pharisees have been portrayed as those who do not comprehend or assent to the principles of a genuine piety. On the other hand, we have the 'sinners' who, although being themselves archetypal evildoers of a sort, invariably respond favourably and show the appropriate attitudes of repentance. The structure of the parable of the Pharisee and the toll collector demonstrates this bifurcation by setting the Pharisee over against the toll collector in stark dualistic terms. For each attribute of the Pharisee there is a corresponding and opposite trait of the toll collector.

We note in the diagram that follows, a series of twofold comparisons: in sections 1 and 2 there are two characters presented (vv. 9, 10; cf. Lk. 15.11); in section 3, two physical positions of prayer, one

---

1. Bultmann's assertion that 14b does not fit the story because the Publican did not 'really humble himself' is incomprehensible in any case (*HST*, p. 179). Surely this is exactly what the toll collector has done. See Schottroff, 'Erzählung', p. 440.

bold and forthright, the other retiring (vv. 11, 13); in section 4, two mental attitudes to prayer, again one bold but the other full of desperation and reticence (vv. 11, 14); in section 5, two prayers, one long and self-justifying and the other brief and self-denigrating (vv. 12, 13); and in section 6, a chiastic logion which delivers the verdict of Jesus on the two characters, one 'justified' the other not (v. 14).

Pharisee	Toll Collector
1. τοὺς πεποιθότας ἐφ᾽ ἑαυτοῖς ὅτι εἰσὶν δίκαιοι καὶ ἐξουθενοῦντας	τοὺς λοιποὺς
2. ὁ εἷς Φαρισαῖος	ὁ ἕτερος τελώνης
3. σταθεὶς	μακρόθεν ἑστὼς
4. πρὸς ἑαυτὸν ταῦτα προσηύχετο	οὐκ ἤθελεν οὐδὲ τοὺς ὀφθαλμοὺς ἐπᾶραι εἰς τὸν οὐρανόν, ἀλλ᾽ ἔτυπτεν τὸ στῆθος αὐτοῦ λέγων
5. ὁ θεός, εὐχαριστῶ σοι ὅτι οὐκ εἰμὶ ὥσπερ οἱ λοιποὶ τῶν ἀνθρώπων, ἅρπαγες, ἄδικοι, μοιχοί, ἢ καὶ ὡς οὗτος ὁ τελώνης. νηστεύω δὶς τοῦ σαββάτου, ἀποδεκατῶ πάντα ὅσα κτῶμαι.	ὁ θεός, ἱλάσθητί μοι τῷ ἁμαρτωλῷ
6. πᾶς ὁ ὑψῶν ἑαυτὸν ταπεινωθήσεται	ὁ δὲ ταπεινῶν ἑαυτὸν ὑψωθήσεται

The correspondence between τοὺς πεποιθότας ἐφ᾽ ἑαυτοῖς and the Φαρισαῖος is readily apparent.[1] The Pharisees are the target of the parable for Luke[2] and we know from the Lucan introduction at 18.9 that the Pharisee is a villain and a negative model of behaviour. Luise Schottroff has drawn attention to a parable of Aesop which

---

1. Jeremias, *Parables*, p. 139.
2. Fitzmyer, *Luke*, p. 1185; Creed, *Luke*, p. 244; cf. Lk. 16.14-15.

demonstrates in a similar way how the reader is led to judge the leading character negatively.[1]

> Praying for Himself Only: A man had the habit of coming late into the church and making this prayer, on his knees: 'Lord God, look thou with favour upon me and my wife and my children—and upon no one else'. Another man in the church who overheard him prayed as follows in the other's hearing: 'Lord, Lord, Almighty God, confound that fellow and his wife and children, and nobody else'.

Because the man habitually enters the church 'late' the reader is alerted at the outset that all is not well. Furthermore, the man prays for 'himself only. . . and no one else'. Were it not for these features the prayer would pass as rather ordinary and acceptable.[2] In the Lucan parable v. 9 serves a similar function of putting the following prayer into a negative perspective. The concluding phrase of the prayer in the fable confirms the negative assessment of his worship when the church-goer asks God to favour him and his family 'and no one else'. This is matched functionally in the Lucan parable by the phrase ἢ καὶ ὡς οὗτος ὁ τελώνης. It is clear from the reader's point of view that the Pharisee is not practising his religion in a legitimate manner. Even if the form of his worship is correct, the reader has already been alerted to the fact that the spirit is all wrong.

The construction of 18.10b, ὁ εἷς Φαρισαῖος καὶ ὁ ἕτερος τελώνης is significant for the way it sets two already well-defined images in sharp ideological contrast.[3] The phrase could not be more economically expressed yet it brings together all that Luke has been developing in his story in a single parabolic confrontation. A graphic mental image is stirred by the contrast of the Pharisee, disdainful of expression and standing forthright in the Temple, compared to the

---

1. Schottroff, 'Erzählung', pp. 448-49. This is Fable 666 quoted here in English from *Babrius and Phaedrus* (trans. B. Perry; London: Loeb Classical Library, 1965), p. 575. The fable is of uncertain date and known from the eleventh century Codex Bruxelensis; see B. Perry, *Studies in the Text History of the Life and Fables of Aesop* (Haverford: Lancaster Press, 1936), pp. 71ff., 204ff. For the Latin text see B. Perry's *Aesopica* (Urbana, IL: University of Illinois Press, 1952), p. 674.

2. Schottroff, 'Erzählung', pp. 448-49.

3. Note how it is preceded by the contrast between the κριτής and the χήρα in Lk. 18.1-8 (which, perhaps not incidentally, is also about prayer). See further J. O'Hanlon, 'The Story of Zacchaeus and the Lukan Ethic', *JSNT* 12 (1981), p. 9.

unnoticed, hand-wringing toll collector standing afar off. The reader is offered a simple choice about whom to identify with: the overdrawn representation of haughtiness and pride or the contrition of the pitiful 'sinner'.[1] There is, of course, no choice at all because no one could possibly find in favour of the boorish Pharisee. The negative representation of the Pharisee forces, as it were, the reader to align him or herself sympathetically with the 'sinner' and the attitude of repentance so represented.[2] This is Luke's purpose and he brings it about with consummate skill.

Structurally, the 'explanation' of the parable is found in v. 14 with the pronouncement of Jesus. Here much of what was left unsaid or merely implied in the parable is given its meaning. It is not the 'Pharisee' but the 'sinner' who has God's approval (cf. 7.30).[3] The reversal of expectation seen previously in Luke[4] is now brought to its ultimate expression. On the one hand, there remains the element of reversal (the toll collector behaves piously, the Pharisee impiously), but it now appears as a justifiable reversal to the reader because of Luke's portrayal of his characters. Thus, the concluding logion declaring the toll collector's justification and the Pharisee's failure (v. 14) is not shocking to its hearers but completely understandable and expected.

The Pharisee
That the portrait of the Pharisee in this parable must be viewed as a negative one has already been suggested above. But to go beyond this and assert that the Pharisee is a 'caricature' requires some explanation. A caricature, so says the dictionary, is a 'deliberate simplification and ludicrous distortion' of negative qualities for the purposes of exag-

---

1.   Bultmann has discussed the characteristic 'antithesis of two types' in Luke (*HST*, p. 192).
2.   There is another, albeit unfortunate, alternative for the Christian reader. H. Mottu has observed that, in practice, a Christian reader's prayer of response to this parable is often: 'I thank you, Oh God, that I am not like this selfish Pharisee. . . ' He quotes Walter Wink who has noted that 'Christians almost invariably take a "Pharisaic" attitude towards Pharisees' (H. Mottu, 'The Pharisee and the Tax Collector: Sartian Notions as Applied to the Reading of Scripture', *USQR* 29 [1973], p. 196). See also Tiede, *Luke*, p. 307.
3.   See Schottroff, 'Erzählung', pp. 456, 458.
4.   Lk. 5.31; 7.47; 13.3, 5, 30; 14.11; 15.7, 10, 32; 16.19-31.

geration. It is a special kind of portraiture that highlights the uncomplimentary so as to draw attention to these qualities. The prayer of the Pharisee should be understood in this way.

He stands apart and prays[1] and we are in the privileged position of listening in. The giving of thanks for his situation is not so odd.[2] There is nothing about the list of evildoers (ἅρπαγες, ἄδικοι, μοιχοί) that marks it out as a caricature.[3] But what is caricatured is that he sees himself in a category unto himself. All the rest are exemplars of unrighteousness. The οἱ λοιποί of 18.11 corresponds to the τοὺς λοιπούς of 18.9. This Pharisee has only one view of οἱ λοιποί: they are ἅρπαγες, ἄδικοι, μοιχοί. The picture is intentionally absurd. The comparison of all of these to the toll collector (ἢ καὶ ὡς οὗτος ὁ τελώνης), as in Lk. 3.12, shows that the toll collector is presented as exceeding and embodying all the qualities of impiety already listed. The portrayal is full of hyperbole and caricature. Just as the man in Aesop's fable prayed for a blessing for himself 'and upon no one else', so the Pharisee would exclude οἱ λοιποί at a single stroke.[4] When the literary nature of this description is appreciated the story can be read for what it is: an illustration that employs exaggeration in order to show how self-dependence and pride (v. 9) stand between the worshipper and God, and that repentance (v. 14) is the remedy. It is only when the parable is read as a source of information on Pharisaism that sight is lost of the real power and intent of the story.

Often mentioned in this connection is the rabbinic prayer at *b. Ber.* 28b. Since it is often cited, it is worth reproducing the passage of

---

1. The Greek is ambiguous: σταθεὶς πρὸς ἑαυτὸν ταῦτα προσηύχετο. Does he 'stand apart' to pray (σταθεὶς πρὸς ἑαυτόν) or pray 'to himself' (πρὸς ἑαυτὸν ταῦτα προσηύχετο)? A number of witnesses removed the ambiguity by changing the reading to σταθεὶς ταῦτα πρὸς ἑαυτὸν 𝔓75, B, ώ, Θ, *f¹*, 892). D has καθ᾽ ἑαυτόν. See Metzger, *A Textual Commentary*, p. 168; Jeremias, *Parables*, p. 140; Marshall, *Luke*, p. 679.

2. See the discussion of *b. Ber.* 28b below, this chapter.

3. μοιχός appears in lists of evildoers in 1 Cor. 6.9 and Heb. 13.4; ἅρπαξ in 1 Cor. 5.10, 11; 6.10. ἄδικος appears at the head of the list in 1 Cor. 6.9 ('Do you not know the ἄδικος will not inherit the kingdom of God?'). Ironically, it is the Pharisees who are charged with being full of ἁρπαγῆς in Lk. 11.39. There Luke has the emphatic 'but inside you (ὑμεῖς) are full of extortion (ἁρπαγῆς)' whereas Mt. 23.25 only refers to the cup and plate as γέμουσιν ἐξ ἁρπαγῆς.

4. See Schottroff, 'Erzählung', pp. 448-49; Fiedler, *Jesus und die Sünder*, p. 229.

which Jeremias and others quote only the second half. The gemara is based on *m. Ber.* 4.2 which deals with how one should pray as one enters the Beth ha-Midrash. It reads:

> Our Rabbis taught: on entering what does a man say? 'May it be Thy will, O Lord my God, that no offence may occur through me, and that I may not err in a matter of halachah and that my colleagues may rejoice in me and that I may not call unclean clean or clean unclean, and that my colleagues may not err in a matter of halachah and that I may rejoice in them'. On his leaving what does he say? [*Jeremias begins his quotation here*] 'I give thanks to Thee, O Lord my God, that Thou hast set my portion with those who sit in the Beth ha-Midrash and Thou hast not set my portion with those who sit in [street] corners, for I rise early and they rise early, but I rise early for words of Torah and they rise early for frivolous talk; I labour and they labour, but I labour and receive a reward and they labour and do not receive a reward; I run and they run, but I run to the life of the future world and they run to the pit of destruction.'

This prayer is cited by some as an example of an authentic rabbinic prayer that shows an attitude towards piety similar to that portrayed in Lk. 18.11-12.[1] This parallel text, it is suggested, shows that Luke's Pharisee prayed in a way which would have been admired and accepted as a laudatory prayer by a reader of the period.[2] So, Jeremias concludes, the ending of the Lucan parable which announces that the toll collector and not the Pharisee went down to his house justified must have 'utterly overwhelmed its hearers'.[3] The unspoken assumption of those who liken the two prayers is that *b. Ber.* 28b, like Lk. 18.11-12, is also an expression of piety fundamentally flawed by an undue pride of achievement.

But to interpret *b. Ber.* 28b as an example of Jewish piety worthy of censure can be done only by reading the second half of the gemara in isolation from its context. I agree this is a genuine prayer which is presented as a model for the proper way to pray.[4] Where it differs

---

1. Jeremias, *Parables*, p. 142-43; Marshall, *Luke*, p. 680; Fitzmyer, *Luke*, p. 1187; Strack–Billerbeck, *Kommentar*, II, pp. 240-41; E. Linnemann, *Parables of Jesus* (London: SPCK, 1966), pp. 59-60.

2. Jeremias, *Parables*, p. 143; Linnemann, *Parables*, p. 60; Perrin, *Rediscovering*, p. 122; Marshall, *Luke*, pp. 677-81. See also Schottroff, 'Erzählung', p. 451 and Fiedler, *Jesus und die Sünder*, p. 230 for others who hold this view.

3. Jeremias, *Parables*, pp. 143-44.

4. Abrahams says, 'This prayer is simply a grateful recognition for good

from the Lucan prayer is in the underlying motivation, i.e. not self-aggrandizement but rather genuine thanksgiving that the worshipper has been spared a life of futile activity.[1] The phrase 'I give thanks to Thee, O Lord my God, that Thou hast set my portion. . .' is categorically different from the self-important boasting in specific deeds of supererogation and the comparison of oneself to οἱ λοιποὶ τῶν ἀνθρώπων in Lk. 18.11-12. The expressions of concern for fellow worshippers in the first part of the gemara show that this worshipper does not set himself apart as better than all others. This prayer is not a caricature and is quite unlike the Lucan prayer in almost every respect. The Lucan prayer intentionally parodies a false way of praying[2] whereas the gemara, when given a fair reading, actually represents a genuinely noble spirit of thanksgiving.

There are many passages in the rabbinic literature that do display extremes of religious bigotry, especially in connection with the relationship between the *talmidei ḥakamim*, and the *'ammei ha-aretz*.[3] But these generally derive, at the earliest, from an Ushan context and reflect the growing enmity for the *talmidei ḥakamim* as a distinct social category. Such distinctions did not exist in the first century and

---

fortune; it in no sense implies (except quite indirectly) that the speaker prides himself on being a better man' (*SPG*, p. 59; also Schottroff, 'Erzählung', p. 451).

1. I would include in this category another rabbinic prayer sometimes mentioned in this connection (e.g. Linnemann, *Parables*, p. 59), *t. Ber.* 7.18: 'Praised [be the Lord], that he did not make me a heathen; for "all the heathen are as nothing before him"; praised be he, that he did not make me a woman, for woman is not under obligation to fulfil the law; praised be he that he did not make me. . . an uneducated man; for the uneducated man is not cautious to avoid sins'. Likewise, two examples mentioned by Strack–Billerbeck (*Kommentar*, II, p. 240): *y. Ber.* 4.7d, 31, the Palestinian Talmud parallel to *b. Ber.* 28b and *b. Erub.* 21b. Their placement of Lk. 18.11ff. in the same spirit as these prayers (p. 241) is an improper comparison.

2. Abrahams does not necessarily view the Pharisaic prayer as a parody, but he does recognize it is not a genuinely pious Pharisaic prayer. He asserts (*SPG*, p. 57) that: 'Luke's Pharisee who thanked God that he was not as this publican must have been an exceptional case, one of the weeds of ritualism, not one of its ordinary or natural fruits'.

3. See above, Chapter 2. A few examples of the many instances of denigration of the *'ammei ha-aretz* by the *talmidei ḥakamim* are: *b. Pes.* 49a-b; *b. Shab.* 32a, 63a; *b. B. Mez.* 85b; *b. B. Bat.* 8a; *m. Ab.* 2.6, 3.6; *ARN* 21.1, 26.2. See further Oppenheimer's section on the *talmidei ḥakamim* in *'Am Ha-aretz*.

b. Ber. 28b no doubt shares this lateness of date.[1] That is not, however, the reason *b. Ber.* 28b should not be likened to Lk. 18.11-12. The reason they are unlike is simply the fundamental difference between that of a genuine expression of thanksgiving and a self-righteous prayer of one who 'trusted in himself that he was righteous and despised others'. Luke's own interpretation of the parable is the decisive factor.

One feature remains to be noted about this caricature of prayer at Lk. 18.11-12. It is a plausible portrayal in many respects. The list of evildoers, as has been noted is not without parallel. The supererogatory deeds of tithing and fasting in v. 12 conform with what we know about Pharisaic concerns in the period.[2] But a caricature must have elements of the plausible in order to be successful. Only by exaggerating actual qualities does a caricature become effective. As Schottroff notes,

> parody and caricature are not often plucked out of thin air— but the difference between an earnestly offered prayer and a caricature of prayer remains discernible.[3]

The Toll Collector

If the Pharisee is a caricature can the same be said of the toll collector? Certain aspects of the portrayal of the toll collector are also exaggerated for effect. He beats his breast and almost begs for mercy, Ὁ θεός, ἱλάσθητί μοι τῷ ἁμαρτωλῷ.[4] He abandons any pretence of religious propriety.[5] Indeed, the very selection of the toll collector for the role as the repentant counterpoint to the Pharisee is an indulgence in caricature for the teller of the parable. The whole juxtaposition of

---

1. So Fitzmyer, *Luke*, p. 1187.
2. Cf. also Didache 12.3; 8.1. See Fitzmyer, *Luke*, p. 1187 n. 12; Leaney, *Luke*, p. 236. Indeed, this Pharisee goes beyond the requirements of the law. *B. Erub.* 21b reveals the underlying sentiment, 'Lord of the universe, I have imposed upon myself more restrictions that Thou hast imposed upon me, and I have observed them'.
3. Schottroff, 'Erzählung', pp. 450-51.
4. On this phrase see further R.G. Hoerber, '"God Be Merciful to Me a Sinner": A Note on Luke 18.13', *CTM* 33 (1962), pp. 283-86.
5. But see a similar attitude: *Pr. Man.* 7-15; *Jos. Asen.* 10.2, 15; 11.1-19; *1 En.* 13.5.

the Pharisee and toll collector is, in itself, something of a parody. But the toll collector differs from the Pharisee in that his actions commend themselves to the reader as being the more appropriate way to address oneself to God in his Temple; common sense demands a verdict in favour of the toll collector.[1] The reader may perhaps even respond to the parable by proclaiming, 'The toll collector—it is I!'[2] It is not 'logical judgment' (*logische Urteil*) which adjudicates the decision but 'understanding' (*Einverständnis*).[3]

The most important aspect of the role of the toll collector relates to the overall programme of Luke in his Gospel. The toll collector was first seen as a social pariah who, nevertheless, responded positively to John when others who should know better do not (Lk. 3.10ff.). The humble toll collector reappeared again as the one who left all to follow Jesus (Lk. 5.27) and then his associates received Jesus as well (Lk. 5.29; 7.29; 15.1-2). But whatever social significance the figure of the toll collector has in the mind of the reader, the term becomes restructured, in Luke's treatment, as a religious metaphor for those who display the proper spirit of contrition and repentance.[4] This demonstrates how the 'historical' melds with Luke's ideological agenda to produce an appealing presentation of Jesus. By means of a 'complete reversal of premises' says Schottroff, the toll collector has become a 'metaphor for humble piety'.[5]

Schottroff also notes that she has been unable to find any parallel in ancient fables which 'elevates a member of a universally hated group to a positive figure'.[6] While the possibility of forgiveness is not new or unique only to Jesus' message, the Gospel development of the 'sinner' into a prototype of one who is 'justified' certainly is new and unique. This is due to the use of the word 'sinner' in reference to those who will in fact be saved, an occurrence only rarely observed prior to the traditions of the Christian literature.[7] Schottroff has provided corroboration for our earlier finding that the 'sinner' as a positive figure of repentance is a rare occurrence in the literature running

1. *Contra* Linnemann, *Parables*, p. 60.
2. Schottroff, 'Erzählung', p. 453; Linnemann, *Parables*, p. 61.
3. Schottroff, 'Erzählung', pp. 441-42.
4. Schottroff, 'Erzählung', p. 454; but cf. Linnemann, *Parables*, pp. 58-60.
5. Schottroff, 'Erzählung', p. 454.
6. Schottroff, 'Erzählung', p. 454.
7. See above, Chapter 3.

up to the Christian period. Indeed, not until the post-destruction period, and then most likely under the influence of Christian tradition, does the 'sinner' figure emerge as a positive model of repentance and the proper object of God's mercy in literature outside the canon. The genius of this literary reversal of roles in the Gospel of Luke is profoundly effective in drawing the reader or hearer into sympathy with the one who has a need for repentance. The identification of the reader with the 'sinner' figure in Luke is almost complete.

Chapter 8

THE STORY OF ZACCHAEUS

In the analysis of Luke's 'sinner' material we turn finally to the narrative of Zacchaeus in Lk. 19.1-10. This passage represents the culmination of our theme in Luke and is, as we shall see, paradigmatic for Luke's unique treatment of the 'sinner' motif.

The story of Zacchaeus is an engaging one and its simple charm and dramatic tenor are without equal in Luke's Gospel. This is due, in part, to the story-telling style in which the account is narrated. At times Luke unveils the inner thoughts and intentions of his characters. We saw this in the parables of the lost son (Luke 15) and the Pharisee and the toll collector (Luke 18), and the story of the sinful woman (Luke 7). In an even more intimate way, Luke here tells the story of Zacchaeus with his emotions and movements fully revealed to the reader. We seem almost to be looking over Zacchaeus's shoulder as the drama unfolds (καὶ ἐζήτει ἰδεῖν τὸν Ἰησοῦν τίς ἐστιν, καὶ οὐκ ἠδύνατο ἀπὸ τοῦ ὄχλου. . .,v. 3). A sense of excitement and anxiety at the approach of Jesus is communicated by the eagerness of the diminutive Zacchaeus (καὶ προδραμὼν εἰς τὸ ἔμπροσθεν, v. 4). There is a frantic quest for a vantage point from which to view the approaching Teacher (ἀνέβη ἐπὶ συκομορέαν ἵνα ἴδῃ αὐτόν, v. 4). Then comes the seemingly chance encounter between Jesus and this chief toll collector. As Zacchaeus is perched in a sycamore tree, a lively and good-natured exchange transpires between the two (Ζακχαῖε, σπεύσας κατάβηθι. . ., v. 5). It is, above all, a happy story. It engages the imagination and sets the mind to musing on its colourful setting. These features mark the story as particularly evocative, but its significance for the Gospel of Luke goes beyond this.

The story is found only in Luke. Not only is the vocabulary and style characteristically Lucan,[1] but many favourite themes[2] are met in this single scene: the friendliness towards the outcast, the shepherd motif of seeking the lost, the window into the psychology of the 'sinner'.[3] While the passage has sometimes received abbreviated treatment by commentators,[4] its importance for the Lucan Gospel has still been appreciated.[5] In Zacchaeus we have a story that brings Luke's portrayal of Jesus' ministry to a climax and all that has taken place in this Gospel is summed up in the relationship between this chief toll collector and the Galilean.

The Story in its Lucan Context

The location of the story of Zacchaeus in the overall Lucan narrative has two important features: physical location and chronology. Both features, however, relate directly to the fact that the days have now drawn near for Jesus to be 'received up' (Lk. 9.51).

The encounter with Zacchaeus occurs in Jericho on the very doorstep of Jerusalem. This is significant since, for Luke, Jerusalem serves as the goal of all Jesus' movements and is the city of his des-

---

1. See J. O'Hanlon, 'The Story of Zacchaeus and the Lukan Ethic', *JSNT* 12 (1981), pp. 2-4; Loewe, 'Towards an Interpretation', pp. 321-27; Fiedler, *Jesus und die Sünder*, pp. 132-33.

2. See again, O'Hanlon, 'Zacchaeus', p. 10 and Loewe, 'Towards an Interpretation', pp. 327-29, 331.

3. Compare the very personal view of the sinful woman in Lk. 7.36-50, and especially the lost son in Lk. 15.11-32; the rich man from the story of Lazarus in Lk. 16.19-30 and the toll collector in Lk. 18.9-14.

4. There is a paucity of journal material on the passage and commentators tend to give Lk. 19.1-10 little space. The main journal articles on the passage are Loewe, 'Towards an Interpretation'; R.C. White, 'A Good Word for Zacchaeus? Exegetical Comment on Luke 19.1-10', *LTQ* 14 (1979), pp. 89-96; O'Hanlon, 'Zacchaeus'. In the commentaries it is Fitzmyer, *Luke*, pp. 1218-26 and Marshall, *Luke*, pp. 694-99 who give the most in-depth treatment. See also the lengthy treatment by Derrett, *Law in the New Testament*, pp. 278-85.

5. Lk. 19.10, says Fitzmyer, 'sums up. . . the soteriological message of the entire travel account—and the Lucan Gospel' (*Luke*, p. 1221). The story of Zacchaeus is 'a retrospective summary of Jesus' saving work' says Tannehill (*Narrative Unity*, p. 107). For Marshall it is the 'climax' of the ministry of Jesus and the 'epitome of the message of this Gospel' (*Luke*, p. 695). O'Hanlon says it is a 'fitting summary of the whole ministry of Jesus. . . ' ('Zacchaeus', p. 11).

tiny. As early as the Transfiguration Luke adds the comment that Elijah and Moses 'spoke of his departure, which he was to accomplish at Jerusalem' (Lk. 9.30; cf. Mk 9.4; Mt. 17.3). The travel narrative itself begins with the statement: 'When the days drew near for him to be received up, he set his face to go to Jerusalem' (L material, 9.51). There is also special Lucan material at 13.33 which says 'it cannot be that a prophet should perish away from Jerusalem'.[1] Thus, in dramatic terms, the story of Zacchaeus could not have been set in a more important location.

Chronologically, the Zacchaeus story is the final episode of Jesus' ministry outside Jerusalem.[2] The story occurs at the critical juncture between the end of the ministry proper and the entry to Jerusalem which marks the beginning of his Passion. Thus the incident is, on the one hand, the penultimate event of the whole Gospel of Luke because it precedes and prepares the way for the Passion. At the same time, it functions in its own right as the climax of the non-Jerusalem portion of Jesus' ministry (chs. 4–19).

In the nearer context, two passages in Luke 18 help us understand the story of Zacchaeus. The first is found in the interpretive connection between Zacchaeus and the parable of the Pharisee and the toll collector (Lk. 18.9-14). Zacchaeus and the toll collector in Luke 18 are both called ἁμαρτωλοί. Both display the characteristic behaviour of Luke's paradigmatic 'sinner', that is, they always produce the right response. The toll collector of the parable does so by his attitude of humility and contrition while Zacchaeus does so not only by his attitude but also, significantly, by his deeds. The events of Lk. 19.1-10 are a real-life demonstration of the attitudes set out in parable form in Lk. 18.9-14.[3] We cannot read the one incident without reflecting on the other and thus forming a fuller understanding of Luke's conception of what the 'sinner' must do. The 'sinner' who humbles

---

1. See also Lk. 18.31 (Mk 10.32-24; Mt. 20.17-19); Marshall, *Luke*, p. 689; Conzelmann, *The Theology of St Luke*, pp. 73-74.

2. Compare Luke also to Mk 10.46ff. which places the healing of the blind Bartimaeus on the road out of Jericho. In Luke this is prior to the entry to Jericho (18.35-43) and thus the scene with Zacchaeus occupies primacy of place as the last act of ministry before entering Jerusalem.

3. Grundmann (*Lukas*, p. 358) says the story follows the 'Beispielserzählung' of the Pharisee and the toll collector and functions as a 'Beleg' [proof]; see also Fiedler, *Jesus und die Sünder*, p. 131.

him or herself (Lk. 18.14b) will win Jesus' (and also God's) approval (Lk. 18.14a; 19.9) and this results in works that befit a restoration to right standing before God (Lk. 19.8, 9).

There is also a significant connection between the rich young ruler (Lk. 18.23, πλούσιος σφόδρα) and Zacchaeus (πλούσιος, v. 2). What the rich young ruler cannot bring himself to do, Zacchaeus does gladly by divesting himself of his riches.[1] Once again, by means of a reversal we find the rich and hated chief toll collector does the proper thing and wins God's approval whereas the essentially law-abiding rich young ruler cannot enter the kingdom. It is interesting to see how Luke has wound his characteristic theme of enmity towards the rich into the final stages of his 'sinner' material. Even the rich (cf. Lk. 16.19-31, the rich man and Lazarus) can find the remedy for their plight in the story and example of Zacchaeus.[2]

Zacchaeus Meets Jesus

Luke brings all the essential facts of the story to our attention at the outset (19.1-6). (1) Jesus is passing through Jericho. (2) There is a man named Zacchaeus, whose occupation is chief toll collector and who is rich. (3) He wants to see Jesus but cannot because of the crowd since he is himself short of stature. (4) He climbs a tree and Jesus sees him. (5) What Jesus commands (σπεύσας κατάβηθι) Zacchaeus does (σπεύσας κατέβη) and he receives the Teacher joyfully as his guest.

The toll collector, by now a common feature of Luke's controversy stories, is represented by the ἀρχιτελώνης[3] Zacchaeus. Where our 'sinner' material began with the toll collector Levi in ch. 5, Luke now climaxes Jesus' ministry with a similar encounter.[4] But this time it is the ἀρχι-toll collector and he represents, in a dramatic and culminative sense, all of his kind who have gone before him in the story (Lk. 3.12; 5.27-28, 29; 7.29; 15.1; 18.13-14). The call of the outcast is now symbolized and epitomized in the archetypal figure of Zacchaeus

---

1. See further O'Hanlon, 'Zacchaeus', pp. 9, 19-21; Loewe, 'Towards an Interpretation', pp. 322-23.

2. So Tannehill, *Narrative Unity*, p.132.

3. The only occurrence of the word in Greek literature (BAG, p. 112).

4. Creed (*Luke*, pp. 228-29) and Bultmann (*HST*, p. 34) take the story simply as an expansion of the Levi story (Lk. 5.28; Mk 2.14-17).

and his encounter with Jesus.[1] It is a perfect scene for Luke.[2] Jesus makes his way through the crowds and picks, out of all these people, the eager arch-sinner to honour with his presence in the home. The action of Jesus is more than just typical; it is almost poetic in the way it demonstrates what Jesus' ministry was all about for Luke. How does Zacchaeus act? Like his predecessors in Luke he is eager to see the Teacher and when invited to come down and act as host to the man of God he joyfully complies.

But now the story darkens[3] with the protestation in v. 7 that Jesus has gone in to be the guest of a man who is an ἁμαρτωλῷ ἀνδρί (cf. Lk. 5.8 where Peter is the first ἁμαρτωλὸς ἀνήρ). This time it is πάντες who grumble (cf. Lk. 5.30; 15.2) rather than the Pharisees but the effect is identical; it throws Jesus' behaviour into the limelight and focuses on how he alone takes a favourable stance toward the 'sinner'. In our treatment of Levi's banquet for Jesus we found no adequate explanation for a specific and substantive cause of 'offence' with regard to his dining habits. We are on equally uncertain grounds with respect to Zacchaeus. Indeed, the reason for the grumbling of the crowd is immaterial to the story. As readers, we do not know the specific reason for offence and it does not matter because we understand the scene regardless. The meaning is clear: Jesus alone is receptive to 'sinners'.

Another parable demonstrates the uncertain nature of the taking of offence:

> What do the thief and the robber resemble? Two people who dwelt in one town and made banquets. One invited the townspeople and did not invite the royal family, the other invited neither the townspeople nor the royal

---

1. O'Hanlon says ('Zacchaeus', p. 9), 'The story is not just one event in Jesus' journey to Jerusalem, to be treated in isolation, but is a synopsis. Zacchaeus is not just a tax gatherer, a hated traitor and despised sinner. He is a chief, rich tax collector, the sinner supreme.'

2. While Bultmann calls the incident 'ideal' and 'metaphorical' (*HST*, p. 56), the scene's many details show that it is not an 'ideal' scene. The story remains manifestly believable until v. 7 and the characteristic Lucan πάντες, 'they *all* murmured'. On the whole, the scene should more properly be described as having 'legendary' rather than 'ideal' characteristics (see M. Dibelius, *From Tradition to Gospel* [Cambridge: James Clarke, 1971], pp. 50-51, 118: 'a personal legend fully told').

3. We noted this same device in the story of the sinful woman in Lk. 7.

family. Which deserves the heavier punishment? Surely the one who invited the townspeople but did not invite the royal family.[1]

One gets the impression that the hosts of the banquets in this rabbinic parable were likely to offend no matter what they did. When subjective social and religious sensibilities are at stake such offence is impossible to quantify and equally diffic lt to defend against. Similarly, the umbrage of the crowd against Jesus (or is it Zacchaeus?) is vague, yet it seems somehow irrational and bigoted to the reader. After all, was not Zacchaeus eager to seek out Jesus; did he not respond rightly to Jesus? The offence of the crowd functions as a device for our author to set Jesus' behaviour in a controversy context and highlight how Jesus differs from his contemporaries. The offence works well in a literary context, but as in Luke 5, it strains our interpretation if taken at a strictly historical level.

In past scenes of controversy we have come to expect at this point the introduction of a logion from Jesus to answer and justify the action just undertaken (cf. Lk. 5.31; 7.35, 40; 15.3-32; 18.14). The story here differs in that Zacchaeus rises to speak and so, for the first time in Luke's Gospel, the 'sinner' is able to articulate his own response directly to Jesus, as we shall now see.

Does Zacchaeus Really Repent?

ἰδοὺ τὰ ἡμίσιά μου τῶν ὑπαρχόντων, κύριε, τοῖς πτωχοῖς δίδωμι,
καὶ εἴ τινός τι ἐσυκοφάντησα ἀποδίδωμι τετραπλοῦν.

The speech of Zacchaeus at 19.8 is often interpreted as a vow for a reformed lifestyle in gratitude for Jesus' behaviour towards him.[2] Jesus calls Zacchaeus; Zacchaeus responds with a promise of a change of behaviour and restoration for past wrongs. Jesus then declares his salvation and inclusion among the sons of Abraham. Understood in this

---

1. *B. B. Kam.* 79b.

2. As do, e.g., A. Schlatter, *Das Evangelium Lukas* (Stuttgart: Calwer Verlag, 1960), p. 403; Tannehill, *Narrative Unity*, pp. 123, 126; Marshall, *Luke*, p. 697; Grundmann, *Lukas*, p. 360; Creed, *Luke*, p. 231; Arndt, *St Luke*, p. 389. O'Hanlon represents the common view: 'Overwhelmed by Jesus' act of mercy, or, more properly, restored to wholeness by his graciousness, Zacchaeus embarks on a new moral existence' ('Zacchaeus', p. 16).

way, the story is a concrete example of 'conversion'[1] and Zacchaeus is the ultimate penitent. Ultimately, I believe this to be the correct interpretation, yet there is another position that must be briefly addressed.

A reading of the Greek text suggests another possible interpretation. The verbs are present tense (δίδωμι, ἀποδίδωμι) and a more natural understanding of the statement would seem to be that the giving of his possessions and the restoration of falsely obtained income have already been the habit of Zacchaeus: 'Behold, Lord, the half of my goods I give to the poor; and if I have defrauded anyone of anything, I restore it fourfold' (RSV).[2] Taken this way, our chief toll collector is not repenting and vowing a changed life but defending himself against the charges of the crowd. Richard C. White has summed up the interpretation in this way:

> the story tells of a man who was stereotyped by his job, resented and wrongly accused by his neighbours, who defended himself against the false charge, and whose good name was vindicated by Jesus.[3]

So White calls the passage a 'vindication' story and his argumentation is quite convincing. In particular it removes the necessity of translating the present tenses as 'futuristic'[4] which is described by White as 'tortuous'. Furthermore, one can appreciate the observation that this could well be a case where translation has been unduly influenced by a theological desire to have Zacchaeus repent. After all, a 'vindication' story has far less appeal theologically than one where the repenting 'sinner' finds forgiveness from Jesus through repentance.

In spite of these arguments there are two reasons why I believe the more traditional interpretation to be, in the last analysis, the correct one. The first is based on considerations internal to 19.8. The determi-

---

1. See Conzelmann, *Theology of St Luke*, pp. 228-30.

2. Compare the NIV: 'Lord, Lord, *Here and now I give* half of my possessions. . . and if I have cheated anyone out of anything *I will repay it* four times the amount'. Good News has: 'Listen sir, I will give half. . . I will pay him back. . . ' The RSV is much to be admired for leaving the ambiguity intact.

3. White, 'A Good Word for Zacchaeus', p. 89. This view is also argued at some length by Fitzmyer (*Luke*, pp. 1218-22).

4. As does Marshall (*Luke*, pp. 697-98): 'futuristic and expresses a resolve'; Robertson (*A Grammar*, p. 870) lists it under 'futuristic presents' and says it expresses a 'certainty of expectation'. See further, N.M. Watson, 'Was Zacchaeus Really Reforming?', *ExpT* 77 (1965–66), pp. 282-85.

native factor lies in the second half of the verse, in the comment about restoration of fraudulently taken goods. In order for White and Fitzmyer to say that the charity and restoration professed by Zacchaeus was his customary manner of business, they must say the 'fraud' was unintentional.[1] What Zacchaeus was saying, according to this view, was that he made fourfold restoration when it was discovered that people were inadvertently over-taxed. Obviously, no one (except perhaps a very poor business person!) would intentionally defraud and then make restoration at fourfold the price.

In response to this position, it must be pointed out that the word used to describe Zacchaeus's activity (συκοφαντέω) is far too strong a word to be construed as unintentional wrongdoing.[2] Even if this were not the case, when someone over-taxes a citizen unintentionally it is not 'fraud' at all but simply a 'mistake'. And according to Jewish law fourfold restitution is neither required nor appropriate for a 'mistake', but only for deliberate acts of theft.[3]

On the other hand, neither can the whole of 19.8b be understood as a promise or vow about his future actions, unless Zacchaeus is promising both to defraud *and* to restore in his future activities.[4] The

---

1. White, 'A Good Word for Zacchaeus', p. 92; see Fitzmyer, *Luke*, p. 1225: 'The implication is that he does not do this deliberately'. Or, as Derrett suggests, the extortion may have been work of underlings (*Law in the New Testament*, pp. 279, 283).

2. Lk. 3.14 is the only other use in the NT, and there it is in reference to violent robbery by soldiers. Also Watson, 'Was Zacchaeus Really Reforming', p. 282: 'this verb always refers in classical Greek to deliberate injustice, like vexatious prosecution, blackmail, or extortion'. See also C. Hunzinger, 'συκοφαντέω', *TDNT*, VII, p. 759; J.H. Moulton and G. Milligan, *The Vocabulary of the Greek Testament* (London: Hodder & Stoughton, 1914–1929), p. 596, both of which highlight the sense of intentional wrongdoing in the word.

3. See Exod. 22.1; 2 Sam. 12.6; cf. Lev. 6.5 where a fifth is added; also Num. 5.6-7; *Ant.* 16.1.3. A double penalty is normal with regard to property ('what has a life and what has not life' (*m. B. Kam.* 1.7; *b. B. Kam.* 67b) but offences dealing with the theft of oxen and sheep carry a four to fivefold penalty (as in Exod. 22.1). All these refer to intentional wrong, i.e. thievery. See Derrett, *Law in the New Testament*, p. 284; Fitzmyer, *Luke*, p. 1225; Strack–Billerbeck, *Kommentar*, II, pp. 250-51.

4. Fitzmyer (*Luke*, p. 1221) asks, 'Would a repentant sinner foresee so clearly his new lapses?' More pointedly, would he admit to the possibility in the flush of this moment?

statement 'and if I have defrauded anyone of anything. . .' can only make sense as an admission of past crimes which have remained undiscovered to this point and for which no restitution has been made. The last half of the statement, ἀποδίδωμι τετραπλοῦν, must be a statement of resolve to finally set things aright. Zacchaeus is in fact 'repenting'.[1] The verb, ἀποδίδωμι is not so much a 'futuristic' present (that is, 'I will repay. . .') as a simple statement of 'present resolve'.[2] The NIV may, after all, best capture the meaning of these present tenses: 'here and now' Zacchaeus not only makes right his wrongs but goes beyond this to give half his goods to the poor. For Luke it is repentance in its most convincing form.

In 19.9 we are not explicitly told *why* Zacchaeus has won Jesus' approval, only that he too is a 'son of Abraham'.[3] Luke leaves us to our own devices to derive the significance of Zacchaeus's actions. But this has been characteristic of Luke; he always leaves a certain vagueness about the penitential activities of his 'sinners'. We are given only glimpses of penitent attitudes and never advised of the full or long-term effect on behaviour. Levi simply leaves his toll table and this seems to be enough (Lk. 5.28); the sinful woman (Lk. 7.36ff.) and the toll collector (Lk. 18.9ff.) grieve for their sin but does a change of life ensue? Does the lost son finally become a productive member of the family (Lk. 15.11-32)? Does Zacchaeus switch professions or make other significant changes in response to his encounter with Jesus? Such details are not given, neither are they necessary for the stories to have their persuasive effect. Luke gives us no detailed paradigm of repentance, no programme of deeds; it is more like an ethos of repentance which pervades these passages. Grief over the

---

1.   If later rabbinic practice applies, one who confesses his guilt is exempt from the fine attached to his crime (*m. B. Met.* 3.1; *b. B. Met.* 33b; *b. B. Kam.* 17a). Perhaps Zacchaeus was an astute business man after all. It is also interesting to note that charity could not be accepted from a toll collector at his excise table, but it was acceptable for him to make such a gift from his home (*m. B. Kam.* 10.1; cf. Lk. 19.8). This points to the practical rather than esoteric nature of many rabbinic prohibitions. If money taken directly from the excise table was unacceptable due to the suspicion of being obtained by robbery it was not deemed necessary to extend this suspicion to the money in his home.

2.   So Creed (*Luke*, p. 231) who contrasts these present tenses to those which denote habit in Lk. 18.12.

3.   Cf. Lk. 1.55, 73; 3.8; 13.16.

past, contrition, humility, deeds of restoration, these are all a part of Luke's view of repentance. But the effect is derived cumulatively from all his 'sinner' material, it is never stated in explicit terms in one place.

Finally, Luke has capped the story with the familiar logion of v. 10: 'For the Son of Man came to seek and to save the lost'. Herein lies the second reason why the story of Zacchaeus must ultimately be considered one of repentance and not vindication. From the point of view of the Lucan narrative, v. 10 is determinative for the way in which Luke wishes the incident to be interpreted. Zacchaeus is the 'lost' one. The 'Son of Man'[1] has appeared to rescue this lost sheep of the house of Israel and set him back within the fold. It is the Ezekiel 34 theme revisited once again. We have found it throughout our material and this event is clearly meant by Luke to be the ultimate example of the efficacy of Jesus' ministry as the shepherd who calls the 'lost' back home. Zacchaeus repents and his deeds win him the shepherd's praise. Luke calls forth echoes of 5.30; 15.4-7, 8-10 and especially 15.32 into a single phrase which sums up his view of the purpose of Jesus' mission: 'The Son of Man came to seek and to save the lost'.[2]

Luke's 'Sinners' in Retrospect

The extraordinary aspect of Luke's treatment of the 'sinner' theme is the variety of types of narrative he calls into service to set it out. There is the bare and unelaborated story (Lk. 5.28ff.); the story full of emotion and pathos (Lk. 7.36ff.); parables of exceptional beauty and power (Lk. 15.1-32); a story based on hyperbole and caricature quite unlike any other Gospel passage (Lk. 18.9-14); and finally the charming and personal story of Zacchaeus. Through it all, Luke's Gospel has come full circle from ch. 5. The initial declaration of ministry to the 'sinners' (Lk. 5.32) has now found its fulfilment and

---

1. This is the first time we have encountered the phrase in the 'sinner' material. On this see Loewe, 'Towards an Interpretation', p. 326.

2. This is similar to the way Luke brought 14.11 forward to 18.14b to cap the story of the Pharisee and the toll collector and reiterate that important theme. It is one of Luke's methods of bringing various strands of a theme into a larger stream. We also note with interest how Lk. 19.10 found its way as an interpolation into Mt. 18.11 (D, K, W, X, II).

fullest expression in the person of Zacchaeus. The policy of inclusion and seeking the 'lost' is fully vindicated.

But is this a theme which spans only chs. 5–19? It is now possible to look back to the beginning of the Gospel of Luke and find that this thematic emphasis was anticipated at the earliest stages.[1] Aspects of the 'Benedictus' in Luke 1 demonstrate the agenda which Luke eventually sets out fully in Jesus' ministry to the 'sinners'.[2]

> And you, child, will be called the prophet of the Most High;
> for you will go before the Lord to prepare his ways,
> to give knowledge of salvation to his people
> in the forgiveness of their sins,
> through the tender mercy of our God,
> when the day shall dawn upon us from on high
> to give light to those who sit in darkness and in the shadow of death,
> to guide our feet into the way of peace (Lk. 1.76-79).

As we read it now we cannot help but think of Zacchaeus. In hindsight, we see that the 'sinners' of Luke's Gospel were, in part, the intended targets of this prophecy as well as the proof of its fulfilment. Zacchaeus is not just another story of one who repents but the living proof of the realization of the promise of forgiveness of sin and the dawning of the day of God's mercy. Our 'sinners' were, without exception, those who sat in 'darkness' (Lk. 1.79). Through the 'tender mercy of our God' (Lk. 1.78) they were ushered into the 'dawn' and the 'knowledge of salvation' (Lk. 1.77-78).

This theme also comes to light in the Great Commission at the very end of the Gospel. There we find the statement:

> Thus it is written, that the Christ should suffer and on the third day rise from the dead, and that repentance and forgiveness of sins should be preached in his name to all nations, beginning from Jerusalem (Lk. 24.46-47).

In general, the Gentiles have not been in view in our 'sinner' material; but it is beyond question that Luke has laid the foundation for a philosophy of outreach which will lend itself to the task of the Gentile mission. The purpose he declares here at the end of his Gospel and pur-

---

1. 'The roots of this story [of Zacchaeus] run to the gospel's first pages' (O'Hanlon, 'Zacchaeus', p. 11).

2. So O'Hanlon, 'Zacchaeus', p. 22; also Loewe, 'Towards an Interpretation', p. 327.

sues in Acts with respect to the Gentile mission proceeds naturally and
logically from the work he has done in his Gospel.

Conclusion

Having fulfilled this portion of his ministry Jesus can now truly set his
heart toward Jerusalem and all that awaits him there. Our 'sinners'
disappear after the story of Zacchaeus, never to reappear in Luke's
writings. The Pharisees make their ignominious exit in Lk. 19.39 at
the very gates of Jerusalem by calling on Jesus to rebuke his disciples
for rejoicing over all the mighty works they had seen. The new enemies are the 'chief priests and scribes' and the focus of conflict moves
to a higher, more cosmic level. But for Luke the 'sinners' are one of
the most important symbols of the purpose of Jesus' earthly ministry
and their repentance was an essential part of what Jesus was called to
accomplish.

We have seen how the theme of Jesus' ministry to those on the
perimeter has shaped Luke's treatment of the Gospel message. Indeed,
the rescue of the 'lost' sheep has become an important facet of Jesus'
whole mission for Luke. Throughout this process Luke has been shift-
ing the perspective of the reader towards a sympathetic view of the
'sinner' with the express purpose of commending the attitude of his
'sinner' to the conscience of the reader. If Luke's 'sinners' have won
the acceptance of Jesus through repentance then so can the reader.
Luke has been exercising his literary skills in precisely the capacity
which has earned him the name 'evangelist'. His purpose has been a
manifestly religious one: to bring his reader to Jesus and inspire the
right response to this ministry. In a sense, the 'sinner' has become the
one to emulate, and anyone who has read this far in Luke's Gospel
with sympathy cannot help but find a sense of comfort and acceptance
in identifying with the 'sinner' figure. This is why Luke's Gospel, and
indeed the Gospel tradition in general, has enduring appeal. It assures
the reader that even though they may themselves feel excluded and
'lost', there can be hope for them, even for the 'sinner'.

CONCLUSION

The tradition about Jesus' association with 'sinners' is one of the central issues in the Gospel of Luke. In the words attributed to Jesus himself, the purpose of his calling was to seek those who bore this appellation. In recent years scholars have reaffirmed a conviction that this aspect of Jesus' ministry was based on a genuine historical concern by Jesus for those who stood on the margins of religious and social propriety in his day. If there is a scholarly consensus about any feature of the life and work of the historical Jesus, it may well be this matter of his association with outcasts.

Few scholars, however, have sought to probe behind the assumptions and unquestioned images that have grown around the issue of Jesus and the 'sinners'. Few have paused to inquire about the actual form and significance that such associations must have had in Jesus' day. Yet the Gospel tradition about this aspect of Jesus' life is itself so compelling in its appeal, so attractive in its imagery that it has assumed central importance in modern notions about *who Jesus was*: Jesus was, above all, a friend to 'sinners' and outcasts. One of the great successes of the Gospel tradition is that it has so deeply implanted this notion in the Christian story.

The result of our investigation has been to show that some of the long-held assumptions about Jesus' fellowship with 'sinners' must be discarded, and that other perspectives have much to teach about the meaning and importance of this tradition. Chapter 1 demonstrated that in the light of recent advances in the understanding of historical Pharisaism, the simple Gospel 'category' of the 'Pharisees' must be critically re-examined. The Pharisees were not the chief adjudicating religious authority in Jesus' day and their Gospel portrayal as such must be must be understood for what it is: a necessary functional element of the Gospel story, a foil against which Jesus' association with 'sinners' can be cast in high relief.

The findings of Chapter 1 further showed that Jesus' teaching style

was within the scope of the forms and methods of religious expression
of the Judaism of his day. The Gospel representation of the Pharisees
as the rigid purveyors of halakhic Judaism, unable to appreciate the
haggadic wisdom of Jesus, obscures the complexity of ancient Judaism
as a living, functioning way of life. Halakhah and haggadah were two
facets of a single religious ethos and Jesus' teaching must be understood, not as a challenge to and departure from those methods, but as
a voice that spoke through the modes of expression of his day. The
Gospels caricature the difference between halakhah and haggadah because their purpose was to show Jesus' superiority over his opponents.
That Luke or any of the other evangelists fails to give a full and accurate picture of Pharisaism or the general religious milieu of Jesus' day
is neither surprising nor should it be construed as a criticism of the
accuracy of the Gospels. They were, after all, evangelists, not modern
historians. Still, it is best to keep in mind that it is never wise to de-
pend on an enemy for an impartial description of the adversary. A
view of Judaism that attempts to go beyond the Gospel portrayal must
seek to appreciate the richness and vitality of Judaism in the early
centuries of this era, something which just does not come through in
the Gospel texts. The controversy with the 'Pharisees' over Jesus'
treatment of the 'sinners' cannot be taken as a full historical account
of the religious milieu of Jesus' day.

Traditional rabbinic imprecations against the *'ammei ha-aretz* have
also formed a part of the modern understanding of Jesus' relationship
to the 'sinners'. In Chapter 2 it was seen how this subject has found its
way into interpretations of the 'sinner' material in the New Testament.
Tithing and the ritual purity of food, the primary issues relating to the
haberim and the *'ammei ha-aretz*, were the concerns of a sectarian
approach to Jewish observance. The investigation has shown that for
the non-farmer tithing on food was supererogatory, as was the
undertaking to eat ordinary food in a state of ritual purity. These issues cannot have formed the basis of a criticism of Jesus' table-fellowship with 'sinners'. Furthermore, when one scrutinizes the rabbinic
material on the *'ammei ha-aretz* it becomes apparent that those who
suffered rabbinic censure were not guilty of substantive offences that
would have cut them off from the mainstream of Jewish religious
practice. They simply did not conform to the sectarian ideal of some
rabbis and this censure did not create widely recognized class divisions in Jewish Palestinian society. The *'ammei ha-aretz* were a con-

struct of the second-century rabbinic consciousness, not a well-defined social entity. Jesus' association with 'sinners' cannot be construed as a challenge to social conventions based on rabbinic prejudice against the *'ammei ha-aretz* because such social conventions did not exist in Jesus' day and it may well be that a distinct social category of the *'ammei ha-aretz* never did exist in a substantive social form.

The investigation of the 'sinner' motif in the literature of the Second Temple period in Chapter 3 gave us an insight into the nature and usage of the concept in a wide range of literary and historical settings. The notion of 'sinners' arises most prominently in the Greek Psalms but the 'sinner' is never concretely identified with specific individuals. Most often the 'sinners' are simply the representatives of wickedness and opposition to God in the dichotomy of a twofold moral universe. The 'sinners' are the necessary counterpart to the idea of the 'righteous' and, as such, should be understood in terms of an ideological category in the religious world view of the psalmist. They are a religious and ideological distinction, not a social one; they exist, but only in the point of view of the one who forms a judgment of their wickedness.

With some exceptions, the basically ideological function of this language holds true in most of the non-canonical texts of the Second Temple period. The 'sinners' are those who reject God, are destined to judgment, and for whom repentance is generally considered impossible. Only later, in the post-destruction milieu, and most probably under the influence of the Christian corpus, does the term 'sinner' come to refer to one for whom mercy and forgiveness are considered appropriate.

Against this background the role of the 'sinners' in Luke's Gospel has been shown to embody many of the elements of an ideological category that is essential to the telling of the Gospel story. The issues discussed in Part I, the Pharisees, table-fellowship, the despised members of Jewish society, all surfaced in one form or another in the Gospel portrayal of Jesus' relationship with the 'sinners'. Yet, we were unable to find ways to understand the offence caused by Jesus' associations at a strictly historical level. Why was the call of Levi so offensive to the 'Pharisees' when it seems they should have rejoiced? Contrary to expectation, the 'sinners' of Luke's Gospel (the sinful woman, the lost son, the humble toll collector) all exemplified the right response to Jesus in counterpoint to the uncomprehending and bigoted 'Pharisees'.

Luke has brought about a reversal of all expectations with the result
that the 'sinner' is now the one who is 'saved'. The repentance of Zacchaeus, the chief 'sinner' of them all, demonstrated in a climactic way
that Jesus' call to the 'lost' was a proper and justifiable course of ministry. All of the Pharisaic charges against Jesus for associating with
'sinners' were shown to be ill founded and his conduct itself became
an indictment of the 'Pharisees' for their own failed responsibility to
seek the 'sinners'.

  In this book I have not attempted to speculate about the purpose
these 'Pharisees' and 'sinners' might have fulfilled in the context of the
Lucan community. We do not know who the 'Pharisees' were for
Luke nor who the 'sinners' were historically, let alone who they represented in the ideology of Luke's community. Therein lies the genius
of this facet of the Gospel tradition. Every age, every community, every individual has its own 'Pharisees', its own 'sinners'. The univer-
sality of the images provoked by the theme of Jesus and the 'sinners' is
the reason why this facet of the Gospel tradition continues to commu-
nicate effectively. Even centuries later the interaction of Jesus with the
dispossessed still operates as a strong symbol, a metaphor for the crucial relationship of the Christian message to society and its institutions.

BIBLIOGRAPHY

Aalen, S., 'St Luke's Gospel and the Last Chapters of I Enoch', *NTS* 13 (1966–67), pp. 1-13.

Abrahams, I., *Studies In Pharisaism and the Gospels* (New York: Ktav, reprint 1976; first published Cambridge:Cambridge University Press, 1917, 1924).

Alexander, P.S., 'Rabbinic Judaism and the New Testament', *ZNW* 74 (1983), pp. 237-46.

—Review of E.P. Sanders's *Jesus and Judaism*, *JJS* 37 (1986), pp. 103-106.

—*Textual Sources for the Study of Judaism* (Manchester: Manchester University Press, 1984).

Allison, D.C., 'Jesus and the Covenant: A Response to E.P. Sanders', *JSNT* 29 (1987), pp. 57-78.

Alon, G., *Jews, Judaism and the Classical World* (trans. I. Abrahams; Jerusalem: Magnes Press, 1977).

—*The Jews in their Land in the Talmudic Age* (trans. G. Levi; Jerusalem: Magnes Press, 1984).

Anderson, G.W., 'Enemies and Evil-doers in the Book of Psalms', *BJRL* 48 (1965–66), pp. 18-29.

Anderson, A.A., *The Book of Psalms* (2 vols.; London: Oliphants, 1972).

Arndt, W.F., *The Gospel according to St Luke* (St Louis: Concordia, 1956).

Aune, D.E., 'Orthodoxy in First Century Judaism: A Response to N.J. McEleney', *JSJ* 7 (1976), pp. 1-10.

Authorized Daily Prayer Book of the United Hebrew Congregations of the British Empire (trans. S. Singer; 17th edn; London: Eyre & Spottiswoode).

Baeck, L., 'Haggadah and Christian Doctrine', *HUCA* 23 (1950), pp. 549-60.

Badian, E., *Publicans and Sinners: Private Enterprise in the Service of the Roman Republic* (Oxford: Basil Blackwell, 1972).

Bamberger, B., 'The Dating of Aggadic Materials', *JBL* 68 (1949), pp. 115-23.

Baron, S., *A Social and Religious History of the Jews* (16 vols.; New York: Columbia University Press, 1957-76).

Barrett, C.K., *The First Epistle to the Corinthians* (New York: Harper & Row, 1986).

Bauer, W., *A Greek English Lexicon of the New Testament and Other Early Christian Literature* (trans. W.F. Arndt and F. W. Gingrich; Chicago: The University of Chicago Press, 1957).

Baumgarten, A.I., 'The Name of the Pharisees', *JBL* 102-103 (1983), pp. 411-28.

Baumgarten, J.M., 'Qumran Studies', *JBL* 77 (1958), pp. 249-57.

—'The Unwritten Law in the Pre-Rabbinic Period', *JSJ* 3 (1972), pp. 7-29.

Beasley-Murray, G.R., *John* (Waco, TX: Word Books, 1987).

Beck, B.E., *Christian Character in the Gospel of Luke* (London: Epworth Press, 1989).

Birkeland, H., *The Evildoers in the Book of Psalms* (Oslo: Jacob Dybwad, 1955).

Bizer, C., 'Die Geschichte vom Zachäus (Lk. 19.1-10)', *Der evangelische Erzieher* 28 (1976), pp. 217-24.

Blass, F. and A. Debrunner, *A Greek Grammar of the New Testament and Other Early Christian Literature* (trans. R.W. Funk; Chicago: The University of Chicago Press, 1961).

Bokser, B.M., *History of Judaism: The Next Ten Years* (Ann Arbor: Scholars Press, 1980).

Booth, R., *Jesus and the Laws of Purity* (Sheffield: JSOT Press, 1986).

Borg, M.J., *Conflict, Holiness and Politics in the Teachings of Jesus* (New York: The Edwin Mellon Press, 1984).

—*Jesus: A New Vision* (San Francisco: Harper & Row, 1987).

Bornkamn, G., *Jesus of Nazareth* (New York: Harper & Row, 1960).

Bouwman, G., 'La pécheresse hospitalière (Lc., VII, 36-50)', *ETL* 45 (1969), pp. 172-79.

Bowker, J., *Jesus and the Pharisees* (Cambridge: Cambridge University Press, 1973).

—*The Targums and Rabbinic Literature* (Cambridge: Cambridge University Press, 1969).

Boyarin, D., 'Penitential Liturgy in 4 Ezra', *JSJ* 1-3 (1972), pp. 30-34.

Braumann, G., 'Die Schuldner und die Sünderin: Luk. VII. 36-50', *NTS* 10 (1964), pp. 487-93.

Brawley, R.L., 'The Pharisees in Luke/Acts: Luke's Address to Jews and his Irenic Purpose' (unpublished PhD dissertation, Princeton Theological Seminary, 1978. British Library Document Supply Center).

—*Luke–Acts and the Jews: Conflict, Apology, and Conciliation* (Atlanta: Scholars Press, 1987).

Bronner, L., *Sects and Separatism During the Second Jewish Commonwealth* (New York: Bloch, 1967).

Brown, F., S.R. Driver and C. Briggs, *A Hebrew and English Lexicon of the Old Testament* (Oxford: Clarendon Press, 1951).

Brown, R.E., *The Gospel according to John* (2 vols.; Garden City: Doubleday, 1966).

Büchler, A., 'Ben Sira's Conception of Sin and Atonement', *JQR* 13 (1923), pp. 303-35.

—*Der galiläische 'Am-ha' Ares des zweiten Jahrhunderts* (Wien: Alfred Hölder, 1906).

Bultmann, R., *The History of the Synoptic Tradition* (trans. J. Marsh from the 2nd German edn; Oxford: Basil Blackwell, 1972).

Burkitt, F.C.,'Jesus and the "Pharisees"', *JTS* 28 (1927), pp. 392-97.

Buttenwieser, M., *The Psalms: Chronologically Treated with a New Translation* (New York: Ktav, 1969).

Caird, G.B., *The Gospel of St Luke* (London: A. & C. Black, 1968).

—*The Language and Imagery of the Bible* (London: Duckworth, 1980).

Carlston, C.E., *The Parables of the Triple Tradition* (Philadelphia: Fortress Press, 1975).

Carroll, J.T., 'Luke's Portrayal of the Pharisees', *CBQ* 50/4 (1988), pp. 604-21.

Charles, R.H., *The Apocrypha and Pseudepigrapha of the Old Testament in English* (2 vols.; London: Oxford University Press, 1913).

Charlesworth, J.H., 'The SNTS Pseudepigrapha Seminars at Tübingen and Paris on the Books of Enoch', *NTS* 25 (1979), pp. 315-23.

—(ed.) *The Old Testament Pseudepigrapha* (2 vols.; New York: Doubleday, 1983).

—*Jesus within Judaism* (London: SPCK, 1988).

—'A History of Pseudepigrapha Research', in *Aufstieg und Niedergang der römischen Welt* (ed. Wolfgang Haase; Berlin: de Gruyter, 1979), II, 19.1, pp. 54-88.

Chilton, B., *A Galilean Rabbi and his Bible* (Wilmington, DE: Michael Glazier, 1984).

—'Jesus and the Repentance of E.P. Sanders', *TynBul*, 39 (1988), pp. 1-18.

Cohen, S., 'The Place of Jesus in the Religious Life of His Day', *JBL* 48 (1929), pp. 82-108.

Cohen, S.J.D., 'The Significance of Yavneh: Pharisees, Rabbis, and the End of Jewish Sectarianism', *HUCA* 55 (1984), pp. 27-53.

—Review of A. Oppenheimer's *'Am Ha-aretz*, *JBL* 97 (1978), pp. 596-97.

Concordance to the Apocrypha/Deuterocanonical Books of the Revised Standard Version (Grand Rapids: Eerdmans, 1983).

Conzelmann, H., *The Theology of St Luke* (trans. G. Buswell; Philadelphia: Fortress Press, 1961).

Corley, K.E., 'Women in the Context of Greco-Roman Meals', in *Society of Biblical Literature: 1989 Seminar Papers* (Atlanta: Scholars Press, 1989), pp. 487-521.

Creed, J.M., *The Gospel according to St Luke* (London: Macmillan, 1950).

Croft, S.J.L., *The Identity of the Individual in the Psalms* (Sheffield: JSOT Press, 1987).

Cross, F.M., Jr, *The Ancient Library of Qumran* (London: Duckworth, 1958).

Dahood, M., *Psalms I* (3 vols.; New York: Doubleday, 1966).

Danby, H. (trans.), *The Mishnah* (Oxford: Oxford University Press, 1933).

Daiches, S., 'Meaning of 'Am Ha-aretz in the Old Testament', *JTS* 30 (1929), pp. 245-49.

Danker, F.W., *Jesus and the New Age* (Philadelphia: Fortress Press, 1988).

Daube, D., 'Rabbinic Methods of Interpretation', in *Understanding the Talmud* (ed. Alan Corré; New York: Ktav, 1975), pp. 275-89.

—*The New Testament and Rabbinic Judaism* (London: The Athlone Press, 1956).

Dawsey, J.M., *The Lukan Voice: Confusion and Irony in the Gospel of Luke* (Macon, GA: Mercer University Press, 1986).

Denis, A.-M., *Concordance Grecque des Pseudépigraphes D'Ancien Testament* (Louvain-la-Neuve: Université Catholique de Louvain, 1987).

Derrett, J.D.M., 'Fresh Light on the Lost Sheep and the Lost Coin', *NTS* 26 (1980), pp. 36-60.

—*Jesus' Audience: The Social and Psychological Environment in which He Worked* (London: Darton, Longman & Todd, 1973).

—*Law in the New Testament* (London: Darton, Longman & Todd, 1970).

Dibelius, M., *From Tradition to Gospel* (Cambridge: James Clarke, 1971).

Dittenberger, W., *Orientis Graeci Inscriptiones Selectae*, I (Lipsiae: Apud S. Hirzel, 1903).

Dodd, C.H., *The Parables of the Kingdom* (London: Nisbet, 1935; rev. edn 1950).

—*The Founder of Christianity* (New York: Collier Books, 1970).

Doeve, J.W., *Jewish Hermeneutics in the Synoptic Gospels and Acts* (trans. G.E. van Baaren-Pape; Assen: Van Gorcum, 1954).

Donahue, J.R., 'Tax Collectors and Sinners', *CBQ* 33 (1971), pp. 39-61.

Dormeyer, D., 'Textpragmatische Analyse und Unterrichtsplanung zum Gleichnis vom verlorenen Schaf Lk 15.1-7', *Die evangelische Erzieher* 27 (1975), pp. 347-57.

Douglas, M., *Purity and Danger* (London: Routledge & Kegan Paul, 1966).

Drury, J., *Tradition and Design in Luke's Gospel* (London: Darton, Longman & Todd, 1976).

Dunn, J.D.G., 'The Incident at Antioch', *JSNT* 18 (1983), pp. 3-57.

Dupont, J., 'Le Pharisien et la pécheresse (Lc 7.36-50)', *Communautés et Liturgies* 4 (1980), pp. 260-68.

Ellis, E.E., *The Gospel of Luke* (London: Nelson, 1966).

Esler, P.F., *Community and Gospel in Luke–Acts: The Social and Political Motivations of Lucan Theology* (Cambridge: Cambridge University Press, 1987).

Farmer, W.R., 'Notes on a Literary and Form-critical Analysis of Some of the Synoptic Material Peculiar to Luke', *NTS* 8 (1961–62), pp. 301-16.

Fiedler, P., *Jesus und die Sünder* (Frankfurt: Peter Lang, 1976).

Finkel, A., *The Pharisees and the Teacher of Nazareth: A Study of Their Background, Their Halachic and Midrashic Teachings, the Similarities and Differences* (Leiden: Brill, 1964).

Finkelstein, L., *The Pharisees: The Sociological Background of their Faith* (2 vols.; Philadelphia: The Jewish Publication Society of America, 1938; 2nd edn 1940).

Fitzmyer, J., *The Gospel according to Luke* (2 vols.; New York: Doubleday, 1985).

Fletcher, D.R., 'The Riddle of the Unjust Steward: Is Irony the Key?', *JBL* 82 (1963), pp. 15-30.

Flusser, D., *Die rabbinischen Gleichnisse und der Gleichniserzahler Jesus* (Bern: Peter Lang, 1981).

Ford, J.M., *My Enemy is my Guest: Jesus and Violence in Luke* (Maryknoll: Orbis Books, 1984).

Forkman, G., *The Limits of the Religious Community* (Lund: Gleerup, 1972).

Freyne, S., *Galilee, Jesus and the Gospels* (Philadelphia: Fortress Press, 1988).

Gaster, T.H., *The Scriptures of the Dead Sea Sect* (London: Secker & Warburg, 1957).

Gesenius' Hebrew and Chaldee Lexicon to the Old Testament Scriptures (trans. Samuel P. Tregelles; Grand Rapids: Baker Book House, 1979; reprint 1984; originally published by Samuel Bagster and Sons 1847).

Gibson, J., 'Hoi Telonai kai Hai Pornai', *JTS* 32 (1981), pp. 429-33.

Gigon, O., *'Idiotes'*, in *Soziale Typenbegriffe im alten Griechenland und ihr Fortleben in den Sprachen der Welt* (ed. Elisabeth C. Welskopf; Berlin: Akademie-Verlag, 1981), pp. 385-91.

Grundmann, W., *Das Evangelium nach Lukas* (Berlin: Evangelische Verlagsanstalt, 1969).

Guelich, R.A., *Mark 1–8.26* (Dallas: Word Books, 1989).

Gunneweg, A.H.J., *''Am Ha-aretz*—A Semantic Revolution', *ZAW* 95 (1983), pp. 437-40.

Hagner, D.A., *The Jewish Reclamation of Jesus: An Analysis and Critique of Modern Jewish Study of Jesus* (Grand Rapids: Academie Press, 1984).

Hatch, E. and H.A. Redpath, *A Concordance to the Septuagint and Other Greek Versions of the Old Testament* (3 vols.; Oxford: Clarendon Press, 1897–1906).

Heinemann, J., 'Amidah', *EncJud*, II (New York: Macmillan, 1971), pp. 838-45

Hendriksen, W., *The Gospel of Luke* (Edinburgh: The Banner of Truth Trust, 1978).

Herford, R.T., *The Pharisees* (Boston: Beacon Press, 1924).

Herr, M.D. ,'Midrash', *EncJud*, XI (New York: Macmillan, 1971), pp. 1507-14

—'Aggadah', *ETal* , I (Jerusalem: Talmudic Encyclopedia Institute, 1969).

—'Aggadah', *EncJud*, II (New York: Macmillan, 1971), pp. 354-66

Herrenbrück, F., 'Zum Vorwurf der Kollaboration des Zöllners mit Rom', *ZNW* 78 (1987), pp. 186-99.

Hickling, C.J.A., 'A Tract on Jesus and the Pharisees? A Conjecture on the Redaction of Luke 15 and 16', *HeyJ* 16 (1975), pp. 253-65.

Hill, D., *The Gospel of Matthew* (Grand Rapids: Eerdmans, 1972).

Hoerber, R.G., ' "God Be Merciful to Me a Sinner": A Note on Luke 18.13', *CTM 33* (1962), pp. 283-86.

Hofius, O., *Jesu Tischgemeinschaft mit den Sündern* (Stuttgart: Calwer Verlag, 1967).

Horsley, R.A., *Jesus and the Spiral of Violence: Popular Jewish Resistance in Roman Palestine* (San Francisco: Harper & Row, 1987).

Hultgren, A.J., *Jesus and his Adversaries* (Minneapolis, MN: Augsburg Publishing House, 1979).

Jastrow, M., *A Dictionary of the Targumim, the Talmud Babli and Yerushalmi, and the Midrashic Literature* (2 vols.; New York: Pardes Publishing House, 1971).

Jeanrod, W.G., *Text and Interpretation as Categories of Theological Thinking* (trans. Thomas J. Wilson; Dublin: Gill and Macmillan, 1988).

Jeremias, J., *Jerusalem in the Time of Jesus* (trans. F.H. and C.H. Cav; Philadelphia: Fortress Press, 1967).

—*New Testament Theology: The Proclamation of Jesus* (trans. J. Bowden; London: SCM Press, 1971).

—*The Eucharistic Words of Jesus* (trans. N. Perrin; London: SCM Press, 1966).

—*The Parables of Jesus* (trans. S. H. Hooke; London: SCM Press, 1963).

—'Tradition und Redaktion in Lukas 15', *ZNW* 62 (1971), pp. 172-89.

—'Zöllner und Sünder', *ZNW* 30 (1931), pp. 293-300.

Jónsson, J., *Humour and Irony in the New Testament* (Leiden: Brill, 1985).

Kilgallen, J.J., 'John the Baptist, the Sinful Woman, and the Pharisee', *JBL* 104 (1985), pp. 675-79.

Kippenberg, H.G., Review of A. Oppenheimer's *'Am Ha-aretz*, *JSJ* 9/2 (1978), pp. 230-32.

Kissane, E., *The Book of Psalms* (2 vols.; Dublin: Brown and Nolan, 1953).

Klausner, J., *Jesus of Nazareth* (London: Allen & Unwin, 1925; reprinted 1947).

Klijn, A.F.J., 'Scribes, Pharisees, Highpriests and Elders in the New Testament', *NovT* 3 (1959), pp. 259-67.

Koenig, J., *New Testament Hospitality* (Philadelphia: Fortress Press, 1985).

Kraft, R.A. and G.W.E. Nickelsburg, *Early Judaism and its Modern Interpreters* (Philadelphia: Fortress Press, 1986).

Lachs, S.T., *A Rabbinic Commentary on the New Testament* (New Jersey: Ktav, 1987).

Landman, I., ''Am Ha-aretz', in *The Universal Jewish Encyclopedia*, I (New York: Universal Jewish Encyclopedia, 1948), pp. 216-18.

Lauterbach, J.Z., 'The Pharisees and their Teachings', *HUCA* 6 (1929), pp. 69-139.

Leaney, A.R.C., *The Gospel according to St Luke* (London: A. & C. Black, 1958).

Legault, A., 'An Application of the Form-Critique Method to the Anointings in Galilee (Lk 7.36-50) and Bethany (Mt. 26.6-13; Mk 4.3-9; Jn 12.1-8)', *CBQ* 16 (1954), pp. 131-145.

Leroy, H., 'Vergebung und Gemeinde nach Lukas 7.36-50', in *Wort Gottes in der Zeit: Festschrift für K.H. Schelkle* (ed. Helmut Feld and Josef Nolte; Patmos: Verlag Dusseldorf, 1973), pp. 85-94.

Lindars, B. (ed.), *Essays on the Place of the Law in Israel and Early Christianity* (Cambridge: James Clarke, 1988).

Linnemann, E., *Parables of Jesus* (London: SPCK, 1966).

Loewe, W.P.,'Towards an Interpretation of Lk.19.1-10', *CBQ* 36 (1974), pp. 321-31.

Maccoby, H., *Early Rabbinic Writings* (Cambridge: Cambridge University Press, 1988).

Mann, J., *The Bible as Read and Preached in the Old Synagogue*, I (New York: Ktav, 1971).

Manson, T.W., *The Teachings of Jesus* (Cambridge: Cambridge University Press, 1931).

Marcus, R., 'The Pharisees in the Light of Modern Scholarship', *JR* 23 (1952), pp. 153-64.

Marshall, I.H., *Commentary on Luke* (Grand Rapids: Eerdmans, 1979).

—*Luke: Historian and Theologian* (Exeter: Paternoster Press, 1970).

Mekilta De-Rabbi Ishmael, I (trans. Jacob Z. Lauterbach; Philadelphia: The Jewish Publication Society of America, 1933 and 1961).

Metzger, B.M., *A Textual Commentary on the Greek New Testament* (London: United Bible Societies, 1975).

Meyer, B., *The Aims of Jesus* (London: SCM Press, 1979).

Meyer, R. and H.F. Weiss, 'Φαρισαῖος', in *Theological Dictionary of the New Testament*, IX (ed. G. Kittel and G. Friedrich; trans. G. Bromiley; 10 vols.; Grand Rapids: Eerdmans, 1964–76), pp. 11-48.

Meyers, E.M., 'The Cultural Setting of Galilee: The Case of Regionalism and Early Judaism', in *Aufstieg und Niedergang der römischen Welt* (ed. Wolfgang Haase; Berlin: de Gruyter, 1979), II, 19.1, pp. 686-702.

Michel, A. and J. Le Moyne, 'Pharisiens', *Dictionnaire de la Bible*. Supplément 7 (Paris: Letouzey & Ané, 1966).

Michel, A., 'τελώνης', in *Theological Dictionary of the New Testament*, VIII (ed. F. Kittel and G. Friedrich; trans. G. Bromiley;10 vols.; Grand Rapids: Eerdmans, 1964–76), pp. 88-105.

Milik, J.T., *Ten Years of Discovery in the Wilderness of Judaea* (trans. J. Strugnell; London: SCM Press, 1959).

Montefiore, C.G., *Rabbinic Literature and Gospel Teachings* (New York: Ktav, 1970).

—*The Synoptic Gospels* (2 vols.; London: Macmillan, 1927, 2nd edn).

Montefiore, C.G. and H. Loewe, *A Rabbinic Anthology* (Cleveland: The World Publishing Company, 1963).

Moore, G.F., *Judaism in the First Centuries of the Christian Era: The Age of the Tannaim* (3 vols.; Cambridge, MA: Harvard University Press, 1927; reprinted 1946).

Morris, L., *The Gospel according to St Luke* (London: Inter-Varsity Press, 1974).

Mottu, H., 'The Pharisee and the Tax Collector: Sartian Notions as Applied to the Reading of Scripture', *USQR* 29 (1973), pp. 195-213.

Moulton, J.H. and G. Milligan, *The Vocabulary of the Greek Testament* (London: Hodder & Stoughton, 1914–29).

Mourlon-Beernaert, P., 'The Lost Sheep: Four Approaches', *TD* 29 (1981), pp. 143-48.

Mowinckel, S., *Psalmstudien* (2 vols.; Amsterdam: Verlag P. Schippers; 1966 reprint of 1922 original).

Moxnes, H., *The Economy of the Kingdom* (Philadelphia: Fortress Press, 1988).

Mussner, F., 'Der nicht erkannte Kairos, (Mt. 11.16-19 = Lk. 7.31-35)', *Bib* 40 (1959), pp. 599-612.

Navonne, J., 'The Lucan Banquet Community', *Bible Today* 50 (1970), pp. 155-62.

Neusner, J., *A Life of Rabban Yohanan ben Zakkai* (Leiden: Brill, 1962).

—' "Judaism" after Moore', *JJS* 31 (1980), pp. 141-56.

—*From Politics to Piety* (Englewood Cliffs, NJ: Prentice-Hall, 1973).

—'The Fellowship in the Second Jewish Commonwealth', *HTR* 53 (1960), pp. 125-42.

—*The Rabbinic Traditions about the Pharisees before 70* (3 vols.; Leiden: Brill, 1971).

—'The Formation of Rabbinic Judaism', in *Aufstieg und Niedergang der römischen Welt* (ed. Wolfgang Haase; Berlin: de Gruyter, 1979), II, 19.2, pp. 3-42.

Bibliography 201

Neusner, J. and R. Sarason (eds.), *The Tosefta: Zeraim* (New York: Ktav, 1986).

Newman, J., *Halachic Sources: From the Beginning to the Ninth Century* (Leiden: Brill, 1969).

Nicholson, E.W., 'The Meaning of 'Am Ha-aretz in the Old Testament', *JSS* 10 (1965), pp. 59-66.

Nickelsburg, W.E., 'Riches, The Rich, and God's Judgment in 1 Enoch 92–105 and the Gospel According to Luke', *NTS* 13 (1966–67), pp. 324-44.

O'Hanlon, J., 'The Story of Zacchaeus and the Lukan Ethic', *JSNT* 12 (1981), pp. 2-26.

Oesterley, W.O.E., *The Psalms* (London: SPCK, 1953).

Ogg, G., 'The Central Section of the Gospel According to St Luke', *NTS* 18 (1971), pp. 39-53.

Oppenheimer, A., 'The Am Ha-aretz', *EncJud*, I (New York: Macmillan, 1971).

—*The ʿAm Ha-aretz: A Study in the Social History of the Jewish People in the Hellenistic-Roman Period* (Leiden: Brill, 1977).

Patte, D., *Early Jewish Hermeneutics in Palestine* (Missoula, MT: Scholars Press, 1975).

Peli, P.H., 'The *Havurot* That Were in Jerusalem', *HUCA* 55 (1984), pp. 55-74.

Perrin, N., *Rediscovering the Teaching of Jesus* (London: SCM Press, 1967).

Perry, B., *Aesopica* (Urbana,IL: University of Illinois Press, 1952).

—*Studies in the Textual History of the Life and Fables of Aesop* (Haverford: Lancaster Press, 1936).

Pesch, R., 'Das Zöllnergastmahl (Mk 2.15-17)', in *Mélanges Bibliques* (ed. A. Descamps and André de Halleux; Gembloux: Duculot, 1970), pp. 63-85.

Pfeiffer, H., *History of New Testament Times* (New York: Harper & Brothers, 1949).

Porton, G., 'Diversity in Postbiblical Judaism', in *Early Judaism and Its Modern Interpreters* (ed. R. Kraft and G.W.E. Nickelsburg; Philadelphia: Fortress Press, 1986), pp. 57-80.

Quell, G., 'πατήρ', in *Theological Dictionary of the New Testament*, V (ed. F. Kittel and G. Friedrich; trans. G. Bromiley; 10 vols.; Grand Rapids: Eerdmans, 1964–76), pp. 945-1014.

Rabin, C., 'The Novitiate', in *Qumran Studies* (Oxford: Oxford University Press, 1957).

Ramaroson, L., 'Le coeur du troisième évangile: Lc 15', *Bib* 60 (1979), pp. 348-60.

Raney, W.H., 'Who Were the Sinners?' *JR* 10 (1930), pp. 578-91.

Rengstorf, K.H. 'ἁμαρτωλός', in *Theological Dictionary of the New Testament*, I (ed. F. Kittel and G. Friedrich; trans. G. Bromiley; 10 vols.; Grand Rapids: Eerdmans, 1964–76), pp. 317-35.

Riches, J., *Jesus and the Transformation of Judaism* (London: Darton, Longman & Todd, 1980).

Ringgren, H., *The Faith of the Psalmists* (London: SCM Press, 1963).

Rivkin, E., *A Hidden Revolution* (Nashville: Abingdon, 1978).

—'Defining the Pharisees: The Tannaitic Sources', *HUCA* 40 (1969), pp. 205-49.

—'Scribes, Pharisees, Lawyers, Hypocrites', *HUCA* 49 (1978), pp. 135-42.

Robertson, A.T., *A Grammar of the Greek New Testament* (Nashville: Broadman Press, 1934).

Rosenbaum, S.N., 'The Concept "Antagonist" in Hebrew Psalm Poetry: A Semantic Field Study' (PhD thesis, Brandeis University; Ann Arbor: Xerox University Microfilms, 1974).

Safrai S. and M. Stern (eds.), *The Jewish People in the First Century*, (2 vols.; CRIANT,

Sec. 1; Philadelphia: Fortress Press, 1974).

Saldarini, A.J., ' "Form Criticism" of Rabbinic Literature', *JBL* 96/2 (1977), pp. 257-74.

Salom, A.P., 'Was Zacchaeus Really Reforming?' *ExpTim* 78 (1966–67), p. 87.

Sanders, E.P., *Jesus and Judaism* (Philadelphia: Fortress Press, 1985).

—'Jesus and the Sinners', *JSNT* 19 (1983), pp. 5-36.

—*Paul and Palestinian Judaism* (Philadelphia: Fortress Press, 1983; reprint).

Sanders, J.T.,'Tradition and Redaction in Luke XV.11-32', *NTS* 15 (1968–69), pp. 433-38.

—*The Jews in Luke–Acts* (London: SCM Press, 1987).

Sandmel, S., 'The Haggada Within Scripture', *JBL* 80 (1961), pp. 105-22.

—'Parallelomania', *JBL* 81 (1962), pp. 1-13.

Schlatter, A., *Das Evangelium des Lukas* (Stuttgart: Calwer Verlag, 1960).

Schnider, F., 'Ausschliessen und ausgeschlossen werden Beobachtungen zur Struktur des Gleichnisses vom Pharisäer und Zöllner Lk. 18, 10-14a', *BZ* 24 (1980), pp. 42-56.

—*Die verlorenen Söhne: Strukturanalytische und historisch-kritische Untersuchungen zu Lk 15* (Göttingen: Vandenhoeck & Ruprecht, 1977).

Schottroff, L., 'Die Erzählung vom Pharisäer und Zöllner als Beispiel für die theologische Kunst des Überredens', in *Neues Testament und christliche Existenz: Festschrift für Herbert Braun* (ed. Hans Dieter Betz and Luise Schottroff; Tübingen: Mohr [Paul Siebeck], 1973), pp. 439-61.

Schürer, E., *The History of the Jewish People in the Age of Jesus Christ* (ed. G. Vermes, F. Millar and M. Black; 3 vols.; Edinburgh: T. & T. Clark ; rev. edn, 1979).

Schürmann, H., *Das Lukasevangelium* (2 vols.; Freiburg: Herder, 1984).

Schwartz, D., 'Josephus and Nicolaus on the Pharisees', *JSJ* 14 (1983), pp. 157-71.

Schwarz, G., 'Lukas XIII.1-5', *NovT* 11 (1969), pp. 121-26.

Scott, B.B., *Hear Then the Parable* (Minneapolis, MN: Fortress Press, 1989).

Simon, M., *Jewish Sects at the Time of Jesus* (trans. James H. Farley; Philadelphia: Fortress Press, 1967).

Sjöberg, E., *Gott und die Sünder im palästinischen Judentum* (Stuttgart-Berlin: Kohlhammer, 1938).

Smith, D.E., 'Table-Fellowship as a Literary Motif in the Gospel of Luke', *JBL* 106/4 (1987), pp. 613-38.

—'The Historical Jesus at Table', in *Society of Biblical Literature: 1989 Seminar Papers* (Atlanta: Scholars Press, 1989), pp. 467-86.

Smith, M., 'A Comparison of Early Christian and Early Rabbinic Tradition', *JBL* 82 (1963), pp. 169-76.

—*Jesus the Magician* (San Francisco: Harper & Row, 1978).

—'Palestinian Judaism in the First Century', in *Israel: Its Role in Civilization* (ed. M. Davis; New York: Harper & Brothers, 1956), pp. 67-81.

Soggin, J.A., 'Der judäische 'Am-Ha'areṣ und das Königtum in Juda', *VT* 13 (1963), pp. 187-95.

Sola Pool, D. de and T. de Sola Pool (eds.), *The Haggadah of Passover* (South Brunswick: Tomas Yoseloff, 1975).

Stanton, G.N., *The Gospels and Jesus* (Oxford: Oxford University Press, 1989).

Steele, E., 'Table-Fellowship with Pharisees: An Editorial Analysis of Luke 7.36-50, 11.37-54, and 14.1-24' (unpublished PhD dissertation, University of Notre Dame, 1981; Ann Arbor: University Microfilms International).

Stone, M.E., *Jewish Writings of the Second Temple Period* (CRIANT, Sec. 2, II; Philadelphia: Fortress Press, 1984).

Strack, H.L., *Introduction to the Talmud and Midrash* (New York: Atheneum, 1969; reprinted from 1931 edition of the Jewish Publication Society of America).

Strack, H.L. and P. Billerbeck, *Kommentar zum neuen Testament aus Talmud und Midrasch* (Munich: Beck, 1924).

Tannehill, R.C., *The Narrative of Luke–Acts* (Philadelphia: Fortress Press, 1986).

Tajfel, H. (ed.), *Social Identity and Intergroup Relations* (Cambridge: Cambridge University Press, 1982).

Thackeray, J., *The Septuagint in Jewish Worship: A Study in Origins* (London: Oxford University Press, 1921).

Tiede, D.L., *Luke* (Minneapolis, MN: Augsburg, 1988).

Trever, J.C., *The Untold Story of Qumran* (London: Pickering & Inglis, 1965).

Tyson, J.B., 'Conflict as a Literary Theme in the Gospel of Luke', in *New Synoptic Studies* (ed. W.R. Farmer; Macon, GA: Mercer University Press, 1983).

—(ed.) *Luke–Acts and the Jewish People: Eight Perspectives* (Minneapolis, MN: Augsburg, 1988).

—'The Jewish Public in Luke/Acts', *NTS* 30 (1984), pp. 574-83.

—'The Opposition to Jesus in the Gospel of Luke', *Perspectives in Religious Studies* 5 (1978), pp. 144-50.

Urbach, E.E., *The Sages: Their Concepts and Beliefs* (trans. I. Abrahams; Cambridge, MA: Harvard University Press, 1987).

—'The Sages', *EncJud*, XIV (New York: Macmillan, 1971), pp. 636-55.

Vermes, G., *The Dead Sea Scrolls in English* (New York: Penguin, 1962; reprinted 1986).

—*Jesus and the World of Judaism* (London: SCM Press, 1983).

—*Jesus the Jew* (Philadelphia: Fortress Press, 1973).

—'Jewish Studies and New Testament Interpretation', *JJS* 31 (1980), pp. 1-17.

Völkel, M., 'Freund der Zöllner und Sünder', *ZNW* 69 (1978), pp. 1-10.

Vogels, W., 'Structural Analysis and Pastoral Work: The Story of Zacchaeus (Luke 19.1-10)', *Lumen Vitae* (English Translation) 33/4 (1978), pp. 482-92.

Volz, H., 'Zur Überlieferung des Gebetes Manasse', *ZKG* 70 (1959), pp. 293-305.

Walker, W.O., 'Jesus and the Tax Collectors', *JBL* 97 (1978), pp. 221-38.

Watson, N.M., 'Was Zacchaeus Really Reforming?' *ExpTim* 77 (1965–66), pp. 282-85.

Weber, M., *Ancient Judaism* (trans. H.H. Gerth and D. Martindale; Glencoe: The Free Press, 1952).

Weber, J.C., Jr, 'Jesus' Opponents in the Gospel of Mark', *JBR* 34 (1966), pp. 214-22.

Wengst, K., *Pax Romana and the Peace of Jesus Christ* (trans. J. Bowden; London: SCM Press, 1987).

Wernberg-Moller, P., *The Manual of Discipline* (trans. P. Wernberg-Moller; Leiden: Brill, 1957).

Westerholm, S., *Jesus and Scribal Authority* (Lund: Gleerup, 1978).

White, R.C., 'A Good Word for Zacchaeus? Exegetical Comment on Luke 19.1-10', *LTQ* 14 (1979), pp. 89-96.

Whitelock, L.T., *An Analytical Concordance of the Books of the Apocrypha* (2 vols.; Washington DC.: University Press of America, 1978).

Wild, R.A., 'The Encounter Between Pharisaic and Christian Judaism: Some Early Gospel Evidence', *NovT* 27/2 (1985), pp. 105-24.

Wilson, S.G., *The Gentiles and the Gentile Mission in Luke–Acts* (Cambridge: Cambridge University Press, 1973).

Young, B., *Jesus and His Jewish Parables* (New York: Paulist Press, 1989).

Young, N.H., ' "Jesus and the Sinners": Some Queries', *JSNT* 24 (1985), pp. 73-75.

Young, F.W., 'Luke 13.1-9', *Int* 31 (1977), pp. 59-63.

Youtie, H.C., 'Publicans and Sinners', *ZPE* 1 (1967), pp. 1-20.

Zeitlin, S., 'The 'Am Ha-aretz', *JQR* 23 (1932–33), pp. 45-61.

—'The Pharisees: A Historical Study', *JQR* 52 (1961–62), pp. 97-129.

Zerwick, M., *Biblical Greek* (Rome: Scripta Pontificii Instituti Biblici, 1963).

Ziesler J.A., 'Luke and the Pharisees', *NTS* 25 (1979), pp. 146-57.

Zimmerli, W., *Ezekiel* (trans. R.E. Clements; 2 vols.; Philadelphia: Fortress Press, 1979).

Zimmerman, F., *The Book of Tobit* (New York: Harper & Brothers, 1958).

INDEXES

INDEX OF REFERENCES

OLD TESTAMENT

NEW TESTAMENT

INDEX OF AUTHORS

JOURNAL FOR THE STUDY OF THE NEW TESTAMENT

Supplement Series